Over 300 Years of Masonic Ritual

MARTIN GANDOFF

CW00821155

Lewis Masonic

Front cover: *The Library and Museum of Freemasonry, London and the Library of the Provincial Grand Lodge of Norfolk*

First published 2017

ISBN 978 0 85318 543 7

All rights reserved. No part of this book may be reproduced or transmitted in any form or by any means, electronic or mechanical, including photocopying, recording, scanning or by any information storage and retrieval system, on the internet or elsewhere, without permission from the Publisher in writing.

© Martin Gandoff 2017

Published by Lewis Masonic

an imprint of Ian Allan Publishing Ltd, Addlestone, Surrey KT15 2SF.
Printed in England.

Visit the Lewis Masonic website at www.lewismasonic.co.uk

Copyright
Illegal copying and selling of publications deprives authors, publishers and booksellers of income, without which there would be no investment in new publications. Unauthorised versions of publications are also likely to be inferior in quality and contain incorrect information. You can help by reporting copyright infringements and acts of piracy to the Publisher or the UK Copyright Service.

Picture Credits
Every effort has been made to identify and correctly attribute photographic credits. Should any error have occurred this is entirely unintentional.

Contents

List of figures

Credits
(A) Courtesy of A. D. Skinner
(B) Courtesy of Grand Lodge of British Columbia and Yukon
(N) Courtesy of the library of the Provincial Grand Lodge of Norfolk
(U) Courtesy of the London Library of the United Grand Lodge of England

Preface

I have been trying for over 30 years to get Brethren interested in the history and development of the Craft and its ritual **and failed miserably**. I thought that a book on the subject might help and during my research and preparation, I felt there were several probable reasons for my earlier failure. Traditionally, the LOI should be the place in which Brethren are instructed and helped in their daily advancement of Masonic knowledge. Our history and tradition has been to do ceremonies well, support charities and good works, and run social activities.

Our LOIs have to spend time and effort with learning and rehearsal leaving little room for much else. I have also found that Past Masters often have little knowledge of, or interest in the history of the Craft and its ritual, so are not inclined to push it to younger Masons.

There is a vast amount of material to be read for a detailed knowledge of the subject and chasing around it to find a recipe for a basic grounding is not exactly easy.

Occasionally a learned Mason will give a lecture to a lodge and sometimes 'we do the Lectures'. Preston's Lectures extend and improve the ritual of the day, but I think you might gain a better understanding of the ritual if you looked at material from the early parts of the 18th century, simpler, but showing you where it came from.

'This history stuff is all very well, but you need to learn your ritual first.' Such a pity because to understand properly what we do, you need to see where it came from and why, but with the pressure to do your job in lodge, together with pressures from family, work and hobbies, it is not surprising that masonic history takes a back place.

The book makes reference to books written up to about 1980 and documents going back to 1400 AD (or earlier). To decide just how much of this is needed to back up a readable but informative book is a nightmare. I have tried to produce a book which will be as suitable for those Masons who have just passed the Third Degree and perhaps have taken a junior office, as well as for Brethren who are much more experienced but nevertheless not really familiar with where the Craft and its ritual came from.

In this year of 2017, we have an opportunity to go back rather more than 300 years and think about the formation of the Premier Grand Lodge, what led up to it and what happened next.

I have tried hard to ensure the book has not been dumbed down as to facts and sources. Some ideas are mine, but many more from others will be expressed, which will make you think and quite often totally disagree - we are looking at someone's opinion or interpretation of what they see as fact (possibly!).

Because there is a lot to read, I have left out all but the most important references within the text and Chapter 11 explains where to do further reading if you want to go deeper.

I hope that you will take the book in the spirit in which it is intended –

A basic, readable book, which will help you to understand why 1717 was so important, give you a good working knowledge of what happened and why, and encourage you to do much more reading and discussion.

You can even think of it as 'A student's guide to the Craft' if you wish. All Brethren are students in some respect and I am not ashamed to admit that having researched for the book, I think I am a better student of the Craft than I once was.

My thanks to Martin Faulks of Ian Allan for his encouragement and to Ian Allan for allowing me to quote from several books; to Quatuor Coronati Lodge for 130 years of wonderful and vital material; to Norfolk Province for access to the Provincial library; colleagues from Montgomerie and Unanimity Lodges and many others in the UK and abroad for help in research and in imparting to me knowledge gained over the years.

I am particularly grateful to the Grand Lodge of British Columbia and Yukon and the London Library of the United Grand Lodge of England for permission to reproduce their copyrighted images.

Martin Gandoff
Norfolk 2017

Introduction

Shortly after my Initiation, I asked my Preceptor where the ritual came from and he said 'It's all in the Bible'. Later I asked a Grand Officer a question about Craft history and he said 'Go and learn your ritual. Don't worry about things like that!' Another said 'Well! That's up to you to find out – I had to. You know that every Mason must find his own way.' Not much help unless you know where to look and how to find out.

Well, over 30 years have passed and as was said to me, I **could** say to you: Learn the ritual first. Don't worry if it doesn't make much sense now. You can always find out what it means later (if you really want to).

What I **must** say however is:

> Do a bit of reading, ask a few questions, have a few discussions and arguments, get a feel for what the Craft is about and why there is some ritual. **Then** you can learn as much of our wonderful ritual as you can and try to work out some of its meaning and significance for you.

This knowledge will help you to appreciate what is good about our Craft and help you with the words.

The book shows that the history of the ritual is actually a history of the Craft and although this year is especially exciting for the 300th anniversary of 1717, the formation of the Premier Grand Lodge, we need to go back much further in our history to get things into place.

> I hope this is a book for three kinds of Mason:
> • any new Mason wanting to gain initial knowledge and looking for a basic source of information on a range of Masonic subjects
> • one who wants to extend his knowledge of some aspects of Masonry and find out how to go further in his studies
> • one trying to help a young Mason at the start of his career.

There are many books, journals, web sites and magazines that you can use and spend a lot of time on. Five books are the most rewarding and are referred to as *HC1, HC3, BJ1, KJH1* and *KJH2* (see Chapter 11 for details of these and other books and sources). All are remarkable in the historical information they provide, but not particularly easy for the beginner. Similarly, there is a wealth of web sites, but a real job to go in and extract enough to start with. Many of the books are out-of-print and getting difficult to find – in a second-hand bookshop (if you can find them) *HC1 or BJ1* will cost about £25 but you will be very lucky to get hold of *KJH1* anywhere except your Provincial library or a County library, or a good research institute.

I hope you will understand what I have done as you go through it. I have concentrated on history and I say little about the government and regulation of the Craft. Nor have I much to say about Masonic symbols. All of these are important to a good all-round knowledge of the Craft, but I have restricted the book to history.

The book was written partly because I wanted to get my own ideas straight and fill in some major gaps in my knowledge, but also because I and the publisher felt that, to recognise the importance of 1717, a book is needed that covers the development of the ritual, as well as the history of the Craft before and after this date.

I have always felt that the history of the Craft and its ritual are inseparable and in a book limited in size, I have decided to minimise details of organisation, management and the overall activities of Grand Lodge and its subsidiaries.

Throughout the book, I have included what I call 'Pause for thoughts'. These are little breaker-uppers that either ask a question or give you a chance to stop and think about things. If they annoy or confuse you, **just ignore them**. Sometimes they are a quote or reference, but they are often me giving an opinion and, as I have said, one opinion may be as valid (or invalid) as another.

I must admit to the worst sin of a historian (I was actually trained as a scientist!). Any serious book of history tries to base ideas on **primary** sources (you can actually read the material) or **secondary** sources where you are relying on someone else's having read it, but you have good reason to trust their views. In the interests of ease and general convenience, I have not always followed this and there are places where I offer my unsupported opinion. Shame!

A detailed and wide-ranging study of Craft history is murderously difficult. The difficulties come from the of lack of evidence in most cases, but theories about the origins of who we are and what we do, covering some 600+ years, have been attempted by innumerable Masons for over 300 years. Many resulting estimates, guesses or pure fantasies have often become set in stone as if they really happened.

This is complicated because what we call Freemasonry, based on the work of the stonemason, almost certainly existed in some form from the 12th century, while what we do today probably dates from the mid- to late-17th century.

Scholars have been arguing for years as to whether the latter (speculative masonry) developed from the former (operative masonry). Much of the early English and Scottish material available is about the building industry but it is very difficult to say how much particularly relates to the Craft and where and how these different documents are related (if at all!).

I ask you to trust me to an extent and do without some references, except where it is essential. I am trying to justify both the apparent vagueness of many ideas and sources and the apparently casual approach in throwing out my ideas, so where I say that 'a particular author was of the view that …', if it relates to a specific reference, I will tell you, but if it is just the way the book or paper is written, I don't.

You will see 'probably', 'perhaps' and so on. This is not always me making a guess. It could be where I am summarising several opinions for simplicity. You can read the publications and form your own opinions.

After centuries of Masons just believing how the Craft developed from the Old Charges and a lot of traditional stuff, there finally developed what we can call the 'authentic school' of Masonic research and looking at evidence, rather than just imagination and the fancies of others in the past, and from the middle to the end of the 19th century onwards, some superb writers emerged.

I have tried to keep my style light but still put in a lot of Masonry, which I hope will help you. Some of it will be almost subliminal – you may not spot what I am doing until you have done some further studies.

I hope I have not dumbed things down. The book is not for idiots. It's just that many Masons don't know (*idiotes* – Greek for one who 'does not know') many of the basic historical facts because no-one has ever told them how **important** and how **exciting** they are.

The order of the book is not entirely linear. Some of the Chapters are slightly out of time sequence. I felt that later material was needed before the earlier could be fully appreciated. You may want to look at Chapter 11 before you read the remainder of the book. Don't be put off by the range of material – you don't have to read all of it.

When I had been in Freemasonry about five years, I made up a list of questions to which I needed answers. They were:

Why and in what form did Masonry start?

Why was it based on building?

Why were early rules and regulations so detailed?

Why did they have a 'moral' content/significance?

What was the content of the early ritual/ceremonial and how did it develop?

How did Masonry become more non-operative and hence speculative?

How did this trend affect the ritual up to 1730?

What happened in the UK and France from 1730-1760?

What did the Antients do to the ritual before and after 1751?

How and why did Preston and others expand the ritual?

What was the ritual prior to the Union in 1813?

How did Logic, West End, Taylor, etc. workings evolve from Stability/Emulation? Were they just minor local variations or more structured?

Are there any English rituals that are very different from these?

I hope the book will go a long way to answering these questions and many more. I will be satisfied if it makes you want to read any or all of Harry Carr, Bernard Jones, Knoop, Jones and Hamer, the Prestonian Lectures and the papers in *AQC*.

Finally, you will see many quotes in their original spelling and grammar. Sometimes it makes them difficult to read, but I feel that they deserve the respect of seeing what they actually looked like. You will also see a number of abbreviations used. They are explained as they occur, but some may be put off by references to *PrGL*, *TDK*, OCs, etc. It's not to save paper. I have always found that an acronym is easier to remember and handle than the full wording.

Good luck with your reading. I hope the book helps to make you a better Mason.

1
Short overview of English history

Introduction

What is history and why does a book that should fascinate you about our ritual start with a musty old chapter on history? History is here to collect and record all the events and changes over time in what we do and why we do it – ie. our society and our culture.

The development of our Craft, from say 1400 to 1825, was to a large extent dependant on the history and development of the life of Britain during this period.

This Chapter quickly skates through this 400+ year period, mainly picking out 'happenings' which may have had a direct or indirect effect on the Craft. Some of this material will come up again in Chapter 3, but we will try to keep this Chapter as general as possible.

Sorry again (not really!) that a book on ritual starts with a history lesson, but for a solid understanding of where Craft ritual came from, we need to trace it through the period and we need a basis of general history for this – well, that's my excuse. There is a difficulty for Masonic historians because many Masons feel that there is something deep-seated and esoteric in our customs and ritual which goes back to 'time immemorial'. There is not much proof until about 1600, apart from a number of mentions of masons, their characteristics and their work, in various obscure documents. We have a constant battle between 'this is what I believe' and 'what I can prove'.

For the greater part of the last millennium, 'life is rotten' is what 99.something% of the population would have said. No proper doctors or dentists. You rely on herbs, snake venom, magic spells to cure typhoid, cancer, etc. Living conditions are dreadful and working conditions not much better. Often rubbish food (mouldy or maggoty). Harsh laws. Brutal punishment. All of this, knowing that you were probably a serf to some high-and-mighty lord (obviously a bloated capitalist) and watch your daughter or wife – 'droit du seigneur' – big man grabs any woman he fancies!

Most of the population were in some state of serfdom - virtually slaves - and they and their family (and their possessions, if they had any) were entirely owned by their employer. On top of all this, the Church breathing fire and damnation and everywhere watching for evil-doing and heresy, with terrible punishments, both physical and spiritual. Shudder!

Note that the Church was a major player in commissioning many religious buildings – churches, abbeys, etc. and had a great deal of control over the style of building and the management of the building process. Fortunately, because there are so many detailed records of the costs and finances associated with buildings, we do have some little evidence of early masonry with which we can try and generalise as to what actually was going on in the mason trade. The nobility, royalty and other 'big men' were probably better off than the serfs in some ways, in their stone castles and abbeys rather than wattle-and-daub or thatched sheds, and had better (at least more) food.

Pause for thought

Much of the early history of masonry is linked to working conditions and laws and regulations to control wages and prevent workers from forming the equivalent of trade unions. We will come back to this later.

We have no really clear idea of what happened to Freemasons and Freemasonry in the 14th-16th centuries. Fortunately we know a lot about the 17th and a lot more about the 18th and 19th centuries.

In reality, there is much doubt as to the connection, **if any**, between the old operative mason and the Speculative Mason of the early to mid-17th century onward. To get a feel for the three or four main stages in the history of the Craft, this history overview will help you to gain an understanding of how working masonry and then non-operative Masonry developed. So, in as painless a way as possible, this opening Chapter picks up some of the main points in our history. This can then springboard us into Chapters 3 to 5, where we cover Craft history up to 1717 and Chapters 6 to 9 up to 1817, where we bring it up to the formation of the United Grand Lodge of England in 1813 and review the ritual, which by then became almost what it is today.

Before 1066
The legacy of the Romans

Pause for thought
https://en.wikipedia.org/wiki/Roman_Britain gives a very good overview of the Roman occupation.

We all know that they came in 55 BC (although the actual conquest was not until 43 BC) and were in Britain for about 500 years (up to about 410 AD). They occupied a large part of the country and forced Roman laws, their culture and way of life on the population. However, their influence may have been less than in other parts of Europe, partly because of England being on the fringe of the Empire and also because it was occupied relatively late in the Roman period.

The Romans built cities and roads that still exist (conceptually) today, such as the Fosse Way and Watling Street – roads that spread over most of the country. In spite of this, there was little major settlement of Romans and no apparent organisational connection between the various centres of administration and it seems likely that the Celtic inhabitants largely retained their tribal existence. For our short and potted history, we can say that Rome left the remains of cities and a culture largely to be destroyed by the indigenous population, the Anglo-Saxon invasion and their settlement. However, some aspects of Roman law and administration (and way of life), after so many years of the existence of the Empire throughout Europe and Asia, left a legacy on Britain.

Many Roman words entered the vocabulary of all the various nations that lived in Britain, and also into the building trade, such as 'cementarius' meaning a builder or mason in Roman times, which remained in use right up to the 13th century. (The first Provost of Aberdeen was Richard Cementarius, a major architect of the time. He was also known as 'Richard the builder'.) It has been said that the word is the origin of 'cement'!

Emperor Constantine, who reigned over the Roman Empire until 337 AD, shuffled the whole of it around. Originally based in Rome, Constantine moved the capital to the Bosphorus Straits between the Sea of Marmara and the Black Sea – between Europe and Asia – calling it Constantinople (obviously).

Possibly for political reasons or perhaps because of the alleged miracle of the sign in the sky, which made him become a Christian, he encouraged Christianity in the Empire.

The conversion of Constantine is well documented. During battles with other Roman leaders, just before the 'Battle of the Milvian Bridge' against Maxentius in 312 AD, he was said to see the 'Chi-Rho' sign in the sky together with words meaning 'Through this sign you shall conquer'. He then dreamt of a vision telling him to put the sign on his battle equipment, which later he did.

He went on to set up Christianity as a very successful state religion, although others were allowed. He allegedly adopted Christianity himself It is very interesting to me that only after the reign of Constantine did halos start to appear on religious paintings and other representations. Perhaps this reflects the fact that Constantine was reputably a follower of Apollo the sun god. Constantine the hypocrite?

The Anglo-Saxons

For reasons which are fascinating but beyond our scope, the Roman Empire started to crumble. Its influence in Britain waned, leaving the country wide open to external attack and it was fairly soon hit by the Scots (Irish) and the Picts (from Scotland).

The Saxons, coming mainly from Germany about 450 AD, started their grab for Britain, bringing their culture, ways and pagan religion.

There then follows nearly 600 years during which our nation starts to form. This was not a dark period even though called the Dark Ages. During the period, we see the formation of kingdoms, such as Mercia, Wessex; and various kings such as Oswy, Aegfrith and possibly King Arthur (one set of legends) and King Athelstan, the son of Edward, the son of Arthur (a quite different set of legends – see the Old Charges in Chapter 3).

Anglo-Saxon Christianity soon developed in England from about 600 AD, both from the strong hand of Rome and also from Ireland, where Celtic Christianity had flourished since 432 AD. There were Bishops and Archbishops. Monasteries and abbeys were built. Augustine, the first Archbishop of Canterbury, took office in 597 and sometime before 601 he baptised the first Christian Anglo-Saxon king, Aethelbert of Kent.

Art developed and there are many examples of Saxon jewellery – buckles, brooches and even more valuable items.

Pause for thought
On the land of one of my neighbours researchers have uncovered a complete gold and jewel necklace, which has been estimated as belonging to a Saxon queen of the time. A very valuable find.

Generally wood was used for building. The foundations of a large building would probably be laid using stone but the bulk would be of wood with thatched roofs. The usual style was 'sunken floor'. Posts were driven in at the corners, a shallow pit was dug and either lined with planks, making a floating floor above the pit, or the pit was covered with materials (such as compressed earth) to make a floor.

It has been suggested that the Anglo-Saxons treated wood almost with some awe. They used it extensively even if stone could have been employed and they seemed to have treated wood with respect, perhaps reflecting their pagan origins.

From about 600 AD, we see the advent of some stone in cathedrals, etc., generally built in the style of the Romans, and it is reported that sites have been excavated showing that they were built on Roman ruins. Anglo Saxons sometimes used these to build communal sites at typically important places, such as near to their farming and agriculture working.

The Vikings

These gentlemen came from Sweden, Norway and Denmark. They are said to have landed in 787 in Dorset and then set themselves up in the Scottish islands.

> Pause for thought
> There is very recent evidence (2016) showing the existence of settlements in Iceland, Greenland and even Canada, all with just sailing boats. What navigators they must have been!

The first major attack in Britain was in 793 at Lindisfarne monastery and then they went on to break up the structure of England with numerous successful battles. Only after some 100 years was the Anglo-Saxon King Alfred able to defeat them and kick them out. The remainder of the period involved various Scandinavian attacks on England until the end of the 10th century. Interesting names of the period include Ethelred who ruled for a long reign and his grandson King Canute who managed to control a kingdom including Scandinavian countries.

Later (1042), Edward the Confessor reigned. He was not a direct descendant of Ethelred and after problems associated with claims against his sovereignty and particularly with the Normans, whom he had used as part of his struggle, he died leaving no heir and hence a consequent fight for the throne.

King Harold was probably recommended by Edward the Confessor and on the 25th September 1066 he beat off an invading army of Norwegians who had landed in Yorkshire (battle of Stamford Bridge). On the 14th October, his exhausted army had to run south for him to meet his death against the Norman invaders under William the Conqueror at the Battle of Hastings.

1066-1456

The Normans

The Normans came from an ill-assorted bunch of North Europeans who eventually settled in France in what became Normandy and pledged allegiance to the King. Originally rather thuggish, over the many years of contact with the 'native' French, they gradually developed a culture of their own which, though warlike, was Christian. They merged politically with various well-established kingdoms, adopted the local language and eventually became a major force in Europe.

Duke William, on behalf of the Duchy of Normandy, came over to England, conquered, and completely changed the face of the country after the Battle of Hastings, where, allegedly, King Harold failed to keep an eye out for an arrow. This is always referred to as 'the Norman Conquest'.

William I

William (the Conqueror) reigned over England for 21 years until 1087. The Normans, to start with, had opposition from Denmark and rebel English attacks, but eventually stabilised the situation. They even managed to get some authority over Wales and Scotland. One of William's great achievements was the ordering of the production of the Domesday Book. Its purpose was tax-orientated and attempted to cover major parts of the country and sort out the financial mess left by Edward the Confessor.

It had two separate parts known as the 'Little Domesday' covering East Anglia and the 'Great Domesday' covering most of the remainder of England, apart from the North-Eastern counties and certain tax-exempt areas such as London. For reasons not known, not all the country was surveyed. The 'Little' was very detailed, covering fees due not only on land and fixed property but even on ownership of cattle. It is said that the 'Great' had rather less detail.

Once an irrevocable base assessment was made, any attempt to challenge it led to rather severe penalties – from a contemporary writer:

the sentence of that strict and terrible last account cannot be evaded by any skilful subterfuge, so when this book is appealed to ... its sentence cannot be quashed or set aside with impunity.

The Plantagenets

William and his legacy had about 50 years before there was more trouble over the succession, which eventually led (via William II and Henrys I and II) to the rise of the house of Plantagenet, starting with Henry III. This set of kings had sovereignty over part of France, leading to many wars between England and France. The Plantagenets included King John, who succeeded Richard I (the Lionheart) after his death in 1199.

Our principal interest in King John is that on the 15th June 1215, near Runnymede (where the author went to school and has unhappy memories of being forced to do cross-country running across part of Runnymede), a party of Barons, having staged a rebellion against John, forced him to sign the *Magna Carta*. In effect, it was a claim for justice, such as against imprisonment without trial and fairness about payments to the Crown, etc. and drastically reduced the power of the king, attempting to eliminate his 'random powers' (under the God-given right of kings, I can do what I like).

The agreement was quickly ignored, and eventually resulted in the 'Barons War', a declaration of war on John by the Barons, with the assistance of the French. It was broken with the aid of collusion between John and Pope Innocent III.

Pause for thought

As a matter of interest, Henry III, successor to John, signed the *Charter of the Forest*, something like the Magna Carta. Its purpose was to define the areas of forests and the rights of people to use the forests (say) for cutting down trees, allowing animals to roam, etc. It also specified what could **not** be done – 'keep off Crown land and don't even think about the King's deer'.

The throne and the country went through a range of problems, with attempts against the Crown and its involvement with wars on the continent, losing Normandy and other lands gained by King Richard.

The Black Death

This spread throughout Europe peaking from 1346 to about 1353. During the reign of Edward III, England was cursed with what was probably pneumonic plague (rather than bubonic). The first signs of the plague were lumps in the groin or armpits. After this, livid black spots appeared on the arms and thighs and other parts of the body. Few recovered. Almost all died within three days, usually without any fever.

It is often suggested that the disease was actually bubonic plague, spread by rat fleas. Recent medical opinion seems to suggest that the speed of infection and the death rate of about 40% (more in the cities) implies airborne infection and more chance of it being pneumonic plague. The curse was appalling. No treatment known. Very quick onset of symptoms and rapid descent into death (three to four days). Life in close and unhygienic contact, with rotten diet and infected bodies lying around until disposed of. Also, lots of workers dying off which was to cause a major upheaval. Fields weren't ploughed. Animals weren't looked after. Families broke up in despair. People fled from their villages in spite of owing allegiance to a local lord. Perhaps the three biggest effects were the desperate shortage of food, inflation of its price, and the massive shortage of workers.

Skilled workers took advantage by travelling to places where they could ask for inflated wages. With this migration of workers (and their families probably), control by the 'big men' started to crumble; their idea had always been to keep the peasants down economically and tie them to their village. This was falling apart and in 1351, to forbid general assemblies of workers, the *Statute of Labourers* was introduced. It was an attempt to reduce wages and bring people back to the village. Eventually the enforcement of the statute and the heavy imposition of taxes caused the 'Peasants Revolt' in 1381. Led by Watt Tyler, a near-army of rebels forced its way through Kent to London where they did much damage and actually murdered several high-ranking officials. The revolt was eventually put down by King Richard, killing many of the rebels.

This general trend to revolt and the need to expand was to have a great influence on the spread of masonry.

Rise of the Guilds

The word 'mystery' crops up in various areas and it is worth solving this mystery now. From the earliest times, a skilled craft or trade was called a mystery and in a Masonic context it has nothing to do with secrets or things of arcane origin, being derived from the Latin 'mysterium', meaning occupation or trade. Alternatively, it is said to come from Old French 'mestier' meaning master.

People have always got together for social, protective, warlike and trade (or craft) reasons.

It is believed that the Greek 'Eranos' and the later Roman 'Collegia', which were associations of workers, may have passed their traditions through the Middle Ages to Italy, France and hence to Anglo-Saxon England. This may have been why the Saxons started to form trade-oriented groups.

Pause for thought

Of interest was the very early formation of a different group called a 'frith' or 'peace' group. They started as something like a neighbourhood watch but eventually became more like police forces before proper central authorities made them redundant.

Guilds were also formed for social reasons (getting/keeping together) and for trade reasons – communication/networking and job protection.

After the Vikings made their visit, the word 'guild' (coming from a word meaning 'payment') came to be applied to groups of people (families, tribes) who came together, or were directed to do so, for reasons largely related to work, ie. different crafts. What we think of as the craft guilds began in England soon after 1100 – groups related to particular trades (or mysteries), associations wanting some control over how they were organised, what they did and how they could survive. They formed groups something like trade unions. It is likely (for financial reasons) that they were often under the control of the king or other high authority, who would maintain tight control over tools and building stock. The authority would also direct work or trade to members of the guild.

Over time, the guilds would develop specific objectives, both as to the organisation and the quality of their work. They would keep out those unskilled in the trade and they probably made set rules for the taking on and handling of apprentices and for sorting out disputes, and so on.

At the same time, keeping up the customs of earlier guilds, they maintained some welfare – helping the sick and needy and burying the dead. The charity aspect led to the concept of a charity 'box', under the control of a 'box man'.

Guilds probably started in London, but by the mid-14th century they had spread to many cities, covering crafts such as Blacksmiths, Weavers, Saddlers, and Coopers. The Weavers claim to have received a Royal Charter in 1155. The Pepperers or spice merchants (later apothecaries) started in 1180 and the company was incorporated as the Worshipful Company of Grocers in 1428. The Coopers are first mentioned in 1298.

There is strong evidence of the confirmation of the London Company of Masons in 1481 and we will see in Chapter 3 how written rules for the mason trade (the 'Old Charges') soon came to be essential and remnants of them can still be seen in their descendants in our Book of Constitutions. The guilds increased in power and eventually were the focal point for a group of people for welfare and insurance (helping the needy, whether sick or widows and orphans, burying the dead, etc.), worship, comradeship, entertainment and so on. As trade and trading developed, there evolved a separation between the 'merchant' (banker, entrepreneur, distributor, employer, etc.) and the 'craftsman', who actually produced carved stones, jewellery, saddles, wheels, arrows, etc. This of course led to separate merchant and craft guilds.

Guilds gradually increased in respectability and were accepted by the authorities, to such a point that a craftsman could not work or ply his trade without belonging to a guild. A tradition developed whereby in guild processions senior members were clothed with their own distinctive material or 'livery' and eventually the major guilds became referred to as 'livery companies' (which exist today).

Chapter 3 tries to explain why masons' guilds might have been different, largely because a typical guild would exist within a town (although there would obviously be relations with similar guilds in other towns), while masons worked on large buildings out in the sticks, for long periods. There was never really a need for a guild exactly like other trades. In fact, there is no real evidence for a masons' guild until about 1356. In Chapter 3, you will see part of the *London Regulations for Masons* covering a dispute between 'real' and 'other' masons. The preamble asserts that the mason's trade 'has not been regulated in due manner by the government of folks of their trade, in such form as other trades are'.

We also know that in 1376 the masons were eventually recognised as one of the 'mysteries' of London.

Many guilds recognised the need for ensuring that members were fully trained and the apprentice scheme slowly evolved. (Note that term we now use as Masons, the 'entered apprentice', did not appear until much later and in Scotland). There is also evidence that some guilds required a full craftsman to travel around, working as a 'journeyman', gaining necessary experience. We will see in Chapter 3 that the early Old Charges allow for the reception and welfare of a journeying mason arriving at a building site.

Pause for thought

The author recently attended a stone masonry workshop under the guidance of the Guildencraft Stone Masons in Norwich. The guild has a basis in trade and offers a range of services, but in particular, traces its origins back to King Athelstan. Young people are tested for a while, as 'trialists' and if sutible, are accepted for a 7-year apprenticeship. On completion, they become **journeymen** and spend two years travelling to gain further experience, before returning to execute a test piece to see if they are qualified for mastership.

All apprentices and qualified masons wear a square paper hat – it falls off if you don't stand properly, or try to lift a weight at the wrong angle.

The authorities of London issued a law organising the formation of trade companies from the guilds. The masons did not have a guild as such, but two of the companies that came into existence were the 'Company of Free-Masons' and the 'Company of Masons' (they eventually merged under the latter name.) There is a theory that there only ever was one company, a mistake being made in the interpretation of certain historic documents (*BJ1* p.70-71).

Pause for thought

Just as a matter of interest, here is a list of some of some of the trades that existed at the time:

Painter/stainer, Sadler, Horner, Fletcher, Layer, Setter, Mason, Smith, Wheelright, Shipright, Brushmaker, Paviour, Pepperer, Sword smith, Bell-grinder, Cooper, Slater.

Randle Holme, one of the earliest recorded men to become a Mason as we know it, in *The Academy of Armory,* published in 1688, listed a whole range of jobs that probably went right back to Saxon times and earlier. Here are some:

- The *Fundator*, a Digger of the Earth to lay a Foundation, or make a ground work to Build upon.
- The *Cuniculator*, a Miner, or digger under the Earth, such are all them that dig in Mines of Silver, Gold, Brass, Iron, Tin, Lead,

Coal, and the like. Such are termed Pioneers that undermine Forts, Towers and Castles, to Blow them up.
- The *Munginato*r, is such as blend Clay and Water, of these kind of Labouring Men, are the Daubers, Mortar Temperers, Plaster makers, and the like.
- The *Manufactor*, or Workers with the hand, and such as follow handy Craft labouring, as Trowel Men, Axe Men, and seilers and coverers of Houses either with Straw, Shingles, Tiles or Slate

That's enough!

Wars of the Roses

The next highlight is the local 'Wars of the Roses'. This was a very unpleasant set of skirmishes starting in 1455 with a feud between the rival Plantagenet Houses of York and Lancaster. The country was not entirely happy at the time, partly because of troubles resulting from the 100 Years War and because Henry VI was not the strongest of kings. The 100 Years War was a set of battles and general aggravation bubbling along between Britain and France from 1337 to 1453. After the Norman Conquest, England, as such, owned much of France and the War had a lot to do with the French recovering their 'lost' provinces.

There was constant, if not continuous, warfare and lawlessness reigned. After some vicious battles (such as Wakefield and Bosworth), years of fighting, the death of various kings and very complicated movement backwards and forwards, Henry VII, ie. Henry Tudor, the first of the Tudors, finally managed to emerge on top.

Repressive laws and regulations

As a little interpolation, let us look at a set of rules and regulations, all geared to repress the workers, obviously to reduce costs but perhaps also to regain the supremacy held over the serfs by the ruling class. Workers after the Black Death now expected that they could keep control over their own affairs, selecting employers and negotiating rates. Not so! The Crown deliberately trod on this freedom with a whole range of measures. Here is a selection:

1350 Edward III   Statute of labours - wages fixed
1356 Edward III   Regulations for Mason trade
1360 Edward III   Prohibition of annual gatherings

1389 Richard II   All organisations to supply full information about
                     'liberties, privileges, statutes, ordinance, usages
                     and customs and accompanying documents'
1423 Henry VI   Reinstatement of penalties for excessive wages
1424 Henry VI   Prohibition of annual gatherings
1495 Henry VII   Regulated wages of free mason, master carpenter and
                     rough mason
1514 Henry VIII   Limit wages of a free mason
1548 Edward VI   Prohibition of meetings for the purpose of fixing
wages and setting qualifications.

If you, the working class want socialism, you will have to wait 500 years
or so!

1457-1624

Henry VII
This King in 1485 inherited a rather bad legacy from the Wars of the Roses.
The government was very weak, almost non-existent, and the Treasury
was just about empty. The King by very vicious means (draconian taxes
and just downright seizure of property) managed to collect much of what
had been lost. His eldest son Arthur died early, leaving his younger son
Henry as his heir. When Henry VII himself died in 1509, the position of
the Tudors was firmed up, and his son (as Henry VIII) succeeded him
unopposed.

The Schaw Statutes
Not entirely appropriate within a sequence of English history but the date
comes in at the right time.

We do have strong evidence of the situation in Scotland after 1599
relating to the mason trade in Kilwinning and other areas in Scotland. There
is no evidence of a Kilwinning lodge (a purely operative lodge) before this
date but it seems to have been highly respected and later on spawned further
lodges. At this time, William Schaw, an employee of James IV of Scotland
(Master of Works to the Crown of Scotland and General Warden of the
Masons), recognised the importance of the lodge in its trade-controlling
powers and he issued two codes of regulations referred to as the 'Schaw
Statutes'. These were directed to the Mason Craft throughout Scotland and
consisted of three groups of regulations:

1. To define the status of Kilwinning lodge in relation to the rest of Scotland.
2. To define the status and powers of the lodge in relation to other lodges.
3. For the proper management and good order of the lodge.

The text confirms '... the existence of the lodge in 1599 as a headquarters of mason trade control on the west coast of Scotland, exercising its powers by sanction of the highest authority ...'.

The oldest Minutes of the lodge are dated 1642. Nothing is known about the lodge before this date. Subsequent Minutes refer, among other items, to apprentices and fellows of the craft, to men having sworn an oath, elections and the barring of some members from work until they had paid fines for disobedience.

Some of the material looks like some of the rules and regulation of the Old Charges, but with no indication of any ritual – this was a management document. There is, however, a reference somewhere in an apprentices' 'ceremony' to the giving of the 'Mason word' although this has no really obvious parallel in pre-1717 Masonic ritual. It is also believed that some lodges accepted honorary members (non-operatives?) in the 16th to 17th centuries.

We see more being put into the later versions of the Old Charges, but until the end of the 17th century there is little else we can say about Masonic procedures. We do not even know whether there was a difference between English and Scottish ritual, although it is believed that the Schaw Statutes were not treated by Scottish Masons in quite the same way that English Masons made use of the Old Charges. We will say more in Chapter 3.

Henry VIII

This selfish, proud and insanely cruel man lived a lavish life raiding the Treasury quite heavily. His marriage to Catherine of Aragon produced only one child, a daughter Mary, about whom we will hear later on. In 1512 Henry started a war with France, and while this was going on James IV of Scotland declared war on England with French allies. James and his army were completely defeated and largely slaughtered at the Battle of Flodden in September 1513.

In 1527 Henry petitioned the Pope in order to divorce Catherine of Aragon because she had not given him a male heir. The Holy See refused to grant this of course. Henry became somewhat peeved and started plans to split off from Rome. This was not just a bit of pique on Henry's part. It was probably motivated for political reasons as the drift to Protestantism was beginning to spread all over Europe, particularly after Martin Luther. In 1517, Luther published his '95 theses', clearly defining his objections to certain aspects of Catholic dogma and teachings, signalling a major drift away from Rome. Henry appointed Thomas Cranmer as Archbishop of Canterbury who quickly annulled the marriage, thereby making the daughter Mary retrospectively illegitimate. The next wife was Anne Boleyn and their daughter was Elizabeth (who eventually became Elizabeth I).

In 1533 the Pope finally decided to excommunicate the King. In spite of this, Henry had passed the *Act of Supremacy*, which gave him the elaborate and highly political title of 'Supreme Head on earth of the Church of England'. This in fact marks the height of the Reformation. The Church continued with little change for quite a few years, but Henry could now do what he wanted to and from 1536 onwards, as a measure of his spite against Rome, he took great steps to damage Roman Catholicism with the 'dissolution' or 'sacking' of the monasteries in 1538 – in which not very amusing interlude, religious buildings such as monasteries and convents were shut down and their assets appropriated by the Crown. He also managed to execute various abbots and, conveniently, a few others for treason.

Henry got rid of Anne and married Jane Seymour, whose son later became Edward VI. Anne's marriage annullment and death made Elizabeth retrospectively illegitimate as well. After various marriages and other measures, Henry finally died in 1547, to be succeeded by Edward VI who reigned until 1553, supporting the drift away from basic Roman control. Jane Grey was made queen for a very short time, but the establishment was not happy with her as the head of state and they arranged for Catherine of Aragon's illegitimate daughter Mary to take the throne.

Mary

Mary was a devout Catholic and probably allowed as many religious assassinations against Protestants as Henry VIII had actually organised against Catholics. It was not a very happy time and as we will see later, it had great influence on people's behaviour**, especially in regard to secrecy and maintaining silence about one's religious views**. Amongst other anti-Protestant measures, she renounced Henry's 'Supreme Head of the Church'.

Elizabeth I

Anne Boleyn's daughter Elizabeth I reigned from the death of Mary in 1558 until 1603. In fact she was very lucky because she was not exactly in amity with her half sister Mary, who actually imprisoned her at one time, and it is surprising that she escaped with her life. After setting up her 'management and advisory' team, she established the English Protestant church which eventually became the Church of England. Henry had set up the Act of Supremacy in 1534 which confirmed the King's supremacy over the Church. This was revoked by Mary and then reinstated by Elizabeth in 1558, calling herself the 'Supreme Governor' of the Church. Elizabeth I was cooler than her predecessors – her reign was in some respects, less oppressive than others had been and in her reign we see much literature and art flourishing.

Regnans in Excelsis ('reigning on high') was a papal bull issued on 25th February 1570 by Pope Pius V after declaring her illegitimate. It said:

Elizabeth, the pretended Queen of England and the servant of crime, to be a heretic and releasing all her subjects from any allegiance to her, even when they had 'sworn oaths to her', and excommunicating any that obeyed her orders.

We charge and command all and singular the nobles, subjects, peoples and others afore said that they do not dare obey her orders, mandates and laws. Those who shall act to the contrary we include in the like sentence of excommunication.

This, in effect, told the people that obedience to Elizabeth was at an end and throughout her life various conspiracies were put down by her supporters. Nonetheless, she reigned for 45 years. Her reign shows that she seemed to have been quite tolerant of people's religious beliefs, unlike some of her predecessors.

Pause for thought

She was relatively easy-going about religion, but not about secret societies or anything that could be thought of as tainted with conspiracy. However:

In 1561 '… hearing also that the Masons had some secrets that they could not or would nor reveal to her, she became jealous of their assemblies and sent an armed force to break up their annual communication … Sir Thomas Sackville … send some of the great officers of the Queen, that were Masons who then joining their assembly, made honourable report to the Queen who ever after esteemed them as cultivators of Peace, Friendship … and never meddled with those who were given to change'.

Elizabeth kept England out of various wars with France, Spain and the Netherlands. She will always be remembered for being on the throne at the defeat of the Spanish Armada in 1588.

Pause for thought

Probably worth mentioning here that resulting from the less elaborate approach to religious behaviour, buildings and masons were starting to carry out different work and we have the signs of architectural change. Buildings tended away from the Gothic style and there was less demand for the large buildings that had formerly been required (abbey, monastery, etc.).

Also, bear in mind that the swapping back and forth in allegiance to Rome led to much major discontent and violence, especially in the next century.

James I/IV

After Elizabeth departed, there was no appropriate or acceptable descendant of Henry VIII for the throne and in March 1603, James VI of Scotland, the son of Mary Queen of Scots, became James I of Great Britain, leading to the 'Union of Crowns', which brought the two thrones together, both for general administration but also to provide a greater measure of authority in foreign adventures. It was not a complete merger as such, with two separate parliaments and legal systems.

James was a Protestant and had been fairly successful in ruling Scotland but quickly came into conflict with English Parlimentarians who were looking to extend the power of Parliament (which was enhanced during the reign of the next king - Charles I). James was bit of a writer and produced several big works. He also oversaw the production of a new version of the Bible, the 'King James Bible'. He died in 1625.

The London Company of Masons

This may not be quite the right place but the date is approximately right. We saw earlier the introduction of the trade guild. As time went by, guilds became more affluent. They all showed strong religious control, offered charity and sickness benefit and generally protected their trades. There is some little evidence of mason organisation at the beginning of the 14th century. In 1356, masons appeared before the authorities in a dispute with non-masons, who claimed that the mason trade 'has not been regulated in due manner' implying that no masons' guild existed at the time.

We have already said that a guild for the mason trade would not have arisen (at least to the same extent) as for other trades, except in large cities, especially London, mainly because of the wide geographic spread of the trade. There is evidence of a London Freemason and Mason Company, whose origins might have been as early as 1376 (a masons' company furnished members to sit on the City of London Council) and similar organisations in other cities. These do not seem to have had links with each other, presumably being set up to help local traders only, unlike other guilds which operated country-wide.

In its early years, it was quite different from a lodge. It was however, governed by a Master and two Wardens and there appear to have been ceremonies for 'entered' and 'accepted' members. A set of 1621 Minutes indicate that there was a separate ceremony by an 'inner fraternity' of the Company. In the mid-17th century, the name of the company was 'The Company of Masons'. The assumption we can make is that it had become much closer to today's lodge and *BJ1* says it is possible that the company contained:

> on the one hand operative members who were skilled masons and
> on the other non-operatives who were made up of two classes: (a)
> those who had joined for social and similar reasons and (b) those
> who had become 'accepted' or 'speculative' or 'symbolic' Masons.

It is likely that the Company was becoming less and less connected with the building trade and the suggestion is that working masons and non-operatives would not join just for social reasons – if the company was declining, presumably there would have been less seedy and much more agreeable places to go for jolliness and conviviality. It has been suggested that there was an inner circle in the company that was beginning to become involved with the philosophical, moral and spiritual aspects of behaviour. Non-operatives might have sought to join, in order to be part of this inner fraternity, called the 'Acception' (or Accepcon in the spelling of the day). In joining this 'Society of Accepted Masons', the new member was said to 'come on the Acception'. Hence 'to be accepted'! This almost certainly is the origin of free and **accepted**.

By about 1680, the company had ceased to exist. Again, with little evidence to back it up, it seems quite likely that, although there is no indication that the London Company actually contained a lodge, it may well have been the inspiration for the formation of a number of lodges. If this is the case, then surely these new lodges would have drawn on the speculative tradition of the Acception?

1625-1687

Charles I

In 1625, Charles I succeeded James I as king of England, Scotland and Ireland. He was high Anglican, while his wife was Catholic, with much of the country going Protestant (even Puritan). An unpopular king, always insisting on the 'Divine Right of Kings' (even the healing royal touch). He constantly played with the rule and authority of Parliament, which he eventually decided to abolish and to rule without it. Finally, unrest grew and with the assistance of the Scots, the Civil War began.

Oliver and Richard Cromwell

By now, there was a very considerable trend towards Puritanism and this helped the 1642 Civil War. This was a series of intrigues and actual small battles which really were a difference of opinion between the Royalists (the Cavaliers), who felt that the position of the Crown was to an extent holy under their High Church (similar to the Catholic church), and the Parliamentarians (the Roundheads), who favoured a much more democratic approach to the government of the country. The results of all this trouble were the arrest of Charles for treason and his execution in 1649, the exile of his son (the future Charles II) and what we call the Commonwealth period. Once Charles had gone to his Maker and until May 1660, when Charles II came to the throne, England went through a dreadful period known as 'the Commonwealth' of England. To start with. It was governed by what was called the 'Rump' Parliament.

Then in 1653, our friend Oliver Cromwell barged in and after a certain amount of fighting, declared himself the Lord Protector of the country. In fact he was a complete dictator for the next five years. The 'management' was first called 'the Commonwealth', but was changed to 'the Protectorate' under the direct control of this single individual. Overall, until his death in 1658, a terrible time for England, particularly with regard to the religious persecution that occurred. The Royalists were obviously disgusted by the anti-Catholic and republican government of the country and wanted to see the son of Charles I brought back from France to reign as Charles II.

Cromwell as Lord Protector (and dictator!) had given himself absolute power and this passed to his son Richard when he died in 1658. Richard was much weaker than his father and eventually was forcibly removed. The country then remained almost in anarchy until the monarchy was formally restored.

Charles II

Charles II returned from France in 1660 to accept the throne of England and thereby kill off the Parliament that had been in power with Cromwell. Following the restoration of the Monarchy (ie. after getting rid of Cromwell who allegedly had destroyed the Crown), England came under his rule and the reign was relatively peaceful domestically, given the tumultuous time of the Interregnum years.

1665-6 the Great Plague

Bubonic plague had been around for centuries, in particular with the Black Death of 1346. With several sizeable outbreaks (tens of thousands of deaths) afterwards. London and other large cities of the time were very overcrowded and highly insanitary, there being no drainage or sewerage and much of the population would have been in poor health anyway. A heavy pall of smoke often lay over London, due to unrestricted coal burning, which could hardly help. Hence, excellent conditions for an epidemic.

It became obvious that a dreadful sickness was on its way and steps were taken to minimise the risk, for example, any ship coming into a British port was required to lay up for some weeks until proved clear of infection.

Many of the poor attempted to flee from the infected London, but found no sanctuary in other places because of their fear of infection.

An exact figure for the number of deaths is not known, partly because there was no official law to make recording of deaths notifiable and because the symptoms of TB and plague on a corpse are similar and could have led to mis-diagnosis. There are contemporary estimates of a country-wide death toll of 100,000. Once over, it left London with a 25% reduction in population, and many buildings left unattended until 'the infection had gone'. It has been said that the Great Fire was a godsend that burnt off the final infection!

The Great Fire of London 1666

For five days from midnight on the 2nd to the 5th of September, the 'Great Fire' raged over London. By the end it had burnt most of the old city of London, including St Paul's Cathedral and many municipal buildings, as well as 80% of homes.

Panic ensued, partly from people forced to leave home, plus loads of 'tourist' sightseers coming in to watch the spectacle. Eventually the firebreaks, produced with quantities of gunpowder; the strong winds which had helped the flames died down; and the burning, where there was not much left to burn anyway, finished it off.

Tradition says that there were relatively few deaths, but another opinion is that many were charred beyond recognition and the deaths of many poor were not recorded at the time anyway.

The extreme shortage of homes because of the devastation led to a very unhappy, homeless population and King Charles allegedly tried to force many of them to evacuate the city. His fear was that their situation might lead to rebellion.

The need to rebuild afterwards became critical and almost anyone who could use basic tools could gain employment but a major consequence was that new buildings were eventually erected, replacing many of the old, ramshackle wrecks of the past.

1688-1714
James II, William and Mary
For some 200 years there had been violent religious disputes. Tensions still existed between Catholics and Protestants, although the reign of Charles II was relatively calm. But in 1685 Charles I's second surviving son and brother to Charles II came to the throne. He was the openly Catholic James II of England and Ireland and also James VII of Scotland; the country again returned to religious and political upheaval.

In particular, when his son James was born, it meant that the succession would pass from his daughter Mary (wife of William of Orange) and hence the continuance of a Catholic dynasty. In addition, he re-introduced the appointment of Catholics in military and government positions, in contravention of Acts of Parliament which strictly prevented this.

In less than three years James II was thrown out, in what is now called the *Glorious Revolution*, also called the *Revolution of 1688*. This involved the overthrow of James by a group of English collaborating with the Dutch William of Orange and inviting him to invade. William did invade with a Dutch fleet and army which eventually led to his ascent to the English throne as William III of England, jointly with his wife Mary II, James's daughter.

In the following year a Bill of Rights was passed containing certain rights including:
- no taxes should be levied without the authority of Parliament
- the right to petition the monarch should be without fear of retribution
- no standing army may be maintained during peacetime without

the consent of Parliament
- subjects **who are Protestants** may bear arms for their defence as permitted by law
- the freedom of speech and debates or proceedings in Parliament should not to be impeached or questioned in any court or place out of Parliament
- excessive bail should not be required, nor excessive fines imposed, nor cruel and unusual punishment inflicted.

England was now starting to look a bit more like a democracy **except for the Catholics**, who were denied the vote and could not gain a commission in the army nor become an MP. The *Act of Settlement* of 1701 declared that the monarch could not be Catholic nor marry a Catholic.

Note that in 1690 the Protestant William (King Billy!) defeated Catholic James II at the Battle of the Boyne, an event which had ramifications right up to this century in Ulster and Eire.

Anne

While James and his descendants would continue to claim the throne, all Catholics (such as James and his son Charles) were barred from the throne by the Act of Settlement.

Queen Anne, one of James II's daughters, came to the throne in 1702, succeeding her brother-in-law WIlliam. After the *Acts of Union* of 1707, England as a sovereign state ceased to exist, with England and Scotland being replaced by the new 'Kingdom of Great Britain'. Anne died in 1714, to be succeeded by George I, the first of the Hanoverian kings.

Later

Having skipped through 500 years or so, just to put the rest of the book into perspective, we will skip very quickly through the next 100 years.

Many things happened nationally and internationally and social activity changed. Much of Europe participated in the Protestant Reformation, which had a major effect on how Christianity was practised. The Bill of Rights removed much injustice. The wider use of printing led to more Bibles becoming available. The Age of Reason (Enlightenment) lead to the spread of more reasonable and democratic thinking.

The East India Company, which was originally formed during Elizabeth I's reign, traded very profitably for Britain for well over 100 years, being responsible for a large part of its trade in products such as tea, chemicals and fine cloth. It became large enough to form independent armies abroad, which were involved in the Indian Rebellion of 1857.

English local and international trade was expanding, with developments in science and engineering, much of which was applied to weapons of war, adding to England's reputation.

In 1715, the first *Jacobite Rebellion* by James Stuart (the Old Pretender) was put down and in 1745, the second rebellion led by Charles Stuart (the Young Pretender), with the dreadful Battle of Culloden in the next year, in effect wiped out the Jacobite forces.

The Seven Years War from 1756 to 1763 was a war between England and Prussia on one side and France and other European countries on the other. The net result for England was that it gained a lot of territory in North America. The French lost a lot territory, generating much resentment, which probably helped the cause of Napoleon some 55 years later.

1773 marked the Boston Tea Party, an initial protest against English taxes, which, in 1776, developed into the American Declaration of Independence.

The French Revolution started in 1789 and war with France continued until 1815, with the Battle of Waterloo and the exile of Napoleon.

We have collapsed nearly 1,800 years of history into one broad Chapter. Lots of omissions of course, but I feel that there is enough for a decent basis for the rest of the book.
I think this is a good point to leave.

2
Ritual and ceremonial

This Chapter is perhaps the most theoretical in the book. As Masons, we do lots of strange things. We also say lots of weird things, at least to those outside the Craft. In fact, if we are honest, many of us don't really know why we do and say many things.

To start off an explanation, we need first of all to appreciate the difference between 'ritual' and 'ceremonial'. They are different and the difference is complicated because there is also the chance of confusion with the word 'rite'. To me:

A rite is a ceremony or procedure.

Ritual is the words and forms of words that make up the rite.

Ceremonial is the 'trappings' that in effect, transform the ritual into the ceremony.

We could say that ceremonial is a ritual of forms while ritual is a ceremonial of words. As Masons, we often refer to the 'workings' of a particular lodge. We usually mean the ritual of the degrees and the ceremonial that goes with the ritual. Before giving examples from the Craft, to understand the 'working' of ceremonies in Masonry, it is important to gain an understanding of how ritual and ceremonial are essential to man.

There are many religious, philosophical and other beliefs, with their associated rite or ceremonial, that have contributed to man's spiritual and material behaviour, some of which may have influenced the eventual practice of Freemasonry and some of the beliefs and ceremonies associated with various early trades, including builders and their work.

Let us look at a simple example first. We might consider a rite called 'celebrating your birthday in the pub'. Part of the ceremonial might be the clinking of glasses together accompanied by some ritual – 'cheers and many happy returns'. The next part of the ceremonial might be for everyone else to raise their glass and repeat the ritual. Compare with the traditional Russian toast where after the libation, the glasses are smashed into the fire.

Another example from part of the ceremony of Opening the Lodge:

To the IG - 'Brother IG. Your situation in the lodge?' or

To the Warden - 'The situation of the IG?'

The wording is essentially the same, but the ceremonial is different depending on who answers the question. In some lodges, the explanations of the stations are all explained by the Wardens, while in others, the IG, JD and SD answer for themselves.

A slightly different example, where there is a difference in ritual and ceremonial within the same rite: in the Closing of the Third Degree, the JW carries out a procedure with the SW, in which certain signs are given. During this, some lodges have intermediate stages, where the signs and passwords for all three Degrees are given, while in strict Emulation the signs and words of the first two Degrees are not given.

Another: in most lodges the Charity column (or bag, or offering plate) is passed round in silence, holding the Sign of Reverence, as one of the last items on the Agenda, with the Organist playing something appropriate. In other lodges, it is collected during the singing of the Closing Ode.

One more: before the presentation of an apron, in some lodges the DC makes sure that the apron is under the SW's pedestal and he presents it as ordered. In some lodges, the Chaplain, accompanied by the Deacons, delivers the apron, on a cushion, to the SW for presentation.

Early man must have noticed over the years that there were things beyond his control, which could give rise to dreadful happenings – floods, famine, pestilence, death and so on. This then developed into a fear of, and probably respect for, the' terrible power' behind these disasters. There must have been many occasions, though, when man noticed (perhaps through sheer coincidence) that because he had done or **not** done something, the calamity didn't happen:

Because he dropped a green stone into the river in the spring, there was no flood in the autumn.
The dry-stone magic!
Because by a fluke, he killed two rabbits with one arrow, his gout disappeared, giving rise to the ceremony of 'majestic pain relief', in which the magic arrow is raised to the Great Archer and the words 'arrow take rabbits and my pain too'.

Ridiculous? No! If things are beyond our control, we dream up ceremonies (ritual and ceremonial) to **thank** our God (or gods) for favours received, to **stop them** doing something or begging them **to do something** else.

Pause for thought
This reminds me of Tom Sawyer and Huckleberry Finn. They

were using a dead cat to cure warts if my childhood memory serves me.

Probably for the last 30,000 years man has carried out ceremonies such as these and eventually, certain individuals would no doubt, have become practised in the art of modifying the ritual or the ceremonial to meet different occasions, and putting the fear of the devil into people at the same time, to boost their position as mystic, high-priest, shaman, magician, etc. In addition, the failure of the 'ignorant masses' to understand the significance of the ceremony would mean that a fear would develop both as to the ceremonies, the need for the ceremonies and those who carried them out. The word **magic** seems most appropriate here.

The magical powers possessed by ancient architects because, for example, they could construct a 90° angle, are stated in the 47th Proposition of Euclid (Past Master's jewel) and in the theorem of Pythagoras. Having some knowledge of the 'sacred' mathematics, being able to use 'sacred instruments' to construct a right angle, to make walls horizontal and properly vertical and other 'secrets', must have been a great mystery to those who didn't know how and may well have given rise to the almost mystical 'master builder' concept.

If you ask people about right angles, they will say '3:4:5'. Get three pieces of wood whose lengths are in the ratio 3:4:5 and they will make a triangle containing a 90° angle (the same applies to 5:12:13). This is fine if you have an accurate ruler and a clearly defined standard length (inch, metre, etc.). If you don't and the three pieces of wood are fairly close to the correct ratio, you might get away with a reasonable right angle for a stone or building block, but not much use to a carpenter trying to butt together a table top and leg and needing a very small square, or a mason putting the finish to a perfect ashlar (that's why the square is to 'try and adjust …').

I have always felt that there is another builder's 'old secret' that is easy to prove, but never seems to appear in the literature.

Put a straight-edge on the ground and with a pin and piece of string, draw a semicircle and mark the points X and Y where the circle touches the straight-edge. These two points are the diameter. Pick a point A on the circumference and draw two lines from X and Y to this point. The angle XAY formed will be **a right angle wherever you put A on the circle**. So with a straight-edge, pin and piece of string, anyone can make a right angle. Strange that this is not well known.

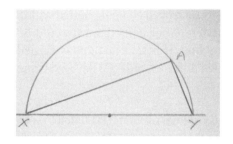

Fig 2.1: Angle in a semicircle

Pause for thought
The proof is simple – I will give you a hint. Draw a line (which will be a radius) from the centre to point A and remember that the angles in a triangle add up to 180^0. Good luck.

Let us look at some more ritual/ceremonial in daily life. Some of these maybe are throwbacks to earlier times, when people believed in not tempting fate, trusting to luck, keeping off bad spirits, etc. We could call some of them just superstitions.

- Spill salt on the table! Take a pinch and with your right hand throw it over your left shoulder into the devil's eyes so he can't see you to harm you
- The song YMCA. Showing my age, but how many people of the 60s and 70s will not start to make the Y, M, etc. when they hear it?
- Taking your time from me. Point …!
- Walk under a ladder. Sensible – nothing falls on you. Symbolic – the triangle could represent the Trinity and you are desecrating it. The solution is to walk backwards under the ladder. Never fails!
- Spit on your hands before lifting the heavy hammer. Could be just to get a better grip, or a sign of contempt to the devil – you can't harm me!
- Step on a crack (in the pavement) and break your mother's back! Cracks also lead to the underworld and by stepping on them, you may release demons. (I wonder if there is a much earlier significance, with the crack loosely resembling a cross – by stepping on it you are desecrating a holy item!)

In early times, there are legends in which the master builder is immured in the building by the Lord who commissioned it, so that he can never again build something as good or better for someone else. In others such as the building of KS Temple, a 'volunteer' was sacrificed by being buried within each cornerstone, so that some of the human or animal spirit could be transmogrified into the 'life' of the building. It is said that this is carried out in modern times, when a coin is buried under a building – the head being a substitute for the real sacrifice.

Protocol

This is a word that is very relevant. In its original meaning, it related to who does what, to whom and when in ceremonial occasions. More recently, in the world of IT, it has come to mean a set of rules that control a conversation as a set of messages in each direction. In our case it is a set of rules (or an understanding) of what items of ceremonial or ritual should be done and by whom and when, eg:

Should the PGM or his representative be applauded in and out of the lodge?

Who should prompt during the ceremony?

Which breast jewels should be worn and by whom?

Who takes part in a precession to welcome in an Official Visitor?

It was not just masons who had initiations, secrets, etc. The following three examples are from a summary of a lecture delivered to Lodge No. 3456 on 14th October 1914 by Dr Thomas Carr (VII ° in the Operatives).

Blacksmiths' guild

The candidate is treated like a piece of rough iron and is ceremonially heated on a forge and afterwards quenched in water. The candidate then takes an obligation on the anvil and is presented with 'working tools'. He is told about the penalty for breaking the obligation and given a password. Finally he is given a lecture about 'King Solomon and the Blacksmith' which shows that the blacksmith is the most important of trades because smiths make tools for everyone else!

Carpenters' guild

This has a legend of King Solomon needing wood for the Temple, which is supplied by Hiram, King of Tyre, brought down 'on floats from Lebanon'. The candidate is treated like a tree and after being symbolically sawed he is felled to the ground. Then instead of taking him to the saw pit, they make him an apprentice, he takes an obligation under certain secrets and finally is presented with a proper wood saw, a mallet, a wood chisel, and a carpenter's apron.

Painter-stainers

The blindfold candidate is brought in and secured on a board and a plumb-bob on a triangular pedestal is suspended ove his navel. With a clasp knife about his throat, he takes an obligation under penalty and a mock 'surgical procedure' is carried out (no more details please!). Apparently this was done until 1881.

> Pause for thought
> The source for this information is authentic, but with just this evidence, we cannot know whether the ceremony and associated ritual developed over the centuries like Masonry, or whether it was borrowed and amended to another trade. A very interesting paper, which confirms some of this and has much information about trade initiation rites etc., can be found by Andy Durr in *AQC* 100:88-108.

Plumbers

In the 1960s Michael Bentine (one of the original Goons) did a mini-play on radio which described the initiation rites of an apprentice bidet installer. There was an obligation, a very painful test and the plumbers' knocks one, two three, one – two three!). Bentine was a Mason and if you can find the piece, it is funny but has a few things you will spot.

So, we are now ready to study the development of Masonic ceremonies - the spoken ritual, the movements etc. associated with the words, and the protocols observed.

3
Craft history 1400-1620

Five terms

We start this Chapter with five important terms. Some will be explained further throughout the book.

The Old Charges

We know that since long before 1380 there existed documents which listed a so-called history of masonry and a set of charges concerning working and moral behaviour. Many examples of this document exist, having been modified and updated over the centuries. We usually refer to these old versions as the 'Manuscript Old Charges'. Towards the end of the 17th century, they started to include aspects of the ceremonies – at least a set of questions and answers explaining the significance of the ceremony. These are perhaps better just described as the 'manuscripts'. For the rest of the book, we will use **OC** to describe both of them.

Free Mason

Lots of arguments about this, with no generally accepted explanation. The term 'free' was used from early times, in the days of serfdom, to mean someone who was not bound to an employer, being free to work, having the liberty not possessed by serfs or slaves. It could also mean having been given, by virtue of experience or some other qualification, the freedom to practice within a city.

Another suggestion is that it is a corruption of the French 'frere maçon' or 'brother mason' – remember that French was the 'official' language of Britain for a long time after 1066.

The term 'freemason' rather than 'mason' came later and even though there are many theories about 'free' in 'freemason', for now we should assume that 'mason' starts to mean not just a stonemason but one who is part of a guild, trade union, secret society or whatever. More later.

The term mason could mean just a stonemason, one skilled in cutting nice square or oblong blocks. But it was also used to mean 'master mason' and this was not just a very skilful stone worker, with experience of intricate stone carving, but could have been a skilled architect and/or clerk of the works (a mixture of HAB and HKT perhaps?).

Another possibility is the fact that English 'freestone' was used when intricate carving was required for cathedrals, etc. Such masons were often called 'masons of free stone', then 'freestone masons' and later 'freemasons'.

In the following example from Scotland we have mason spelt as 'masoun'. (It also appears in early documents as 'masson'.) It is the *Indenture betwix Dunde and its Masoun*, AD 1536. It is said to be the earliest authentic example of a Scottish lodge containing a saint's name, ie. *Our Lady (St Mary's) Luge of Dunde*e:

> This indentit charter party maid at Dunde the xxiii day of Merch in the zeir of God ane thowsand fif hundredth and thretty-sex zeris proportis . . . that it is appoyntit . . .and aggreit betuix honorable men the preuost bailzies counsall and communite of the burgh of Dunde and Andro Barry kirkmaister for the time of the paroche kirk of our lady of the samyn on that ane part, and George Boiss masoun on that uther part, in maner ... as followis,... And he to keip his Interes daily and hourly to his lawbour forsaid at the samyn tymis and houris as the aid vss and consuetud of **our lady luge of Dunde** had and usit befor.... and to his zerly fee the sowm of twenty four pundis usuale money of Scotland.

Another Scottish record from the Minutes of the Lodge of Edinburgh (about 1600) states that the freedom of the Burgh had been accorded to its 'frie mesones', giving them the right to work.

The Prestonian Lecture for 1952, *'Free' in "Freemason" and the idea of Freedom throughout six centuries* by Bernard Jones, offers a detailed review of the term, as does Chapter 10 of *BJ1*.

We must be careful in the use of 'freemason'. I think now we all know that it means something like:

> Someone who adheres to the charges in the Book of Constitutions, who remains faithful to Obligations made in the Degrees, practices moral truth, virtue and uprightness and endeavours to lead a good life, using all aspects of the old building trade as points of focus.

The lodge

We need to discuss the term now. It was obviously in use in 1536 (see above). Masons would need to meet somewhere on the site to give and receive instructions and training, discuss practices and for social reasons. This could be within the stoneyard or in a building set aside for this. The term 'lodge' gradually came to be used both for this building and the group of men involved.

The earliest known reference to a **lodge** as a building occurs in the building accounts of Vale Royal Abbey in 1277, when **logias** and **mansiones** (lodges and households) were erected for the workers, because the site of the abbey was a long way from where they lived. It seems likely that the building (lodge) was used for refreshment and as a repository for tools and other kit. There is not much evidence of the use of the term to mean 'the group of men' until about 1600 in Scotland.

Intimately related to the matter of masons' wages is that of the hours of labour in olden times and on this point some light is thrown by the following (you can just make it out if you work hard!). It is taken from the Burgh Records of Edinburgh:

Statute anent the government of the Maister Masoun of the College Kirk of St Giles, **1491,**

> The quhilk day the prouest, dene of gild, baillies, and counsale of the burgh of Edinburgh, thinkis expedient and also ordanis that their maister masoun … the said maister and his seruandis sail begyn to thair werk ilk day in somer at the straik of v houris in the morning, and to continew … ix houris before none and swa to wirk thairat quhill that xj houris be strikken, and afternone to forgather agane to their wark at the hour of ane, and than to remayne quhill iiij houris, and than to gett a recreatioun in **the commoun luge** be the space of half ane hour … and fra thine furth to abyde at thair lawbour continually quhill the hour of vij be striking.

It mainly refers to rules for workers but is claimed to be one of the first printed references to the lodge (luge). The term 'lodge' has much history associated with it. It probably started as a basic tool shed or workshop, but it would then be expanded as a place of shelter and perhaps meal breaks and later as a dormitory.

As building projects became longer, there would be a need for a more substantial lodge building. It is thought that the 'luge' was a shed for purposes of shelter for the workmen, meals and rest. The term then came to be applied as well to meetings and to the body of craftsmen constituting such assemblies.

People have looked at various languages (including Sanskrit and Latin) to try and find a true derivation of the word. No really satisfactory explanation has been given.

Mystery

The term 'mystery' (and 'misterie') occurs in some of the OC and other documents. It does not mean a secret. It was used to mean the skill and ability associated with a particular trade.

Apprenticeship

Starting around 1200, it became the practice for an experienced tradesman to take on what was called an apprentice, a lad of between 10 and 17 years of age, who was often tested to see if he could show some potential for the skills of the trade. The employer (his master) would undertake to train the boy in the mystery, in return for board, lodging, equipment and general welfare. During the period the apprentice was fully bound to his master. Similarly, a master could not entice an apprentice from another master.

With some trades, depending on the advantages of the training, it might be necessary to pay a premium to the employer for taking him on - no wages being paid for the duration of the apprenticeship.

After a period, usually seven years, the apprentice was hopefully fully trained and able to carry out work on his own. In some trades the term 'journeyman' was applied to mean one who had completed their apprenticeship and could practice anywhere.

In 1563 the *Statute of Artificers* was passed under Queen Elizabeth I. As well as fixing prices and regulating wages, it laid down rules for regulating training and in general made the state responsible for the control that was previously exercised by craft guilds.

The term 'entered apprentice' in various spellings started to appear in Scotland and eventually 'apprentice' and 'entered apprentice' began to mean something different. We believe that the apprentice was as stated above, a youngster just coming in to the trade, while 'entry' implies fitness to enter the fraternity, the assumption being that the full training period had been satisfied and the candidate was entitled to fellowship (there being only two grades, 'fellow' and 'master').,

Pause for thought

Somehow in a rather confused mess of old documents, we are trying to lay a basis for the development of secrets, ceremonies and ritual. No apology for the very early documents - few authors put these in!

Why 1400?

We saw in Chapter 1 that there were many regulations relating to all aspects of the building industry such as it was then, and we know of the existence of the *Regius Poem* or *Halliwell Manuscript* (see below). This has been positively dated to 1380 and many historians believe that it may have been copied from something even earlier. We will see soon that this manuscript and its developments became absolutely fundamental to the Craft and echoes still exist in our Constitutions and the Installation ceremony now.

Probably ever since man made fixed buildings, there have always been certain techniques and bits of knowledge, as with any trade, to keep as trade secrets and one of the commonest examples is the ability to produce a right angle, both to ensure that parts of the building are vertical and to ensure that blocks are square. Most Masons know about the Pythagoras theorem or the 47th Proposition of Euclid and the 3:4:5 triangle and there would be many other secrets known 'only to the enlightened member of the masonic mystery'. (Remember that we looked at another way to produce a right angle in Chapter 2.)

We now return to about 1400 and look at how building and the building industry developed in England and how its practices led to the development of the ritual, ceremonial and charitable activity (and even the beginnings of Speculation?).

1400 is a bit of a lie really, because the oldest of the manuscript OC (more later) is actually dated as being older than 1380. Also, we will need to refer to even earlier documents. However, we end the Chapter about 1620 because there is much evidence that what we call 'non-operative' Masonry was beginning to flourish by then.

From church records such as fabric rolls, regulations and proclamations, etc. we may be reasonably sure that there were masons in the 14th century or earlier, who were something like a closed society. They protected their trade to an extent and had initiation ceremonies with secrets. There is little to show, however, that these masons had anything in common with the Speculative Freemasons of later years.

There seems to have been two classes of mason, the superior class being the 'freestone mason' (mestre mason de franche père) or 'chief mestre'.

There is also evidence that trades often merged (or at least associated), so that masons, thatchers, tilers (and others connected with building construction) could have been linked.

A further problem for the Masonic student is that our ritual contains much that can be attributed (if you really want to) to ancient civilisations and philosophies, the Bible and some ideas from more recent times. To try and link these to what the pre-1400 and later Masons did will lead to much conjecture, opinion and guesswork (perhaps to excess). It is so easy, for example, to take something from an ancient Egyptian ceremony, to which a certain significance has been attributed, and then say that because the ceremony has some similarity with ours, we should assume the same significance!

I must now show a declaration of interest. I delight in performing and listening to Craft ritual and its origin has no effect on this. But, I keep a sense of perspective. I believe that over 75% of the material in our existing ritual has no real basis in fact – its origin is so obscure or so convenient to that which earlier Speculative Freemasons used to reinforce their philosophical ideas, that an origin 'lost in time' and confirmed as being of 'time immemorial' could be rejected. This of course does not mean that we reject the words of the ritual. We hope to gain much joy and spiritual uplift from the words we say, but we must remember that much of their origin is suspect, in that we don't really know who wrote it or why.

Consider our Grand Master HAB. There is no Old Testament 'raising' of someone who died a heroic death. There is some evidence of Huram (and various other versions of the name) being someone with building (masonic) skills. There is also an account of the sons of Noah attempting to 'raise' a body and things 'slipping'. All this was evolved by writers who tried to embellish older ideas into the 'glorious death', that we are familiar with today.

Let us start with one of the biggest controversies in Masonry. We will see shortly that very early in the last millennium there must have been some form of masonry, in which masons were to an extent, organised and had ceremonies of some kind. By definition, they were all connected with building and hence we call them 'operative masons'. Perhaps 400 years later, we find that increasingly more men who were not connected with building joined lodges, for various reasons. We call them 'non-operative' masons and lodges gradually lost any association with building, although their ritual and ceremonies still reflected their masonic origins.

Then, over time, some masons started to think more about the ritual and its significance and bringing in philosophical and religious ideas from many sources. These men were becoming more concerned with the **philosophy**

and meaning of what they did in lodge and less about the **practical aspects of masonry**. We say that they started to speculate on Masonry at large as well as the ritual. We refer to them as 'Speculative Masons'.

To recap:

Operative Mason – practical worker, possibly part of a masonic organisation with certain ceremonies and passwords

Non-operative mason – not a worker, rather someone invited to join an operative lodge, for example, as an honour to the lodge, such as the local squire or parson. These lodges would still carry out the workings kept 'from time immemorial'. (Non-operative masons were sometimes referred to as 'gentlemen masons'.)

Speculative Mason – nothing to do with building work. Masons who work as we do now – using similar ritual and the rest of the workings – tools, symbols and so on, to speculate on good behaviour, etc.

Operative masonry, with simple ceremonies and gradually-evolving traditions, probably started between, say, 1150 and 1250. The trend to non-operative masonry probably was from about 1600 and what we still call 'operative lodges' (ie. those that had chosen not to take on board any of that 'speculative rubbish'), were still in existence well beyond the formation of the Premier Grand Lodge in 1717.

Now the controversy. It seems logical to assume that there was a gradual transition from operative to non-operative and hence to Speculative. This is the famous 'transition' theory, whose greatest exponent was Brother Harry Carr (*HC1*). His paper *600 years of Craft ritual* in *AQC* 81:153-205 really lays out his views. However, the comments on the paper by other equally respected Brethren show that alternative views exist (clearly indicating that even as eminent a Mason as Harry was not immune to having bricks thrown at him).

The mainstream alternative seems to be that Speculative Freemasons developed without any real connection to operative masons. Did Speculative Freemasonry come from operative and non-operative or did it grow independently, and at the same time, and eventually supersede it. The controversy arises because although this would seem to be a logical progression for Masonic development - ie. **all operatives** at first, then bringing non-builders and finally recognising the real values of the Craft, becoming Speculative - there is almost no **real** evidence that it happened that way.

The opposite view is that operative/non-operatives flourished from early in the 15th century and died out, perhaps as late as the 19th century, while Speculative Masonry started almost independently in the early to middle part of the 17th century (or even earlier), making use of traditions, ideas and possibly ceremonies of working masons.

But why did the Craft develop with the emphasis on building rather than, say, woodworking, boat-building or some other mystery? Again, no evidence. We can only assume that Speculative Masonry (Chapter 4), having as a main aspect leading a good life, symbolically building with 'living stones' and aspiring to higher things, has a parallel in the process of building (say) a great cathedral from the foundations right up to the spire, figuratively reaching up to God Himself.

Let us look at building and builders and see how the need for regulation and the documents produced almost certainly form a major contribution to our Craft. Our biggest problem, as always, is the lack of Masonic documents covering 1400-1620. We will see examples of non-Masonic documents related to the legal position of the time.

You will be introduced to the early OCs, which help us to believe that there was some form of organised Freemasonry in the late 14th century, and many writers have brought in all kinds of theories to explain what influenced the development of the Craft. Some of these theories were put forward a long time ago and unfortunately, as we find with much 'Masonic research', age leads to 'time immemorial' – 'as it goes back so far, it must have some relevance'. Unfortunately, we have no lodge Minutes, formal records or anything that shows there was ritual or ceremonial associated with membership of a masonic group until well into the 16th century.

Pause for thought

This applies to England. There is a mass of documents from Scotland, from which we must make the assumption that Masonry developed in a certain way there. We may also assume that much of the Scottish ceremonial practice was similar in England. My big assumption!

If you can understand 16th century Scottish, the oldest preserved lodge Minute in the world is in the first Minute Book of the *Lodge of Edinburgh, No. 1 (Marys Chapel)* of 1599. It has this:

The qlk day George Patoun maissoun grenttit & confessit that he had offendit agane the dekin & mrs for placeing of ane cowane to wirk at ane chymnay heid for tua dayis and ane half day, for the qlk offenss he submittit him self in the dekin & mrs guds willis for qt vnlaw they pless to lay to his charge, and thay having respect to the said Georges humill submissioun & of his estait they remittit him the said offenss Providing alwayis that gif ather he [or] ony vther brother comitt the lyke offenss heirefter that the law sall strvke vpoun thame indiscreta wtout exceptioun of personis. This wes done in prcs of Paull Maissoun dekin, Thoas Weir warden, Thoas Watt, Johne Broun, Henrie Tailzefeir, the said George Patoun, & Adam Walkar.

My partial translation attempt is as follows:

The next day George Patoun Mason, granted and confessed that he had offended against the Deacon and Masters for placing of a cowan to work at a chimney…..

Stone building in England

The Romans had 'colleges' of builders (Chapter 8). They left Britain about 410 AD and much of the formerly conquered land fell back into barbarism. Building of houses and perhaps communal buildings (meeting houses?) continued, and it makes sense to expect them to have retained some of the old styles if not the skills, and there would have been some work in stone. Historians claim however that there is little evidence of the arts and skills of the colleges surviving the Dark Ages and hence influencing Saxon building.

The Saxons invaded before 500 AD and made a few changes, but there were still ruins showing Roman influence in the country. Later Pope Gregory sent missionaries to convert the Saxons to Christianity and this led to the demand for places for worship (churches). (There is evidence that a missionary often took a party of builders, in anticipation of the need to provide a place of worship for the proposed converts).

With little stone-handling skills, most buildings would involve wood and carpenters, joiners and other wood workers would be the main trade, although some stone (such as flints) would be needed for foundations and shoring up walls. The standard small Anglo-Saxon building was a sunken floor with wooden posts all the way round. Planks would then be used to cover the floor, leaving a space below either for storage or for insulation.

Trades like paviours, slaters, and plasterers probably did not start to emerge until after the Normans arrived. When they did come they used freestone, brought from Normandy, and over the years they gradually skilled-up the Saxons into producing finer work.

To start with, it is likely that stone would have been used as wood had been used in the past (carpentry with rocks and stones). However, there would have been some travel to Rome, and maybe Greece, by members of the Church and other building commissioners and they would have seen Graeco-Roman architecture. Ideas from these and contact with European builders would have gradually spread to those who commissioned churches and other buildings, ie. castles, abbeys, cathedrals and royal and private estates. This obviously led to a great demand for builders and the need for stone.

Building (masonic) organisation.

We mentioned guilds in Chapter 1. To remind you, they probably started off about 1000 AD as people grouped for social or religious reasons and only later for trade reasons. They were well established in England in the reign of Henry I in about 1153. They developed into 'organisations', for protecting a particular trade from unskilled workers or outsiders, partly to ensure they had work and partly to protect their reputation as workers.

Guilds generally grew in influence and in London operated a restrictive practice – men of the craft had to belong to the guild in order to be free to work in the city.

A Guild of Masons was established in 1356 (the *Regulations for the Trade of Masons,* below, shows that there was no masonic guild before then).

The London Masons' Company was established in 1472 with a set of ordinances to regulate trade operation. There seems little evidence of the spread of a country-wide masonic organisation and this may be due to the essential nature of the work. With other guilds, the employer might be an experienced trader (jeweller, barber, saddler, etc.) employing a few people. With building, the employer would be the Crown, the Church or other 'rich' body. They would not want workers to be organised, because this of course could lead to demands for pay rises and restrictive practices (remember life was hard at the time). Furthermore, the Crown could 'press' employees, ie. force them to work at a particular location for a pre-determined wage.

With the Guild in existence from 1356 and with probably 200 years or more of working tradition, ordinances and other rules and regulations would be devised and documented, many of which would be included in the *Regius MS* (see below), which is probably one of the earliest guild-oriented documents in existence.

Pause for thought
What follows is an attempt to lay a basis for why the OC arose and what they might have contained. It is purely a matter of opinion, as we have little evidence of what really happened, but to me it makes a lot of sense. Relating this to the modern building site is quite deliberate!

By 1376, the Masons were accepted as one of forty-seven mysteries in London, represented on the Common Council of the city - the earliest British masonic craft Guild of which we have record.

We know that regulations were needed to resolve differences between masters and workmen. In addition, to protect the reputation of the craftsmen, regulations also existed to allow for the inspection of work in progress or completed, with sanctions for 'dodgy' builders. It also seems very likely that there would be mechanisms for collecting alms for welfare, such as for the sick, for burials and perhaps for church fabric update.

The increasing development of large buildings led to a major change in the trades needed and in working conditions on the building sites. Many more staff than before were involved.

Imagine a typical building site of today with cement mixers, dumpers, cranes, etc. Now imagine a similar cathedral building site, with almost no equipment and with perhaps a hundred skilled tradesmen supported by many hundreds of labourers and 'shlappers' (old Hebrew *ish sabbal* – men of burden). Consider the time factor. To lay the basic structure of a large wooden church might take maybe five years before the 'interior decorators' could move in. With an abbey or cathedral the structure might take a whole generation, perhaps 30 or 40 years.

The work became more dangerous. In the earlier days of building it is unlikely that a typical building would be more than, say, 25 feet high (two floors). Cathedrals, abbeys and so on might easily stretch to 200 feet plus and with long ladders, scaffolding and scaffold boards, we are now dealing with much more accident-prone operations.

What about first-aid? No hospitals. No defibrillator kits. In Roman or earlier Egyptian times an injured or unfit working slave would probably have been killed off and dumped somewhere out of the way, but while the medieval period was hard in many ways, there must have been some concern for safety.

Many other logistical problems might have arisen from a lot of people working for a long time, a long distance from any urban centres. How do you handle food and refreshment? What about recreation, night-time accommodation, sewer facilities, etc. Associated with these would be the need for on-going training, as some unskilled staff were 'recruited'. With a major building site and its lack of modern equipment, there would be many low-skill jobs that still needed some degree of training. Tools would be needed and the equivalent of fab. shops would have to be developed and manned.

Another problem was bound to arise that would have serious effects, that of discipline - hundreds of people kicking around in the evenings, doing what?

On the credit side, there were efforts towards efficiency - that is, quality control and better methods of working. By the 16th century, it became recognised that the masons' work would be inspected and work could be rejected if below standard (a fine could be levied as well – the trade policing itself!).

As the building industry progressed it would have been necessary to pass on traditional ways, methods and secrets, and therefore procedures, to ensure that these were only communicated to 'appropriate' people. The traditional building site would be a magnet for workers travelling around the country and it would be necessary to safeguard against the hiring or contracting of journeyman workers who were unable to prove their trade record or skill level.

Bear in mind that at this time the Roman Catholic Church was supreme and any association of people that did not overtly show its faith would be considered as heretic and pursued with the full force of the law. There must have been clerics carrying out administrative and supervisory duties – supervising the work and able to report to the Abbot or whoever, that progress was satisfactory. Surely, part of their work would be preaching the Gospel to workers? Surely no self-respecting person in Holy Orders would not attempt to save this enormous bunch of sinners?

Many rules and regulations stated in the OC address many of these issues while reflecting the religious character of the society of their time. So, in all of this, there evolved **and we don't really know how and when**, sets of rules and regulations, together with a history of masonry, all contained within a Christian framework.

Pause for thought

Here we have perhaps the most agonising problem of any Masonic historian. We know that a lot of building in stone was carried out for several hundred years. During this time, we are pretty sure that some of the more experienced masons must have wanted to see documented, the rules and regulations they felt necessary to protect themselves and their secrets.

The earliest and later OCs, to a great extent based on working regulations of the day, contained a long and confused history, 'fraternity' charges to behave well on and off site in a Christian fashion, together with mystery charges for working, including safety. The history may well have been developed in order to try and add some official sanction and a touch of the exotic to what was done.

The essentially Christian aspect is because all guilds at the time had a religious basis.

So, where on earth did the material come from, and who actually documented it, and how and where did the 'documenters' and the 'masons' get together to work out what to document, and how did the employers feel about all this, and, and … ? We just don't know, so we have to make intelligent guesses.

Possible sources of regulations

We have a few clues in some earlier regulations! There was a *Bologna statute* of 1248, issued in Italy in that city, where masons and carpenters were organised together. The statute is mainly about financial and administrative aspects of the trades – it almost looks like a schedule for the accountants, but it does however contain some interesting lines:

That no Master shall harm another Master in his work. We enact and order: that no Master Mason and Carpenter shall harm another Master of the Union of Masters by accepting a work at a fixed price, after having assured him and promised formally, where he did receive this work in a different manner. Except that, if a Master turned up before the work was formally promised and assured to him and he would ask a part, he then shall give him a part, if the other wishes so.

The Officers shall visit the sick members and give them support. We enact and order: that if one of our members is sick the Officers have the duty to visit him when they learn about it, and to give him support and help. And if he dies and has nothing for the burial, the Union shall have him buried honorably at its own expense.

Nobody besoin of the Union is allowed to work for someone who is in debt to a Master. Very important. We enact and order: that nobody of the Union is allowed to work a day or on accord for someone, who has to give or to pay money to a Master because of his Trade, once he has learned it, or that the case was denounced to him by this Master, or the Officers of the Union.

The next example comes from the *French book of Trades* of 1268:

Masons, Mortarers and Plasterers may have as many helpers and servants in their business as they please as long as they do not show any of them the fine points of their Craft.

Masters with apprentices whose term of apprenticeship is fulfilled must come before the Guild Master and testify to the fact that their apprentice has accomplished his term faithfully and well, whereupon the Guild Master shall ask the apprentice to promise under oath to observe the practices and customs of the Craft loyally and well.

In this era, the trade had clearly defined grades. At the lowest level were the labourers and servants. Then we had apprentices (an apprenticeship lasting five to eight years), craft men who had finished their training but did not have the means to set up in business on their own; and skilled Masters (craft men with money or financial backing).

At the highest level were master builders. These would be the architects of the day, who were highly-skilled in the construction of large buildings but at the same time, in order to run a massive building site, would also be skilled in the management of stock and labour - in other words they would be true site managers as well as being a master architect. So in old documents, when a master builder is referred to, it doesn't just mean a top-class stone worker or a superb painter/decorator, it means somebody who is at the top of his profession, fully skilled and able to direct any aspect of the work on the building site.

Just one more possible source of ideas, from the *York Minster Ordinances* of 1370. The group of masons involved with the building of York Minister swore to certain rules:

And they shall stand there faithfully working at their work all day after that, as long as they can clearly see to work, if it is a full day of work; otherwise until high noon is struck by the clock, when a holiday falls at noon, except within the aforesaid time between Michaelmas and Lent; and at all other times of the year they may dine before noon if they wish, and also eat at noon where they like.

… It is also ordered that no Mason shall be received at work on the work of the aforesaid church unless he is first tested for a week or more as to his good work; and if after this he is found competent for the work, he may be received by the common assent of the Master and the keepers of the work and of the Master Mason, and he must swear upon the book that he will truly and carefully, according to his power, without any kind of guile, treachery, or deceit; maintain and keep holy all the points of this aforesaid ordinance in all things that affect or may affect him, …

And let whoever goes against this ordinance and breaks it against the will of the aforesaid chapter have God's curse and Saint Peter's. Shudder!

Note that the *York Ordinances* imply some degree of trade organisation. We cannot assume, however, that this would be representative of some country-wide set-up. It must have been specific to the York Minister work. No doubt other sets of regulations were set up for the masons employed on other work.

So, we see some of the material that **might** have been available to the assemblers of our OC and when we look at them shortly, you will see a similarity of language.

Pause for thought

This might be a good time just to list many of the various trades associated with the craft that were around at the time:

Mason, Layer/Setter/Cementer, Slater, Paviour, Scrabbler, Painter/stainer, Brushmaker, Smith, Wheelwright.

Some of these were organised into guilds.

The Scrabbler (or Scrappler) was a low grade stoneworker whose job was to make use of a maul, taking largish stones and bashing them down to various sizes, closer to those ashlars needed for the building.

This is also a good time to introduce the 'cowan': primarily a term of Scottish origin, a worker who has no training or professional qualifications, who tries to obtain work as if he had.

(There is a very challenging early Scottish definition, namely 'one who does not have the Mason's word' - see the oldest preserved Minute above). Another name for a cowan was 'dry stone worker' - someone who could pile stones to make a wall, but had no carving or cementing skills.

Regulations for the Trade of Masons 1356

Before we look at the earliest OC, we will look at parts of an English item which shows early regulations relating to masons. Note that the language and general details are not dissimilar to those in the OC.

At a Congregation of Mayor and Aldermen holden on the Monday next before the purification of the Blessed Virgin Mary (2 Feby.) in the thirtieth year of the reign of King Edward III, etc., there being present Simon Fraunceys the Mayor, John Lovekyn, and other …, certain Articles were ordained touching the trade of Masons, in these words:

1. Whereas Simon Fraunceys, Mayor of the City of London, has been given to understand that divers dissensions and disputes have been moved in the said City, between the Masons who are 'hewers' on the one hand, and the light-Masons and 'setters' on the other; because that **their trade has not been regulated in due manner by the government of Folks of their trade in such form as other trades are**. Therefore the said Mayor … caused all the good folks of the said trade to be summoned before him, to have from them good and due information how their trade might be best ordered and ruled, for the profit of the common people …

4. Also, that good folks of the said trade shall be chosen and sworn every time that need shall be, to Oversee that no one of the trade takes work to complete, if he does not well and perfectly know how to perform such work, on pain of losing, to the use of the commonality, the first time that he shall by the persons so sworn be convicted thereof, one mark; and the second time two marks; and the third time he shall forswear his trade for ever …

6. Also, that **no one shall set an apprentice or journeyman to work, except in the presence of his Master, before he has been perfectly instructed in his calling**; and he who shall do

the contrary, and by the person so sworn be convicted thereof, let him pay the first time to the commonality half a mark, and the second time one mark, and the third time 20 shillings; and so let him pay 20 shillings every time that he shall be convicted thereof.

7. Also, that no man of the said trade **shall take an Apprentice for a less time than seven years**, according to the usage of the City; and he who shall do the contrary thereof, shall be punished in the same manner …

10. Also, that no one of the said trade shall take the Apprentice of another to the prejudice or damage of his Master, until his term shall have fully expired, on pain of paying, to the use of the commonality, half a mark each time that he shall be convicted thereof.

Note that Article 1 clearly show it was recognised that there was **a need for some kind of Mason organisation**.

The Old Charges

By the 1300s masonic guilds (or at least groups or associations) were becoming established. With material such as the above that might have been available; the pride felt by masons with an alleged craft history going back thousands of years; and knowing that there were secrets that they would need to keep, we may guess that at some time **well before 1400**, some masons (or perhaps employers) hoping to streamline things, must have decided that the rules and regulations needed to be documented.

These OCs must have originally been written to define the ceremonies that were offered and their historical and trade-related basis. They give almost no clues as to what went on! Fortunately for us, over the centuries the OC manuscripts changed and were developed, eventually giving clear evidence of the origins of our early ritual. Before looking at them, let us first look at what the ceremony was in, say, 1400.

We believe that the candidate apprentice had probably served a seven year term of apprenticeship and the ceremony was really to enter him formally (accept) into the trade. It probably consisted of not much more than a prayer, the giving of secrets of some kind and an obligation, with some or all of the OC being read to him.

The first OC, called the *Regius Poem*, was written somewhere between 1350 and 1450, but is generally accepted as about 1390. There is some evidence that it was written later than this and there is an apparent mention of it in later documents. It was first published by James Halliwell in 1840 and is also called the *Halliwell manuscript.* It is a poem written by who knows who, as we have said earlier. The manuscript is one of the oldest Masonic documents to be discovered and very clearly shows an Initiation ceremony. To give you an idea of what a poor author has to contend with, here are the first few lines in their original text:

Hic incipiunt constituciones artis gemetriae secundum Eucyldem
1. Whose wol bothe wel rede and loke,
2. He may fynde wryte yn olde boke
3. Of grete lordys and eke ladyysse
4. That hade mony chyldryn y-fere,y-wisse
5. And hade no rentys to fnde hem wyth
6. Nowther yn towne, ny felde, nr fryth ….

And here is its translation:

Here begin the constitutions of the art of Geometry according to Euclid.

Whoever will both well read and look

He may find written in old book

Of great lords and also ladies

That had many children together certainly

And had no income to keep them with

Neither in town nor field nor frith …

Both the *Regius* and its later derivatives have the same basic structure:

1. A dreadful legendary history of Masonry – not because it is full of dread, but because whoever wrote it had no idea of time at all – Euclid comes to England and teaches Geometry to medieval kings etc, etc.
2. Articles for the Master, such as:

The third article forsooth it is,

That the master takes to no 'prentice,

Unless he have good assurance to dwell

Seven years with him, as I you tell,

His craft to learn, that is profitable;

Within less he may not be able

To lords' profit, nor to his own

As you may know by good reason

The fourth article this must be,
That the master him well besee,
That he no bondman 'prentice make,
Nor for no covetousness do him take;
For the lord that he is bound to,
May fetch the 'prentice wheresoever he go.
If in the lodge he were ty-take, (taken)
Much disease it might there make,
And such case it might befal,
That it might grieve some or all.
For all the masons that be there
Will stand together all y-fere. (together)
If such one in that craft should dwell,
Of divers diseases you might tell;
For more ease then, and of honesty,
Take a 'prentice of higher degree.
By old time written I find
That the 'prentice should be of gentle kind;
And so sometime, great lords' blood
Took this geometry that is full good
The fourteenth article by good reason,
Sheweth the master how he shall don; (do)
He shall no 'prentice to him take,
Unless diver cares he have to make,
That he may within his term,
Of him divers points may learn.
The fifteenth article maketh an end,
For to the master he is a friend;
To teach him so, that for no man,
No false maintenance he take him upon,
Nor maintain his fellows in their sin,
For no good that he might win;
Nor no false oath suffer him to make,
For dread of their souls' sake,
Keep it well to great honour,
Lest it would turn the craft to shame,
And himself to very much blame.
3. Points for the Craftsmen, such as:

The third point must be severele, (severely)
With the 'prentice know it well,
His master's counsel he keep and close,
And his fellows by his good purpose;
The privities of the chamber tell he no man,
Nor in the lodge whatsoever they don; (do)
Whatsoever thou hearest or seest them do,
Tell it no man wheresoever you go;
The counsel of hall, and even of bower,
Keep it well to great honour,
Lest it would turn thyself to blame,
And bring the craft into great shame.
The sixth point is full given to know,
Both to high and even to low,
For such case it might befall;
Among the masons some or all,
Through envy or deadly hate,
Oft ariseth full great debate.
Then ought the mason if that he may,
Put them both under a day;
But loveday yet shall they make none,
Till that the work-day be clean gone
Upon the holy-day you must well take
Leisure enough loveday to make,
Lest that it would the work-day
Hinder their work for such a fray;
To such end then that you them draw.
That they stand well in God's law.
The fourteenth point is full good law
To him that would be under awe;
A good true oath he must there swear
To his master and his fellows that be there;
He must be steadfast and also true
To all this ordinance, wheresoever he go,
And to his liege lord the king,
To be true to him over all thing.
And all these points here before
To them thou must need be y-swore, (sworn)

And all shall swear the same oath
Of the masons, be they lief be they loath.
To all these points here before,

(In other words, **you all must swear the Mason's oath – like it or lump it**)

That hath been ordained by full good lore.
And they shall enquire every man
Of his party, as well as he can,
If any man may be found guilty
In any of these points specially;
And who he be, let him be sought,
And to the assembly let him be brought.

4. An ordinance relating to assemblies as laid down by King Athelstan.
5. The legend of the Four Crowned Martyrs, who were slain because they would not produce 'idols'.
6. Some more history and some explanation of the Seven Liberal Arts.
7. Matters relating to worship and Christian behaviour.

It would seem that groups of masons and employers, seeing guilds being formed to help the regularising of other trades and maybe knowing about regulations such as the ones referred to earlier, might have arranged for a scribe to document rules both for activities on site, such as for safety, but also as guidelines for personal behaviour and to protect the honour and good name of the craft of mason.

The fourteenth point is exciting because it clearly points out that, whatever might be involved with what masons might have done in ceremonies, the oath was considered 'important'.

Pause for thought

If the workers didn't arrange for a scribe to produce the documents, then who did?

The only possible answer for me is that a kind of consortium of members of the Church and building commissioners (princes, lords, etc.) over the Gothic period eventually decided to promote efficient and profitability in the business of building by producing documents, with regulations giving the workers what looked something like a bill of rights, (perhaps giving them the impression that their employers really cared for them!). This could then lead to better labour relations, safer work and perhaps something for the builders to adopt as the equivalent of a 'trade bible' or 'union rule-book'.

The next OC that was discovered is the *Cooke Manuscript* of the early 1400s. It is longer than the Halliwell and is not poetical. Its structure is slightly different, in that it has a much longer dreadful history, the Articles and Points are expanded and the English is closer to today. Compare these with the above (the third point seems to be a mix of the Halliwell third and fourth points):

The third point - He shall hele the counsel or his fellows in lodge and in chamber, and wherever Masons meet.

The fourth point - He shall be no traitor to the art and do it no harm nor conform to any enactments against the art nor against the members thereof: but he shall maintain it in all honour to the best of his ability.

The sixth point - In case of disagreement between him and his fellows, he shall unquestioningly obey the master and be silent thereon at the bidding of his master, or of his master's warden in his master's absence, until the next following holiday and shall then settle the matter according to the verdict of his fellows; and not upon a work-day because of the hindrance to the work and to the lord's interests.

Pause for thought

This one, for you to think about, comes from a different manuscript:

And also that no Mason shall be no comon player at hassard or at dyce nor at none other unlawfull playes wherby the Crafte might be slaundred And also that no Mason shall vse no leachery nor be no baude wherby the Crafte might be slandred And also that no ffellowe goe into the Towne A nights tyme there as is A Lodge of ffellowes wthout that he haue A fellow wth him that might beare him wyttnesse that he was in honest places.

From these two manuscripts, which experts have said come from even earlier versions, many others were subsequently produced with their range of variations, changes and additions, but until the late 17th century (Chapter 4) we do not know anything about how they affected or indeed defined the ritual.

We believe that there was an initiation ceremony for what we know call an 'entered apprentice'. This would probably be a lad who had started say at the age of 12 and had worked (slaved?) for his master for seven years or so, picking up various aspects of the trade, but perticulary in carving and sculpture and was now sufficiently experienced to be received into what must have been something like a brotherhood of masons. After more years of experience, he would be accepted as a 'fellow' of the craft, a fully experienced builder and entitled to run his own site if he could afford it.

The later *William Watson MS* of 1535 is similar to the *Regius*, except the history is slightly different. It starts with a detailed review of the Seven Liberal Arts and Sciences and a detailed description of why geometry is so important. The charges are now at the end and have become more streamlined.

The Schaw Statutes

We do have strong evidence of the situation in Scotland after 1599, relating to the mason trade in Edinburgh, Kilwinning and other areas in Scotland. In common with most trades, a city would lay down rules to govern the working of the trade, in order to protect the 'customer' as well as for the maintenance of good order and its reputation.

William Schaw held the office of Warden-General, appointed by James VI. This was an administrative position (also called 'Chief Master of Masons')

On 28th December 1598, as the 'general warden of all the Masons' and with the approval of the main lodges, he issued the first of two sets of enactments, known as the *Schaw Statutes,* directed to the Mason Craft throughout Scotland.

The 1598 set are similar to the working and social requirements of the *Regius Poem* we looked at above. For example:

… statutes and ordinances to be observed by all the master Masons within this realm, set down by William Schaw, Master of Work to His Majesty and general warden of the said Craft, with the consent of the masters afterspecified.

First that they observe and keep all the good ordinances set down previously concerning the privileges of their craft by their predecessors of good memory and especially that they be true one to another and live charitably together as becomes sworn brothers and companions of the Craft.

… That there be one warden chosen and elected every year … and that by the votes of the masters of the said lodges, and the consent of their Warden-General … that such a warden has been chosen for such a year to the end that the Warden-General may send directions to the elected warden.

… That all masters undertaking any work be very careful to see that their scaffolding and footways be surely set and placed, to the end that **through their negligence and sloth no hurt or injury may come to any person working on the work**, under the pain of prohibiting them thereafter from working as masters in charge of any work, but ever to be subject **all the rest of their days** to work under another principal master having charge of the work.

The Lodge of Kilwinning had claimed that it had privileges going back into antiquity, which the statute did not allow for and at the end of 1599, Schaw issued a second Statute. Its main purposes were:

- To define the status of Kilwinning lodge in relation to the rest of West Scotland
- To define the status and powers of the lodge in relation to other lodges
- To ensure that the lodge was properly managed.

Here are first three items:

- Edinburgh shall be, in the future as in the past, the **first** and principal lodge in Scotland; Kilwinning, the **second** as is established in our ancient writings; and Stirling shall be the **third** lodge, conformably to the old privileges thereof.
- The warden within the bounds of Kilwinning and other places subject to their lodge, shall be elected annually by a majority of the masters of the lodge, on the twentieth day of December, in the Kirk of Kilwinning. Immediately after election, the Warden General must be notified who was chosen warden.
- Agreeably to former ancient liberties, **the warden of Kilwinning shall be present** at the election of wardens within the limits of the lower ward of Cliddisdale, Glasgow, Ayr, and the district of Carrik. Furthermore, the warden and deacon of Kilwinning shall have authority to convene the wardens within the indicated jurisdiction, when anything of importance is to be done …

Two further items of interest are:

- The warden of Kilwinning shall appoint six worthy and perfect masons, well known to the craft as such, to inquire into the qualifications of **all the masons within the district**, as regards their skill and knowledge of the trade and their familiarity with the old traditions, to the end that the warden-deacon may be answerable thereafter for all such persons within his district and jurisdiction.
- Authority is given to the warden-deacon of Kilwinning to exclude from the lodges of the district **all persons who wilfully fail to live up to all the acts and ancient statutes set down from time immemorial**, also all who are disobedient to their church, craft, council and other statutes and acts to be promulgated hereafter for good order.

The wording of the statutes confirms that the three head lodges were in existence in 1599 with Kilwinning controlling the mason trade on the west coast of Scotland. The position of Schaw within the hierarchy meant that the statutes had the highest of authorities behind them. The Statute gave the right of Kilwinning to oversee the appointment of lodge deacons and wardens and to add further ordinances if needed.

> Pause for thought
> No such clear organisation nor the ordinances to control it ever existed in England.

Grand Lodge No. 1

The *Grand Lodge No. 1 Manuscript* (1632) is interesting because, although is it similar to the *Watson*, it contains the following piece of history:

... King of another region that men called Hiram, who loved King Solomon well and gave him timber for his work. And he had a son named **Aynone** who was **a master of geometry** and a chief master of all his masons as he was **master of engravings carvings and all manner of masonry** connected to the temple....

This is the first and probably only appearance of HAB until the late 18th Century.

From the *Grand Lodge MS* and later in the *York MS* we see that part of a ceremony included (first in Latin as a tribute to the early writers) then in

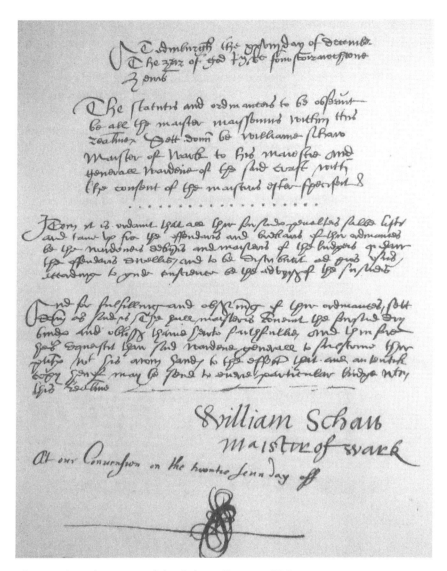

Fig 3.1: Opening page of the Schaw Statutes 124

English:

   ...Tunc unus ex senioribus teneat librum ut ille vel illi potiat vel
   potiant manus sup librum et tunc precepta deberent Legi.
   ...Then let one of the elders hold the book out to him who is taking
   the oath, and let him place his hand on the book or on top of the

book, while the Articles and Precepts are read.

I think that this, a posture for an oath, might have been part of the initiation ceremony for many years before these manuscripts were written. We will see soon that a ceremony existed whereby the candidate is taken out and terrified (for whatever reason), and when he comes back he places his hand on the book (the Bible, rather than the lodge copy of the OC) and makes an obligation. Then certain secrets are imparted. We don't know what, but there is certainly a word and from the early Scottish manuscripts allegedly the word is whispered round the members of the lodge, finishing with the candidate (or master).

Remember that we are dealing with the early birth of our Craft and virtually nothing is known about the ceremony. Much later manuscripts contain a set of questions and answers as a catechism and we have to assume that these are a retrospect of what happened in the ceremony. We know almost nothing about the ceremony of the 15th and 16th centuries.

So that you don't feel entirely negative about all this negativity, if we anticipate Chapter 4, in the *Edinburgh Register House manuscript* of 1696, we begin to get some ideas. Bear in mind that this is a Scottish manuscript, which may not necessarily reflect the jolly English masons. It starts with 15 Qs and As, which will make some sense:

Some Questions that Masons use to put to these who profess to have ye Mason Word before they will acknowledge them.

These are just two:

Q. - What is the first point?

A. - Tell me the first point ile tell you the second, The first is to heill and conceal, second, under no less pain, which is then cutting of the throat, for you most make that sign, when you say that.

Q. - Are there lights in your Lodge?

A. - Yes three the north east, south west, and eastern passage. The one denotes the master Mason, the other the warden The third the setter croft ….

In a later part it asks questions for the **fellow** including:

Q. - Are you a fellow craft?

A. - Yes.

Q. - How many points of the fellowship are ther?

A. - Fyve viz foot to foot Knee to Knee Heart to Heart, Hand to Hand ear to ear. Then make the sign of fellowship and shake

hands you will acknowledged a very mason. The words are in
I of Kings Ch 7, v, 21, and in 2 Chr: ch 3 verse last.
Then there is a description of what happens (Chapter 4).

Pause for thought
We don't have a 'blue book' and we only have some idea of the
ceremonial and the wording. From this Scottish manuscript we
know there is a secret word and we have a clear description of
the ceremony but where is the ritual? You can't just have a load
of leaping about with some questions at the end, or can you?
Perhaps that is all there was between 1400 and 1696.

The following (in modern English) is from the *Dumfries No. 3 manuscript*
of about 1570:

Then let the person that is made a mason choose out of the lodge, a
mason who is to instruct him in those secrets which must never be
written and he is to call him **tuter**. Then his tuter will take him
aside and show him **all the whole mystery**, that at his return he
may exercise with the rest of his fellow masons.

Was he just learning the answers to a number of questions (like our
candidates have to do for the Passing and Raising ceremonies) **or was there
more to it?**

The 'traditional history' in the charges up to the early 17th century tells
that Edwin the son of King Athelstan:

Set up a great assembly of Masons:

… and made a proclamation that all masons who had any writings
or understanding of the Charges and manners which had been
made before in this land or in any other, should bring them forth;
and when it had been done, some were found in French, some in
Greek, and some in English, and some in other languages, but the
same intent was found in all of them. He made a Book there of
how the Craft was founded, and he himself commanded that it
should be read when any masons should be made. From that day
until now the manners of masons have been kept and observed in
that form, as well as men might observe and govern it.
EVERY man that is a mason take right good heed to these Charges,
and if any man find himself guilty of any of them, that he amend
himself before God. And in particular, you that are to be charged,
take good heed to keep these Charges right well, for it is of great

peril and great danger for a man to forswear himself upon a Book. Perhaps you can see now why lodges kept a copy of their OC (often as a vellum roll) and treated it as the 'be all and end all' of their Masonry.

Secrecy

The poor masons of the 14th and 15th centuries, all of whom were Roman Catholic because this was the only form of Christianity practiced in England, must have been terrified if they were ever informed of the *Concilium Avenionense* or the *Papal Avignon Decree* of 1326. This is a small part (in modern English):

> In some districts of our provinces, there are people, mostly
> noblemen, sometimes commoners, organizing leagues, societies,
> conspiracies that are forbidden by the ecclesiastic law as well as by
> the civil law; under the name of brotherhoods.
>
> They gather once a year at places where their secret assemblies and
> meetings are being held; having entered the room, they take an
> obligation according to which **they must support each other**
> **against everybody except their Masters** and assist, advise and
> help each other in any situation.
>
> Sometimes, having put on a uniformed costume and using tokens
> and distinctive signs, they elect one of theirs as leader; to whom
> they swear complete obedience: therefore justice is suffering as a
> result and murder and robbery follow ...
>
> ... We resolve that the oaths to be taken by the aforesaid persons
> are prohibited, valueless, and that nobody may feel bound to
> observe them. Under our guarantee, we do absolve them. However,
> they shall get a salutary punishment from their confessors, for
> those imprudent and rash oaths.

Shudder!

We have a group of skilled masons, some of whom are highly qualified (with the special knowledge known only to the few), all of whom want to protect their secrets from those not entitled. Similarly, as we will see, many masons travelled about and needed to prove their ability. This explains why masons have always been secretive and in the early days it would have led to signs, etc. that would prove 'something'.

This is the 10th item of the *'Eucladus Charge'* in *Kilwinning No. 3* MS (1675-1725) and states:

You shall at all times receive strange masons and fellows and cherish and relieve them when thy come, if upon examination they appear to be such, & set them on work, as ye manner is.

If **you have no mould or stone at ye place where you meet**, you shall **refresh him and assist him with money to carry him to ye next lodge**.

Just a small but important aspect of secrecy. There are many places where you can get full details of all ceremonies of all Masonic Orders. Nevertheless, it is important to ensure that these details are kept secret from our Candidates.

In view of the seriousness of some ritual and the associated dramatic parts, it is a great pity for the Candidate to have pre-knowledge – it must spoil the effect for him.

We look in Chapter 4 at later OC, which have clear evidence of an obligation (which might have had a word and sign associated).

Review of the ritual in 1620

We are getting close to the time where the next Chapter will cover the likely emergence of Speculative Freemasonry. Certainly, in 1620, we have little evidence of Masons and their ceremonies (if more than one), other than what can be gleaned from the OC. We think it might have gone like this:
  • The candidate is brought in, probably blindfolded, is probably roughed up a bit, and terrified
  • A prayer is then read
  • The legendary history part of the OC is read out (sometimes?)
  • The candidate and an elder put their hands on the VSL and the articles from the OC are read
  • The candidate makes an obligation
  • The secrets are given.
Between say 1620 and the end of the century, our suggested scheme above eventually developed into fairly clear ceremonies for Apprentice and Fellowcraft/Master, but there is no evidence of more than this yet.

The next Chapter traces the development of the Degrees throughout a century of major change in England.

4
Craft history 1620-1716

Non-operatives

This is a difficult Chapter and contains the probable origins of the Speculative Masonry we practice today.We can only scratch the surface in one Chapter – it needs a whole book.

It will be hard work for you, but I strongly recommend that whatever other reading you do, you should try to become familiar with the works of three outstanding Masonic scholars:

AQC 91: 77-100 *The Birth of Free-Masonry* — Eric Ward

AQC 95:120-169 *Some thoughts on the origins of Speculative Masonry* — Colin Dyer

AQC 96:170-183 *The Origin of the Craft* — Andrew Durr.

We had lodges consisting of original operative lodges and those of non-operatives, who had been brought into lodges partly because of the influence that they could bring to bear and also to enhance the authority of the lodge. From quite early in the century, we believe that upper-class non-operatives were being accepted or adopted as masons and in token of their supposed 'superiority', they would come in as an EA and be immediately passed up to FC.

We will see shortly that the earliest documented Initiation of a non-operative was of Elias Ashmole in 1646. There is a Scottish Minute record of the entry of a non-mason in 1600 and another in 1634 when John Boswell, Laird of Auchinleck, entered the Lodge at Edinburgh.

We can't be sure when, but before very long, certainly before the end of the 17th century, there would probably have been lodges **with no operative members at all**. Again, there is no strongly persuasive evidence as to whether Speculative Masonry evolved smoothly and logically from purely Operative Masonry via Non-operative Masonry, or whether it was born independently of the building trade. This Chapter tries to show how an age of 'thinking' might have helped either the creation or the spread of Speculative Masonry.

'Esoteric' subjects

We continue this Chapter, after the terrible 16th century with all its religious strife, with the period 1620 to 1716, with equally terrible events. It is generally agreed however that this may well have been one of the most important centuries in our history. There are several buzzwords that can be seen to define the period – 'the Scientific Revolution', 'the Age of Enlightenment', 'the London Company', 'Elias Ashmole', 'The Royal Society' and the 'Premier Grand Lodge', with the *Edinburgh Register House MS 1696* being an important document. We examine this, one of the most important periods in the development of the Craft and its ritual, when many major changes occurred.

Before looking at the significance of the buzzwords, we should spend just a little time dealing with what are often referred to as 'esoteric' subjects with a brief mention of 'Hermeticism', the 'Kabbala' and 'Rosicrucianism'. They deserve mention not because there is much evidence to suggest that they had anything to do with Freemasonry or its development but because they are esoteric, meaning 'restricted to the few', Many have been attracted to them because of their mysterious (or mystical) flavour and have used them to try and support weird and wonderful inner meanings and inner significances within the Craft. This seems especially so in relation to explanations of Masonic symbols, often referring them back into the distant mists of time.

Hermeticism

This comes from Hermes Trismegistus (Thrice-Great Hermes), the Greek name for Thoth, the Egyptian god who allegedly invented writing and was regarded as a scribe, teacher and god of magic. Its philosophical tradition was that of the importance of inner enlightenment or 'gnosis' (self-knowledge), rather than that of pure rationalism or doctrinal faith. Until relatively recently Christianity, as the major western faith, had tended to be 'faith-oriented', with great reliance placed on the Bible and other holy writings within the interpretation and teachings of the Church.

Greek philosophy was said to be 'rational' with greater emphasis on 'thinking out things' rather than accepting common doctrine, and hermetic thinking was an approach that was not comfortable with pure rationality or pure 'faith'.

Although not entirely related, a slightly different approach started to appear and was particularly important in the 13th to 14th centuries. It is called 'Gnosticism' and, something like hermetic thought, approaches oneness with God by inner contemplation. There have been numerous suggestions that Hermeticism was, in effect, re-born in the Age of Enlightenment.

Kabbala

The Kabbala was a Jewish tradition, later taken up by Christian philosophers. It attempts to determine (explain?) the relationship between the eternal, everlasting God and the material and finite universe created by Him. It offers the means of obtaining spiritual development by understanding this relationship, defining the universe, man and the nature and purpose of existence.

Fundamentalist Jewish scholars use the teachings to look for the inner meaning of both the Hebrew Bible and traditional Rabbinic literature, together with associated Jewish religious observances.

Emphasis is placed on evaluating the perceived hidden biblical meanings, especially in Genesis and Ezekial. (The Kabbala is the basis for Jewish movements such as the Lubovichi and Hasidics.)

Some obscure aspects of the Kabbala relate to 'gematria', covering the mystical significance of numbers. (It is not too difficult to try and link this, if you wish, to Masonic 3,5,7 etc.!)

Rosicrucianism

A certain fictional Christian Rosenkreutz goes from Germany to the Middle East and starts to develop his philosophies. He returns to Germany and sets up a small society around 'the Temple of the Holy Ghost'. His aims seem to have been to further the quests of alchemy, such as finding 'the philosopher's stone' - to turn base metals into gold - and the 'elixir of life' (eternal life and health).

Some Rosicrucian thinking has links to the Kabbala and the Masonic order *Societas Rosicruciana in Anglia*.

Science

Francis Bacon developed and popularised what we now know as 'the scientific method'. It relies on observing phenomena, collecting data and then trying to determine a mechanism or theory behind the phenomenon. This is in contrast to the traditional approach, which, in many cases, used so-called 'logic' and theological thinking (such as the literal interpretation of the words of the Bible), in which any argument against could be considered as heresy - many of the early scientists suffered at the hands of the Inquisition. One of Bacon's well-known quotations was:

The corruption of philosophy by the mixing of it up with superstition and theology, is of a much wider extent, and is most injurious to it both as a whole and in parts.

Astronomy had as its model the early Greek scheme, where the earth was the centre of universe, with the sun and the planets revolving round it. Copernicus in 1514, published his idea of the sun being at the centre, and this work was extended by him and other famous astronomers of the time (Tycho Brahe, his assistant Johannes Kepler, Galileo Galilei and Isaac Newton); and with Newton's major developments in the design of the telescope, the universe came into view.

Until the end of the 16th century, medicine was largely a mixture of luck, with diagnosis and treatment having little or no structured knowledge behind them. Interesting that Leonardo da Vinci, around 1500, secretly dissected human corpses (at the express risk of excommunication), in order to determine the internal structure of the body – probably one of the few westerners of the time to do so.

Science was nearly all black magic, spells and alchemy - attempts to find the 'philosopher's stone' and the 'elixir of life'.

A certain William Harvey in 1599 enrolled at Padua University to study medicine and anatomy (at this time Galileo was there teaching sciences). Harvey was a very skilled surgeon, practising from 1590-1657 and in 1628, after pioneering work in dissection, published his *Anatomical Studies on the Motion of the Heart and Blood in Animals*, which as one of the most important of medical treatises so far, clearly identified the flow of blood to and from the heart.

As thinking developed, it widened, so that bodies started to be set up to look at science in a more rational way and develop it in astronomy, biology, mathematics and physics. Many of the prominent scientific thinkers, such as Hooke, the well-known physicist (Hooke's Law – 'the extension is proportional to the tension') were also deeply religious and their scientific and religious ideas helped to establish new ideas about the universe and the laws of nature.

The Age of Enlightenment

From about 1620 onwards, we know there had been an expansion in the number of lodges and we are also pretty sure that lodges were admitting non-masons. A number of OC manuscripts had been written and were in the hands of many lodges. But we still have no idea of ritual or ceremonies other than what we can deduce from them.

The Speculative Mason probably arose in this period, many feel, as a response to the philosophies deriving from the 'Age of Enlightenment'. We have seen that the first 200 to 300 years of operative masonry contained military, civil and religious strife. Events around the two King Charles, the Civil War, the Great Fire, etc., were to make the next 100 years just a little bit stressful too.

Nevertheless, from ideas developing about religion, the gradual trend to international trade, internationalisation, greater contact between different cultures and thinkers and a slightly less difficult world to live in, people started to think in liberal terms. This showed up as a desire for freedom of speech and discussion, free trade and general democracy, including the desire to finish with the 'divine right of kings' – not being subject to the will of the people or the Church (or anyone else for that matter!).

Apart from during the Civil War, free discussion seems to have been the most important aspect of the Age. People exchanged ideas in the smart salons of the cities as well as in taverns. Coffee houses, from about 1650, started to become common and were an ideal place for people of different social classes to meet, swop theories and (to an extent) educate each other, especially with ideas on nature, religion, politics, literature and the arts.

Yet another source of free thinking were the debating societies that evolved. Some were for specific audiences, such as doctors, scientists and actors. Others were much more open and gave audiences a chance to hear many views on many subjects by many people (open-ness to the masses?).

It was also the time of clubs, where gentlemen could relax away from the woes of life and perhaps extend their knowledge of matters that piqued their imagination, especially relating to older mythologies and philosophies. It seems likely that this very atmosphere had something to do with the way 'speculative' lodges were bubbling up.

The Age probably extended into the 18th century, the very time when Masonry changed completely from a basic trade-oriented, semi-organised body into a thinking and largely tradesman-free body that eventually started to show some organisation. Another factor from the Age that must have profoundly affected Masonry was the Royal Society (coming up next).

The Age did have some opposing views - it allowed promiscuous association among people from different rungs of the social ladder, from the artisan to the aristocrat, and was therefore compared to Noah's Ark, receiving all types of animals, **clean or unclean**.

Knoop and Jones in *Genesis of Freemasonry* (QCC, 1947) said:

the meetings of the lodge provided a convenient opportunity for that compound of refreshment, smoking and conversation, in circumstances of ease rather than elegance, and undisturbed by the society of women, in which many men can take a rational pleasure.

Royal Society

The Royal Society had its beginnings around 1645. A group of mathematicians, philosophers, scientists and others started to meet with the theme of the scientific method (see above), using experimental evidence to draw conclusions. Meetings were originally in London, but later were held in Oxford too. One of the early members, John Wallis, gave the following description:

> About the year 1645, while I lived in London (at a time when, by our civil wars, academical studies were much interrupted in both our Universities), ... I had the opportunity of being acquainted with divers worthy persons, inquisitive natural philosophy, and other parts of human learning; and particularly of what hath been called the New Philosophy or Experimental Philosophy. We did by agreements, divers of us, meet weekly in London on a certain day and hour, under a certain penalty, and a weekly contribution for the charge of experiments, with certain rules agreed amongst us, to treat and discourse of such affairs.

The first members included men such as mathematicians Robert Moray, John Wilkins and John Wallis, the chemist and physicist Robert Boyle and the architect Christopher Wren. The Society quickly gained a reputation for the genuine search after knowledge and members were responsible for the publication of many scientific and mathematical papers in what became *The Philosophical Transactions* of the Society.

The Society had to keep a low profile during the Civil War but with the restoration of the Monarchy in 1660, it resumed activity and members decided to form themselves into a 'Society of Philosophers'. The first meeting of the original twelve men agreed to invite forty further members, most of whom joined as fellows, including statesmen, soldiers, antiquarians, administrators, and writers. The meeting also agreed to seek a more formal structure and within two years obtained a Royal Charter from Charles II and became the *Royal Society*. The number of fellows rose to 150 by 1663 and over 200 by 1675.

The London Company

We introduced the guilds in Chapter 3. We know that a Masons' Company of London existed in 1375 (and probably earlier) and later received a coat of arms in 1472. The company regulated the mason trade in and around London. In 1621 the accounts of the London Company of Masons show the admission of 'operative masons', and then later of some men described as 'made masons.' The few records available don't suggest this was something new and it could have been going on for years.

As time went on, the Company became more sophisticated and perhaps less directed to the support of working masons, bringing in people with no connection with the trade at all. The Company records can only be traced back to about 1670, but there is clear evidence that going back to 1620 and underneath its 'official' operation, there was what can only be called a speculative **lodge** at a 'secret' level. In its original spelling, it was called the 'Accepcon' (acception!) and it brought in its initiates as 'Accepted Masons'.

Non-operatives probably became increasingly attracted to the Company because it offered an extra or alternative way to meet like-minded people. Also, the 'strange' legends, with all their antiquity, might have appealed to the more speculative thinkers.

Pause for thought

At the time, the word 'speculative' was increasingly being used to mean rather more than 'non-operative' and once accepted, the 'mason' could then apply for membership of the Company.

In our Working Tools we say '… but rather free and accepted or speculative…'.

We discussed the derivation of 'free' in Chapter 3. Perhaps now you can see where the rest came from – a Mason was 'accepted' because he showed some inclination towards the 'speculative', ie. he was perhaps a 'child' of the Age of Enlightenment.

There were two routes into the Company, either by having carried out good works such as in charity, or in being 'accepted' by other members (old school tie?). The first was the 'traditional' way, either by 'good works' or by election. The other seems to have been used as an unusual way for Company membership. (We have no record of when the 'Accepcon' was dropped.)

Eventually (about 1680), the Company had lost all ability to control the building trade. By 1682, it was a lodge only and had no further regulatory functions.

Four important names

Elias Ashmole

It was once thought that the first record of the entry of a Speculative Mason in England was that of the Scottish General Moray in Newcastle in 1641 into a Scottish lodge. But we have already seen that the London Company was 'making Masons' perhaps 20 years earlier, even if we don't know if such ceremonies were regular in the Masonic sense of the time (if there actually was one!). We also referred to earlier entries in the Lodge of Edinburgh.

We have good reason to believe that Elias Ashmole, initiated in October 1646, was probably the first Initiate whose entry is documented. His diary says:

> I was made a **Free Mason** at Warrington in Lancashire with Col, Henry Mainwaring….. Mr. Richard Penket Warden, Mr. James Collier,…

Some of the other names mentioned are said by *BJ1* and *PK1* to have been 'gentlemen' – according to etiquette at the time, 'Mr' implied gentleman of some kind, while omitting it implied tradesman, merchant or some other 'non-gentle person' - Mr Jones the lawyer, but Bill Smith the carpenter! Then in March 1682, Ashmole went to another lodge meeting and *BJ1* says quite definitely that some of the names mentioned in his diary are those of the London Masons Company. It does however seem very unlikely that Warrington was the only place where non-operatives met (Messrs Plot, Holme and Aubrey would surely have recognised this from their observation of what Masons did!).

Robert Plot

The writer of *A Natural History of Staffordshire* of 1686, a curious but very significant piece of writing. Plot was an assistant of Ashmole and his book, written about 40 years after Ashmole's Initiation, contains a section with his comments and views on Masonry. He starts with a resumé of the 'traditional history' and explains some of the activities. He then goes on to blast off at the history and the Craft. Nevertheless, the book, if his observations are correct, goes a long way to filling a hole in our knowledge about 17th century Masons:

> To these add the *Customs* relating to the *County*, whereof they have one, of admitting Men into the *Society* of *Freemasons*, that in the moorelands of this *County* seems to be of greater request, than any

where else, though I find the *Custom* spread more or less, all over the *Nation*; for here I found persons of the most eminent quality, that did not disdain to be of this *Fellowship*.

Nor indeed need they, were it of that *Antiquity* and *honor*, **that is pretended in a large *parchment volum* they have amongst them, containing the *History* and *Rules* of the craft of *masonry*.** Which is there deduced not only from *sacred writ*, but *profane story*, particularly that it was brought into *England* by *St. Amphibal* ... Whereupon he caused them to assemble at *York*, and to bring all the old *Books* of their *craft*, and out of them ordained such *charges* and *manners*, as they then thought fit: which *charges* in the said *Schrole* or *Parchment volum*, are in part declared: and thus was the *craft* of *masonry* grounded and confirmed in *England*. It is also there declared that these *charges* and *manners* were after perused and approved by King *Hen.* 6. and his *council*, both as to *Masters* and *Fellows* of this right Worshipfull *craft*.

Into which *Society* when any are admitted, they call a *meeting* (or *Lodg* as they term it in some places) which must consist at lest of 5 or 6 of the *Ancients* of the *Order*, whom the *candidats* present with *gloves*, and so likewise to their *wives*, and entertain with a *collation* according to the Custom of the place:

This ended, they proceed to the *admission* of them, which cheifly consists in **the communication of certain *secret signes*, whereby they are known to one another all over the *Nation*,** by which means they have maintenance whither ever they travel: for if any man appear though altogether unknown that can shew any of these *signes* to a *Fellow* of the *Society*, whom they otherwise call an *accepted mason*, he is obliged presently to come to him, from what company or place soever he be in, nay tho' from the top of a *Steeple*, (what hazard or inconvenience soever he run) to know his pleasure, and assist him; *viz.*, if he want *work* he is bound to find him some; or if he cannot doe that, to give him *mony*, or otherwise support him till *work* can be had.

Randle Holme

His main work was an encyclopaedic account of heraldry but he also classified plants, diseases, tools for many trades, astronomy, geography, etc. it was called the *Academie of Armory* (see Chapter 1), printed in 1688 and containing the following selection:

… A Fraternity, or Society, or Brotherhood, or Company; are such in a corporation, that are of one and the same trade, or occupation, who being joyned together by oath and covenant, do follow such orders and rules, as are made, or to be made for the good order, rule, and support of such and every of their occupations. These several Fraternities are generally governed by one or two Masters, and two Wardens, but most companies with us by two Aldermen and two Stewards, the latter being to pay and receive what concerned them.

Later, he says:

I cannot but Honor the Fellowship of the Masons because of its Antiquity; and the more, as being a Member of that Society called Free-Masons. In being conversant amongst them I have observed the use of these several tools …

Three of the many tools he describes in the work are as follows:

In this Square are three Free Masons tools very usefull in there trade.

The first is a *Shovel*: It hath a square bottom, and sole; else it is in all other parts like the Spade. With this their Mortar is tempered, and foundations for Walls are digged.

The second is the *Hand Hammer*, which is both long and strong in the head, with an Iron hoop on the end of the handle to keep it from bruising or wearing, because the end is very oft used by them, as well as the hammer part. This may be well termed a Masons Hammer, because there is no other tradsmans like it, haveing the face long, and the hinder part flat and broad to the Halve side.

The third is the *Chissel*, now this is a Chissel Contrary to all others used in joynery or Carpentry; for this is all Iron strong and thick, the edge not very sharp but well made, and of good temperned Steel. Of these they have severall sorts, big and little, according as the nature of the work requireth.

And many others.

Pause for thought

Are they in any way precursors of our Working Tools?

Incidentally, the description of the hammer sounds more like a gavel that a hammer. In an article published in *The Square* in 2016, I explain why the gavel has no proper place in current Craft working, the heavy maul being far more important. Holme doesn't mention the maul!

John Aubrey

Just one more quote, similar to Plot and Holme, taken from *The Natural History of Wiltshire* by John Aubrey, published in 1686:

> ... The Fraternity of Free-Masons (Adopted-Masons). They are known to any other by certayn Signes & Markes and Watch-words: it continues to this day. They have Severall Lodges in severall Counties for their reception: and when any of them fall into decay, the brotherhood is to relieve him, &c. The manner of their Adoption is very formall and with an Oath of Secrecy...

The writings of Plot, Holme and Aubrey seem unanimous in describing the spread of Masonry and the importance of signs and other items of recognition. They also all use the term lodge, apparently as a meeting place.

Fire and plague

Two dreadful disasters that had an effect on building and the building trade. The Bubonic Plague again struck London in mid-1665 and by the time it had passed, nearly 25% of the population of London had died. Many people fled the city to try and escape infection. Other cities suffered, especially York.

In conjunction with the effects of the Great Fire, there would be a need for accommodation, churches, etc., away from the traditional centres of population – a move towards decentralisation.

The Great Fire of London started in September 1666. It destroyed the old City of London and burnt many thousands of houses. There are estimates of over 90% of Londoners being made homeless. Other losses included St Paul's Cathedral, many churches and numerous official buildings.

The king (Charles II) was concerned about riots and destabilisation by those whose homes had gone, and set up measures to encourage them to leave the capital and re-settle elsewhere.

The overall effect of the two disasters is fairly obvious to see. It resulted in a desperate shortage of buildings, so a vast amount of stone rebuilding was required; too much by far for the local masons to undertake and masons from anywhere were encouraged to come in with seven years of freedom (and maybe longer). It was said that anyone who could use a tool (trowel, axe, shovel or whatever), could find work somewhere; and in what became a new epidemic of building and the consequent deregulation (you are likely to cut every corner you can when there are massive profits to be made), the

Masons' Company was hit heavily and lost its influence not long after and hence lost admission fees. In order to survive a bit longer, it introduced a kind of subscription, which it called a 'quarterage', collected quarterly from members

Pause for thought

Illustrations of Masonry by William Preston (1772) actually lists the names of about 50 churches that were re-built by 1697.

Two degrees?

Before continuing with further documents, we should review the situation as to Operative-to-Speculative. This is all very frustrating – we still have no real evidence for two degrees until about 1696. The *Grand Lodge No. 1 MS 1632* shows charges for masters and fellows and then, charges for masons. It is believed that there was just an initiation ceremony for the entered apprentice and the 'promotion' to fellow (and master if you had enough money to go it alone). The ceremonies were probably not much more than an opening prayer with a recital of some or all of the OC; then the obligation or oath and maybe the transfer of 'signs, tokens and words'.

We know from OCs of the 16th and early 17th centuries that there were charges to be obeyed, both related to trade and to moral and religious behaviour, but until we look below at the *Edinburgh Register House MS 1696,* we have no information about ritual or ceremonial. What follows are several more quotes, in 'bad' English! You need to see them, at least in part, because they contain a lot of history and some ritual or ceremonial.

The *Harleian MS 1670* has the following:

No person (of what degree soever) bee accepted a free Mason, unless he shall have a lodge of five free Masons; at least, whereof one to bee a master, or warden, of that limit or division, wherein such Lodge shalbee kept **& another of the trade of Free Masonry**

In other words, we see **absolutely certainly** that 'non-working masons' were present in lodges. (There is a record of an operative lodge, at Aberdeen in 1670, where of the forty-nine members registered, only a quarter were operatives, the Master being a Collector of the King's Customs.)

Incidentally, the *Harleian* contains a charge which starts with:

I, in the presence of Almighty God, & my Fellowes, and Brethren, here present, promise, and declare, that I will not at any time hereafter, by any Act or circumstance whatsoever, Directly or Indirectly, publish, discover, reveale or make knowne any of the

secrets, privileges, or Counsells, of the Fraternity or fellowship of
Free Masonry, which at this time, or any time thereafter, shall be
made known to me, soe helpe mee God & the holy contents of this
book.

If you relate this to our present First Degree oath, you will see that there
are small glimpses of things that will eventually happen.

Harry Carr in *HC1* says that there was an extra document found with
the *Harleian*, with the following (in modern English):

There are **several words and signs** of a free Mason to be revealed
you which you will answer before God at the Great and terrible day
of judgement …

This seems to indicate that there was more than one word/sign in use and a
hint of more than one degree?

The 'modern' manuscripts

Edinburgh Register House MS.

We now look at this, which has been said to date from 1696, the first OC
which really indicates that some ceremonial eventually does get
documented. The document was found in 1930 in the historical department
of the Old Register House, Edinburgh. It is thought that it faithfully
represents Scottish practice. Later manuscripts of English origin do vary
but seem to have much similarity with this one, so we can assume that it
must represent something close to what was being done in England.

It starts with 'some questions that masons use to put to those who have
the word before they will acknowledge them'. (In Scotland, possession of
the 'mason word' was the alleged sign of being a mason.) The first questions
are similar to those of earlier manuscripts, but after question 15, it says:

After the Masons have examined you by all or some of these
questions and that you have answered them exactly and made the
signes, they will acknowledge you, but **not a master mason or
fellow craft but only as an apprentice**, soe they will say I see you
have been in the Kitchene but I know not if you have been in the
hall.

The answer is:

I have been in the hall as well as in the kitchene.

There then follow **two more questions**:

Are you a fellow Craft?

Ans. yes!

How many points of fellowship are there?

Ans. five viz foot to foot Knee to Knee, Heart to Heart, Hand to Hand and ear to ear.

Then make the sign of fellowship and shake hand and you will be acknowledged a true mason.

This last answer ends with biblical references to the two pillar words.

Pause for thought

This surely indicates two degrees must have been in existence, otherwise why have two ceremonies? Note also that the FPOF are becoming more recognisable.

Something for you to think about. Was the sign of fellowship the sign of a **fellow of the craft** or the sign of a **friend,** ie. a sign of **friendship**, rather than that of a masonic 'rank'?

After the questions comes 'the forme of giving the mason word'. This is just some of it:

… You are to take the person to take the word upon his knees and after a great many ceremonies to frighten him you make him take up the bible and laying his right hand on it you are to conjure him, to secrecie …

… After he hes taken that oath he is removed out of the company, with the youngest mason where after he is sufficiently frighted with 1,000 ridiculous postures and grimmaces.

… when he enters again into the company he must make a ridiculous bow, then the signe and say God bless the honourable company …

…. under no less a pain than having my tongue cut out … of being buried within the flood mark …

Then this is part of what follows for the fellowcraft/master:

Now it is to be remarked that all the signes and words as yet spoken of are only what belong **to the entered apprentice.** But to be a master mason or fellow craft there is **more to be done** which after follows.

First all the prentices are to be removed out of the company and none suffered to stay but Masters. Then he who is to be admitted and member of the Fellowship is put again to his knees and gets the oath administered to him of new …

He makes the master's sign and says the same words of entry as the apprentice did leaving out The Common Judge …

Then the master gives him the word and grips his hand after the Masons way **which is all that is to be done to make him a perfect Mason.**

(The reference to the common judge is obscure. Some think it was a template to ease the cutting of stones.)

Now it is very clear that there are two levels of membership (even if not exactly what we now mean by two Degrees). The signs are not that different from ours, so will not be explained, but apart from going out, being frightened and informed about some secrets, we don't really have much information about what happened in the two ceremonies.

The actual format of the ceremony (ceremonies!) is not clear as to the questions. Were they gone through at the end of the ceremony (after he has been given the secrets)? Did they start the ceremony before the candidate was brought in (something like an Opening)?

It seems likely that an entered apprentice taking initiation or a fellow taking a higher oath would presumably have proved themselves at some level professionally qualified, so there possibly would have been more than just an oath and the giving of words and signs - in other words, a sort of inner working to the ceremony (a pure guess on my part!).

The Sloane MS 3329

This is the next significant manuscript, traced to about 1700. It is similar to the earlier manuscripts but there are more questions in the catechism. Some relate to the actual form of the lodge, mentioning the square pavement and the ashlars.

The next few questions are new and start to become both Christian and Speculative (?):

(Q) Where was the word first given

(A) at the Tower of Babylon

(Q) where did they first call their lodge

(A) at the holy Chapell of St. John

(Q) how stood your lodge

(A) as the said holy Chappell and all other holy Temples stand viz east and west.

Finally, the manuscript gives a terrible description of the FPOF, but also makes reference to the two halves of a word – 'M…' and 'B…'.

The Dumfries No. 4

Dated about 1710, this goes back to a very long and extended traditional history. There then follows a 'charge' consisting of 19 points (including 'mental reservation or Equivocation' and then a further discourse:

> Firstly you shall serve the true god and carefully keep his precepts in generall particularlie the Ten words delivered to Moses on mount Sinai As you have them explained in full on ye pavement of the Temple secondly you shall be true & stedfast to ye holy catholick church and shun all herise and shisim or eror to your wnderstanding thirdly you shall be true to the lawfull King of the Realm …

There then follows a review of the trade charges present in 16th and early 17th century manuscripts and an apprentice charge which doesn't have much new in it. It then becomes more biblical. We are given a much expanded catechism:

> (Q) How many steps in Jacobs ladder
> (A) 3
> (Q) what was they
> (A) father son and holy spirit
> …(Q) what meant ye golden dore of ye temple where they went in to sanctum sanctorum
> (A) it was another type of Christ who is ye door ye way and the truth and ye life by whome & in whom all ye entreth into heaven.

Next comes a set of 13 questions, mainly about the temple (tabernacle!) and its contents. Finally, some more history, again bringing in the pillar words, but this time using 'strength' and 'establish'.

This is a Scottish manuscript, but there is no reason to assume that English lodges were in any way less Christian than this seems to indicate. We will see later that the ritual was generally Christian until after the formation of the Premier Grand Lodge.

The Haughfoot 'fragment'

Masonic history tells us that someone found an old Minute Book of the former Haughfoot Lodge (in Scotland), in which almost all of the pages had been ripped out, presumably for secrecy reasons. But a little portion was left at the top of the next page containing the following:

> … of entrie as the apprentice did Leaving out (The Common Judge). Then they whisper the word as before - and the Master Mason grips his hand after the ordinary way.

If you refer back to the Edinburgh Register House MS above, you can see that it is very similar to the 'master's part'. Masonic scholars agree that the fragment unquestionably verifies this and hence, other OCs.

The Trinity College Dublin MS 1711

A very short piece of work, consisting of 11 questions and a discourse on the full signs and words of all three degrees, with explanations. The fourth question and answer are:

Q. What makes a full & perfect lodge? A. three masters, 3 fellow Craftsmen, & 3 enterprentices.

It concludes with detailed descriptions of the EA/FC/MM signs and words, with explanations and the worst possible explanation of the FPOF.

We need to anticipate and look at two more documents. As they come after 1716, they should be in the next Chapter but they follow logically here. Then we can review the situation!

A Mason's examination 1723

This was part of a letter published in a newspaper at the time. It consists of a lot of rubbish, but after the 'M' word is communicated to the youngest master, he apparently says:

An **enter'd Mason** I have been,

B... and **J**... I have seen;

A **Fellow** I was sworn most rare,

And know the Astler, Diamond and Square;

I know the **Master's** part full well,

As honest **M...** will you tell.

The astler, etc. are what we assume were the Working Tools of the three grades. One little point to confuse things – the answer to how many points of fellowship is:

Six; Foot to Foot, Knee to Knee, Hand to Hand, Ear to Ear, Tongue to Tongue, Heart to Heart!

We now have a very clear signal that there are three Degrees although we still don't have details.

The Graham MS 1726

This starts with a long set of questions and then leads into another traditional history, with elements not present in earlier manuscripts. It would seem to be the basis of our Raising ceremony. It concerns the sons of Noah, the 'famous preacher', who were examining his corpse to discover any of his secrets (we don't know what they actually expected!). Finding a largely consumed corpse, after a finger-hold **slipped away**, they reared up the body 'ffoot to ffoot knee to knee Breast to breast Cheeck to cheeck and hand to back'.

Then one said:

Here is yet marrow in the bone.

Another said:

It stinketh.

They then apparently:

Agreed for to give 'it' a 'name' as it is known to free masonry to this day.

Unfortunately, we don't know what 'it' actually is, nor the 'name' it was given.

One other small point, which might have major significance. Further on, there is a reference to Bazalliel and the holding of certain secrets:

The sons of king Alboyne came to him to discover the secrets.

Bazalliel agreed:

conditionally they were not to discover it without another to themselves, **to make a trible voice.**

It is outside the brief of this book to look at Royal Arch ritual, but historians suggest that some of the ritual may have come from earlier Craft Second and Third Degree material and this example could be just a small pointer.

Organisation (if any!)

Now, let us look at the 'day-to-day' running of lodges. It seems likely that:

- There have been masons since medieval times, who originally started as groups of uneducated building workers, employed largely on ecclesiastical buildings.
- They shared customs, regulations, possibly ceremonies, and a legendary history, with one mason as the master.
- As the building industry matured and the construction of large buildings developed, the master mason in effect emerged as the chief architect and probably in control of all the building materials and supplies. Because of his job as master builder he would, of necessity, be in possession of certain builders' secrets, and man being man, claimed the secrets had descended from time immemorial with only the privileged few having access.
- After the Dissolution of the Monasteries and the Reformation the building of large churches and cathedrals started to decrease.

Masons would probably have had to find other craft guilds to join, while trying to maintain the traditions of their old masonic lodges.

- As time went on, in order to keep the lodges viable, they needed to swell their numbers (and fee income) by bringing in people who were not stonemasons. Eventually, the non-operative masons far outweighed the operatives.

- For whatever reason, educated gentleman were attracted to lodges, and seeing the presumably relatively basic nature of the ritual and the associated ceremonial, started to campaign for changes and extensions. By the formation of the Premier Grand Lodge, they had formalised the 'two-degree' system and three degrees could not have been far away.

There had always been some measure of organisation or at least a central source of 'experience' in Scotland. In England, widespread use of some of the later OCs, if not showing organisation, at least points to some degree of conformity. We have little else to show the existence of a country-wide-masonic body but -

Sooner or later, a central 'authority' was likely to evolve?

5
Craft history 1717-1730

Premier Grand lodge starts to bubble up

Three eminent bits of reading for more details of the coverage of this Chapter:

Prestonian Lecture 1926 *The Evolution of the Second Degree* — Lionel Vibert

Prestonian Lecture 1925 *The Development of the Trigradal System* — Lionel Vibert

AQC 112: 91-107 *The Early Years of the Premier Grand Lodge, 1717-1740: a Re-Appraisal* — Geoffrey Markham

I make no apologies for suggesting this extra reading. These two writers are highly respected and reading some of their work will certainly expand your knowledge.

We now come to what is probably the most important era in the life of our Craft. We see the formation of the Premier Grand Lodge of England (we will abbreviatethis to **PrGL** to avoid confusion with **PGL** for Provincial Grand lodge. We see the production of sets of the regulations which governed the Craft and which are reflected in our present Regulations. We see how the Third Degree firmed up and the proof of a three-degree system. We examine some of the later manuscripts and, in particular, look at what could be **the most important Masonic publication of all time**.

We are at the beginning of the period following the dreadful 17th century and its Civil War. We know that after the War, with the need to re-establish the throne and the stability that hopefully would come with it, surely many Masons were hoping their Masonry might offer a means of conviviality and 'clubiness' but at the same time, to give (and receive) charity and to discuss and reflect on philosophical, moral and social issues.

We have had the passage of some 60 years of the Age of Enlightenment to smooth things out, soften attitudes and generally give a background for discussion. Lodge meetings were still fairly basic. It is thought that the actual meeting on a prepared floor consisted of little more than the reading of the OCs (or part of them) and the giving of signs, tokens, words, etc., perhaps with some explanation. The Catechisms were probably treated like lectures, being read at the dinner table (it was to be a while before the lodge ceremonies and the festive board were finally separated and the ceremony no longer done round the dining table).

Many lodges met in inns, especially those containing a high proportion of non-operatives, mainly working men, and it was an important part of the lodge's business to maintain the charity 'box' for death benefit or the relief of distress and illness. This would be funded by small payments by brethren (something like an insurance policy) but hopefully this would be boosted by the 'gentry' brethren!

We ended Chapter 4 with a note about the organisation of the Craft and the fact that sooner or later a central authority was likely to evolve. It could well have been much later rather than sooner - records indicate that by the early part of the century in London there were probably only four lodges actually in established existence, in spite of steps taken to expand the membership of lodges. (**This does not tie in with vague theories that non-operative Masonry was wide-spread and met in general assembly, as per the OC.**)

Pause for thought

Around 1703, the Lodge of St Paul (whose operative masons used to meet in the grounds of the cathedral), to try to increase numbers and enhance the credibility of the Craft, agreed to continue the existence of 'so praiseworthy an institution to be used as the conservator of religion and tradition and perpetuate by the beautiful allegories of its legends and symbols, its eminently humanitarian doctrines'. Therefore they passed the following resolution:

That the privileges of Masonry shall no longer be confined to operative masons, but be free to men of all professions, provided that they are regularly approved and initiated into the fraternity.

Lodges generally were autonomous, each claiming to exist from time immemorial, setting rules for membership qualification, and holding allegiance, not to some higher masonic authority, but probably to certain 'agreed' ancient customs and the OCs, including the right to form new lodges.

With lodges meeting when they wanted to and with no real fraternisation with other lodges, even though their workings might have been similar and

Fig 5.1: Hogarth's 'Night' showing a drunken WM getting home somehow.

with signs and words being widely recognised and accepted, it is very unlikely that there really existed an overall masonic community as such.

These four London non-operative lodges possibility represented one of the lowest states that Masonry had reached and lodges probably were nothing much more than social and boozing organisations where the gentry could get together, do a bit of charity, do some 'leaping about' in ritual and generally behave not particularly reputably – outside the original aims of the accepted Masons that early traditions and the more 'sensible' ideas of the Age of Enlightenment would have fostered.

We can assume however that, with the traditions laid down in the OCs, there was always a perceived need (however little based on real evidence) for regular assemblies of masons. Presumably the London Masons finally decided that there might be a good case for setting up some kind of organisation with a 'grand' master at its head as a 'centre of unity and harmony'. This could perhaps update the Old Charges to make them more relevant to the day and, at the same time, produce rules and regulations that could organise their Craft, encourage a tidy expansion, and give themselves some power.

> Pause for thought
> Yet again we have to moan at the almost complete lack of documentation between (say) 1680 and 1723 as to the state of the Craft and the PrGL in its first years. One of the few sources of information is James Anderson, about whom we will hear very soon. He described the formation of PrGL in the second (1738) edition of the Book of Constitutions. Masonic historians have had reasons to doubt the accuracy of much of his words, although what he said must have to an extent been agreed by senior members of the new lodge.

Into existence

Whatever!

Anderson claims that the four lodges got together and a temporary Grand Lodge was formed in principle at the Apple Tree Tavern in 1716 or early 1717. We don't know what traditions and background these lodges really shared, nor do we know if any other lodges were invited to join in.

At this assembly, the Brethren then present, by a majority of hands, elected Mr Anthony Sayer ('Gentleman, the Master of St Paul's Lodge') to the office of **Grand Master of Masons**.

Then on St John the Baptist's Day (24th June) 1717, the assembly, feast and formal election were held at the Goose and Gridiron Ale-House (formerly the 'Swan and Lyre' – 'Goose and Gridiron' being its nick-name).

The Grand Lodge was styled as **The Premier Grand Lodge of England**, with jurisdiction over London and Westminster. (At the time, the actual area covered was probably not much more than a few square miles, similar to the area covered by the earlier London Company of Masons.)

Two Grand Wardens were appointed and St John's Day was reserved for the Annual Assembly and Feast in the future. The Grand Master introduced the idea of a meeting of all Grand Officers for quarterly communications and dates were specified (although they were never taken up!).

The four lodges involved met:
- at the Goose and Gridiron Ale-House, in St Paul's Churchyard
- at the Crown Ale-House, in Parker's Lane, near Drury Lane
- at the Apple-tree Tavern, in Charles Street, Covent Garden
- at the Rummer and Grapes Tavern, in Channel Row, Westminster

Grand Officers included George Payne, the second and fourth Grand Master, John Desaguliers, the third Grand Master, and several others who became Grand Masters, together with James Anderson. Presumably to give

Fig 5.2: One of several early prints of the Goose and Gridiron.

themselves status by claiming to conform to the old traditions, they agreed to:

- re-instate the Quarterly Communication of the officers of Lodges
- re-institute an Annual Assembly and Feast
- choose a Grand Master from among themselves (lay brethren) until they could convince a **noble brother** to do them the honour.

Pause for thought
The formation of the PrGL was not really a revolution. It was more a definition and cementing of old traditions according to ancient usage, tradition itself being the supreme authority (it's always been this way among Masons!).

Who was involved?

Many Masons have heard of Anderson and that he was the father of our Constitutions, but there is much evidence to show that although he was a very pushy gentleman with strong ideas, some of his comments might not be entirely accurate. In addition, there were others, perhaps more important, involved in the Constitutions.

George Payne

A previous Master of the 'Rummer and Grapes' lodge, Payne was a well-connected man, apparently thought to be very dynamic. His position with the tax office meant that he had many acquaintances in public life. One of the claims about him is that he was an early protagonist of the development of the Craft from the Operative to the Speculative and was particularly instrumental in convincing many operatives that Speculative Masonry was here to stay. He drafted the first set of Constitutions for the PrGL. He was Grand Master twice and remained an active member of Grand Lodge for nearly 40 years.

John Desaguliers

The Reverend John Theophilus Desaguliers was initiated into Freemasonry in the Goose and Gridiron lodge. He was a minister of the cloth, a respected scientist and naturalist, a friend of Isaac Newton and a member of the Royal Society. He published many papers on a wide range of physics, such as water motion, optics and mechanics.

He was installed as the third Grand Master on 24th June 1719, and during his year of office Anthony Sayer held the position of Senior Grand

Warden. At his Installation, he was said to have introduced the custom of drinking toasts (Masons of course didn't drink before that!). He held office as Deputy Grand Master in 1722, 1723 and 1725.

In 1721 Desaguliers made a visit to Scotland. He was well received and his visit is documented in *the history of the Lodge of Edinburgh* published in 1873. (It is quoted because it shows that Scottish and English Masonry of the time were obviously, to an extent, in line.) It says that:

… he was initiated in the Lodge of Antiquity in 1712 and his love of mechanics and the prominent part which science plays in Operative Masonry no doubt induced him to become a member of the Fraternity. He found that the spirit of toleration prevailing amongst members of the Fraternity was particularly grateful to one who had himself suffered from religious intolerance. This inspired him with the idea of reconstructing the society on a basis which should unite together in harmony those who were divided by religious and political schisms. In carrying out his plan he was materially aided by the high position he occupied in society and by the widespread acquaintance he enjoyed. Such was the distinguished person of whom it is recorded i**n the first of several minutes** that having sought a conference with the master Masons of Edinburgh **that body granted his request and received him as a brother into their Lodge.**

Part of one of these Minutes is very significant:

Att Maries Chapell the 24 of August 1721 years – James Wattson present deacon of the Masons of Edinr.,. Preses. The which day Doctor John Theophilus Desaguliers, fellow of the Royall Societie and the Chaplain … and finding him duly qualified in all points of Masonry, **they received him as a Brother into their Societe …**

The book also says that he was the prime mover in instituting the 'English Grand Lodge' and had been engaged with other learned brethren **in the production of a 'master's part' for the catechetical arrangement of its lectures!**.

We will see later that he may have had a lot to do with updating the ritual and his visit to Scotland may have been partly to determine which of the old material had been changed there and where Scottish work was going.

Pause for thought

W. Weisberger *AQC*: 113, 65-96 is an interesting paper on Desaguliers in which he shows how he was responsible for bringing scientists, free-thinkers and nobility into the new lodge. He also gives views on what changes Desaguliers may have made in the ritual towards Speculation.

Now, **a mad theory**. Between 1720 and 1730, the ritual changed from a two-degree system (with some hints of the future), to a full three-degree system. We will meet Samuel Prichard later in the Chapter.

With no evidence whatsoever to back it up, **is it possible that Prichard actually was Desaguliers?**

Shock! Horror!

James Anderson

Not very much is known about this Scottish minister. He received an MA and later a DD. He served in the Church in Scotland but then moved to England and eventually set up a Scottish chapel in London. His entry into the Craft is obscure. Some have said that it was in Scotland, as he seems to have been familiar with certain Scottish craft terms such as 'fellowcraft'. He is said to have been a member of the Rummer and Grapes lodge before the formation of the PrGL.

The 1723 Constitutions

Pause for thought

Note that the presence of operatives in lodges still, is shown by the PrGL selecting as Grand Wardens, among others, Jacob Lamball, a carpenter, in 1717; Joshua Timson, a blacksmith and John Cordwell, a city carpenter in 1718 and Thomas Morrice, a stone cutter in 1718.

As we have said, Anderson did not publish until 1723 and with no Minutes kept by the PrGL, we cannot really know what went on between 1717 and 1723, apart from what Anderson said in the later set published in 1738. It seems unlikely that more lodges joined the PrGL until at least 1721 and Andersons's statistics cannot be verified.

In the year 1721 the Duke of Montagu as Grand Master boosted the credibility and hence the popularity of the Craft and there was then a rash of constituting new lodges (fashionable members of the gentry would see it as a status symbol and clamour to join a lodge).

It was accepted by the PrGL that rules and regulations were needed, but it was not until 1723 that the formal set of Constitutions, produced by Anderson, was actually printed. There is a good chance that the PrGL was really not much more than a gathering of like-minded Masons who wanted to regularise some of their proceedings. It declared itself supreme and as Grand Master in 1718 Payne realised that it was essential to lay down some rules and regulations as to the governing of the Craft. It was clearly apparent to him that the operative system was too crude to serve the practical needs of a compact society of the kind he and his colleagues had in mind.

One of the first things the new Grand Lodge did was to seize control of the machinery for creating new lodges. It had decreed that no Masons might assemble as a lodge without Warrant from the Grand Lodge, although exception was made in case of the original 'Four Old Lodges', which were conceded to exist as of immemorial right.

Payne leapt into the production of the rules efficiently and produced a set of General Regulations, which he had offered at his Installation. He asked Brethren to bring in 'The Old Gothic Constitutions' and any other papers that might be of interest, including lodge Minutes and other records. It is not surprising that many papers were burnt, rather than let them fall into the hands of people who were 'destroying the Craft'. The set of general Regulations was approved by the members of the PrGL in 1721. (It has been said that Payne, with his Constitutions, was the father of Masonic jurisprudence and Desaguliers, perhaps fancifully, was the father of modern ritual.)

Payne soon realised that it would be necessary to have the Regulations printed and published for the Craft. Anderson grabbed the chance and took the opportunity to write a modified (updated?) History of the Craft as an introduction, and to prepare a set of Charges; his intention clearly being to give the new body a work which would in every respect replace the Old Manuscript Constitutions. The work consists of a dedication written by Desaguliers and addressed to Montagu as late Grand Master; a Historical introduction; a set of six Charges; Payne's Regulations almost unchanged; the manner of constituting a new lodge; and songs for the Master, Wardens, Fellow Craft and Entered Apprentice, of which the last is well known in this country and is still sung today in many lodges.

The Grand Masters for the first five years were:

Anthony Sayer	1717
George Payne	1718
John Desaguliers	1719
George Payne	1720
Lord Montagu	1721-1723

By 1723, after Anderson had done his work, the Regulations were made available and the office of Secretary created. The PrGL also started keeping records of all proceedings and a bureaucratic structure was starting to evolve. It soon passed a resolution that had dramatic effects:

It is not in the Power of any person, or Body of men, to make any Alteration, or Innovation in the Body of Masonry without the Consent first of the Annual Grand Lodge.

One of the big problems this caused was over the Royal Arch which was starting to appear. The PrGL insisted of course that there were only two Degrees, and when the precursors of the Antients started working Royal Arch ceremonies there was argument as to whether it was an extra Degree and if so that it breached the 'no alteration' dictat.

It would seem that maintenance of the bureaucracy was of major importance and this was probably a good reason for the dictat, but the Grand Lodge was curiously soft, for example, on the way Anderson seemed to ride rough-shod over other members. Similarly, as we will see later in this Chapter, the possibility of a third Degree was bubbling on the back-burner and PrGL must surely have known that something was going on. However, there is no record that they took any action over what was a fundamental 'alteration **and** innovation'

Payne's Regulations, of which there are 39 in number, are quite similar to our modern Book Constitutions. For example:

III. the *Master* of each particular *Lodge*, or one of the *Wardens* or some other Brother by his order, shall keep a Book containing their *By-laws*, the Names of their Members, with a List of all the *Lodges* in Town and the usual Times and Places of their forming and **all their Transactions that are proper to be written**.

V. No Man can be made or admitted and member of a particular *Lodge* without previous notice *one Month before* given to the said

Lodge in order to make due Enquiry into the Reputation and Capacity of the *Candidate* unless by a dispensation Grand Master or his deputy.

XI. All *Particular Lodges* are to observe the same *Usages* as much as possible; in order to which, and for cultivating a good Understanding among *Free-Masons*, some Members out of *every Lodge* shall be deputed **to visit the** *other Lodges* as often as shall be thought convenient.

The new PrGL had engaged Anderson (some say he forced it on them) to produce a set of Constitutions, based on Payne's, but including a large part of the history from the Old Charges. It is unlikely that Anderson could have rocked the boat very much. He was never a Grand Master and although it is accepted that he was quite forceful and dogmatic, the others were strong enough to prevent him doing too much on his own. (There is some doubt as to whether he was a member of one of the four lodges or present at the formation of the PrGL.) Nevertheless, as we have said, he did make changes to the history, 'sort of' bringing it up to date in covering the 18th century. It seems reasonable to say that Desaguliers got on board the intellectuals of the time, while Payne attracted the heavies - influential people who would 'add respectability to the ranks'.

Whoever was the greater force, together, their efforts in establishing the PrGL soon changed the Craft for ever. The chances are that while Payne was the prime producer of the Regulations, Desaguliers put **his** name to the dedication at the beginning and Anderson then put the whole lot together for publication in 1723. Somehow, in this first edition, Anderson managed to avoid saying **anything at all** about the actual formation of the PrGL or what had occurred since then!

Pause for thought
I apologise for the poor quality of the original copy of the 1723 Constitutions. I went to Norfolk Provincial Library and asked the librarian Allan Morrell if he had a book with pictures. To my astonishment, he climbed up a ladder and came down (from the heavens!) with an **original copy** of the Constitutions. I was almost afraid to touch the book. I took some photos, but the light being poor, they are not the best. However, I offer the pictures with pride and humility and and thanks to Norfolk.

Fig 5.3: The 1723 Anderson's *Constitutions*.

In the later version of his Constitutions (1738), he claims that Lord Montagu, the first noble Grand Master in 1721, told him to 'digest the Old Gothic Constitutions' in a new and better method and after approval by learned Brothers, it was released for distribution in the agreed 1723 version entitled:

> *The Constitutions and Charges of the Free-Masons. Containing the History, Charges, Regulations, &c of that most Ancient and Right Worshipful Fraternity ...*

After the dedication and the history, there follows a set of what Anderson calls 'general heads'. They are:

I. Of God and Religion. (**This one is quoted in full** because it, in effect, was the basis for de-Christianisation.)

*A Mason is obliged, by his Tenure, to obey the moral Law; and if he rightly understands the art, he will never be stupid atheist, nor an irreligious libertine. But though in ancient times Masons were charg'd every Country to be of the Religion of that Country or Nation, whatever it was yet 'tis now thought more expedient **only to oblige them to that Religion in which all Men agree, leaving*** *their particular Opinions to themselves, that is, to be good Men and true or Men of Honour and Honesty, by whatever Denominations or Persuasions they may be distinguish'd;* whereby Masonry becomes the Centre of Union and the Means of conciliating in true Friendship amongst Persons that must have remain'd at a perpetual distance.

Pause for thought

We should note that the Old Charges had always promoted Trinitarian Christianity and deference and devotion to the Church. Ritual in 1724 still contained references to the Trinity (Chapter 4). Anderson certainly was an innovator, 'allowing' Masons to have their own opinions as to their religious persuasion. Very interesting that this went through, in effect breaking well over 300 years of specific doctrine, in leaving Masons 'particular opinions to themselves, by whatever Denominations or Persuasions they may be distinguished'. (Apparently in 1732, the Master of one London lodge was Daniel Delvalle or Dalville **'an eminent Jew snuff merchant'**. Things really were changing for the better.)

Also worth noting that, even after the Union in 1813, many lodges maintained allegiance to the two Saints and kept to Trinitarian prayers in the ritual.

II. Of the Civil Magistrate, supreme and subordinate
   ie. k*eep the peace and don't plot against the state!*
III. Of Lodges
   ie. b*elong to a lodge. Attend and ensure that only fit and proper people come in!*
IV. Of Masters, Wardens, Fellows and Apprentices
   A throw-back to some of the Old Charges relating to progression on merit and that members should be sufficiently healthy to take on responsibilities.
V. Of the Management of the Craft in working
   ie. r*elating to honest working, proper treatment of employees and maintenance of the proper skills.*

Pause for thought

Strange that this appears in the Regulations, considering that by this time and in the London area at least, most lodges were non-operative.

VI. Of behaviour

This six-part section specifies correct and proper behaviour within the lodge, after the lodge (feast!), outside, with Brethren and with strangers, at home and towards a strange Brother.

The general heads finish with an overall admonition to good and peaceful behaviour.

Pause for thought

If you compare the details of these heads with that of our Charge after Initiation, you will not be surprised to see much in common.

Anderson's Constitutions start with the usual history, similar to what we have been suffering from in most OCs. The 39 Anderson Regulations which follow the history are exactly the same as those of Payne, and Anderson actually starts them with the oh-so-generous admission 'Compiled **first by Mr. George Payne** Anno 1720 when he was Grand-Master ...' (the acknowledgement was probably insisted on by the Grand Officers.)

After this comes something new – in a 'Postscript' he gives instructions for the constituting of a new lodge. There then follows his 'Approbation', where he justifies what he has done, especially why the OCs needed changing and updating. This finishes with the names of the Masters and Wardens of 20 lodges which helped to approve the Constitutions. Finally, there are the songs.

An interesting review of the 1723 Constitutions is given in *Spondee's review of Anderson* (1731), published in a journal of the time (see *KJH2* p.274). It waffles on about the history, making various criticisms. It then goes on, and it is difficult to see if the writer (Mr. Spondee) is actually being very cynical – we have no way of knowing why the review was produced – but he says:

By these instances, you will judge of the nature and importance of the *History*. As to its credibility, you may entirely depend on it: for J.T. Desaguliers, L.L.D. and F.R.S. Deputy Grand-master, in the dedication of it to his Brother, the most noble Prince, John Duke of Montagu, the right worshipful Grand-master assures us, that It is a just and exact account &c in which is preserved all that was authentic in the old ones and that every Brother will be pleased with the performance, knowing that it had his Grace's approval and approbation in manuscript ...

The rest of the review is hardly any more sympathetic to the Craft!

A major point about the 1723 Constitutions, which reflects in the ritual of the time (at least until 1730) is the absence of any mention of three Degrees – it is still EA and FC/Master.

One of the original Regulations required the FC/Master's degree to be conferred only in Grand Lodge. It is thought that Payne put this in the original set to keep control over the development of lodges. It became obvious after a while that, firstly, it would restrict the number of Masters and secondly, even after seven years, there were only about 50 lodges on the register. In the early years of the Grand Lodge, how many lodges would have taken any notice of such a Regulation anyway? Being restrictive to the development of the Order and probably in response to 'old Masons' ignoring it, in 1725 it was quietly dropped.

The American Masonic Service Association published in 1924 a copy of the original 1723 Constitutions, with a very learned introduction by Lionel Vibert. Not cheap but available on-line. A historic document that every Mason should possess. (It has been since reprinted – ISBN -07661-0073-1.)

As the influence of the PrGL spread, it ordered the creation of a list of lodges and where they met, and in December 1727, it ordered:

that it be referr'd to the succeeding Grand Master, Deputy Grand Master, and Grand Wardens, to inquire into the Precedency of the several Lodges, and to make Report thereof at the next Quarterly Communication in order that the same may be finally settled and ent'red accordingly.

The list was kept up-to-date and eventually became the Freemasons' Calendar. Over the years, the order of precedence of lodges was constantly revised.

The Picart engraving is taken from his *Ceremonies and religious customs of people all over the world* (1737) and shows a list of lodges at the time.

As agreed, annual feasts were held, first in taverns but later it was realised that with growing numbers, it was necessary to find somewhere bigger and it is believed that one of the livery companies offered its premises. With presumably more sumptuous surroundings and a greater level of formality, it became essential to appoint brethren as Stewards. Eventually, by the end of 1728, twelve men offered their services and were appointed. (By 1732 the twelve serving Stewards had acquired the right to

Fig 5.4: Engraving from B. Picart.

nominate their successors. They were also permitted to have their jewels attached to red ribbons, and their aprons lined with red silk.)

We do not know just how wide were the plans of the founding lodges and what they expected for the future. Did they hope to cover just inner London or were they hoping for wide expansion? The first Minute Book in 1723 showed 52 lodges on the roll with the names of 731 Brethren given from 36 of these lodges. These lodges were all within a limited distance but things got going quickly and by 1725 there were lodges at Bath, Bristol, Chester, Chichester, Norwich and Salford.

During the early years of the PrGL, a number of London lodges ignored it and its 'new-fangled and restrictive regulations'. They were called St John Masons or Old Masons.

By 1730, there were constituted lodges in France, Spain, Gibraltar, India and the Netherlands.

Pause for thought

Rather annoying that detailed records of the PrGL were kept from

mid-1723 onwards but there is no record of how the PrGL was
set up until the second edition of Anderson's Constitutions in 1738
- and for the details, Anderson has never been considered 'totally
reliable'.

We do have another source, though. William Preston, whom we will meet
later, published his *Illustrations of Masonry* in 1772. We look at the first
three 'Books' in another Chapter, but in a later edition, his 'Book IV' is *A
History of Masonry in England* and has sections starting with the Romans
and ending in 1804. Of particular interest for this Chapter are *Section VII –
History of the Revival of Masonry in the South of England* and *Section VIII
– History of Masonry from the Revival in the South of England till the death
of King George I.* They cover mainly 1717 to 1727.

It may be that the 'Grand Lodge' concept had some attraction to other
Masons, because in 1725 the Grand Lodge of Ireland was constituted. A
newspaper article in the *Dublin Weekly Journal No. 13, Saturday, June 26
1726* says:

...about one hundred brethren belonging to the six lodges of
Gentlemen Freemasons who are under the Jurisdiction of the
Grand Master assembled at 11 a.m. on June 24, at the Yellow Lion
in Werburgh Street, and proceeded in coaches to the King's Inns,
wearing 'Aprons, White Gloves, and other parts of the
Distinguishing Dress of that Worshipful Order.'
After a procession round the great hall of the Inns 'with many
important ceremonies, the Grand Lodge 'retired to the Room
prepared for them, where after performing the Mystical
Ceremonies of the Grand Lodge which are held so sacred, that they
must not be discovered to a Private Brother; they proceeded to the
Election of a new Grand Master &c.'

Once formed and up and running, in 1731 it set up a scheme whereby, as a
true mark of its regularity, a 'Warrant' was issued to a lodge.

Not long after the formation of the Irish GL, Scottish Masons began to
wonder whether there was merit in the concept. There is a record in the
September 1735 Minutes of the Lodge of Canongate Kilwinning. This is
the first part:

Att Maries Chapell the 25th day of November 1737. Thomas
Mylne, Master; Samwell Neilson, warden..The which day the

brethren took to their serious consideration a printed circular letter with printed coppies of proposalls and regulations sent to them by the Masters and Wardens of this and the other three Lodges in and about Edr., viz., Kilwinning Scots Armes, Canongate Kilwinning, and Leith Kilwinning (with whom the present Master and Warden of this Lodge had been formerly appointed to concurr), signifieing their intention, **for the promoting of Masonry in generall, to make choise of a Grand Master with two Grand Wardens over all the regular Mason Lodges in Scotland** ...

A committee was appointed and in November 1737, the Grand Lodge of Scotland received its first Grand Master, William St Clair.

All three Grand Lodges started to promote lodges overseas, especially in America. The Irish Grand Lodge came up with the idea of 'travelling' military lodges and from 1732 a number were warranted. (PGL eventually followed suit.)

Finally, for the record, Anderson's revised Constitutions were published in 1756, 1767 and 1784.

The Third Degree?

PrGL is ticking along with lots of lodges completely ignoring it but nevertheless expanding nicely. But what had happened to the Degrees, if anything? We said above that Desaguliers probably developed the ritual but we have little evidence as to how and from where he got his ideas (perhaps some from his Edinburgh visit). He is rated as being the real originator of a more modern ritual, taking a rather disorganised set of questions and answers and sorting it out, making changes and additions in a rather pretentious style of English. His brief (if he ever had one) was to keep undisturbed anything that was 'time immemorial' but to look for something like a 'Speculative' meaning for what had been basic operative items.

We met *A Mason's examination 1723* and *The Graham MS 1726* in Chapter 4. From these we know that there were definitely the FPOF with a two-part ('M' and 'B') master word. Soon we will find that Prichard produced a three-degree publication in 1730, with a fairly detailed Third Degree 'traditional history', including the murder of HA.

The *Wilkinson* manuscript of 1727 has a very detailed First Degree catechism, similar to Prichard's, with little reference to other degrees except for the last question:

When you are Asked how old you are When an Apprentice under Seven;- fellow Craft under 14: When a Master, three times Seven.

Now, if we go back to the Regulation in the Constitutions, 'It is not in the Power of any person ...', it clearly states that no innovations are possible without PrGL consent. But we know that between 1723 and 1730, a Third Degree appeared, as did changes to the other two. This **surely was innovation** and was apparently allowed (even if not officially sanctioned). Could this be because the person(s) responsible were either too respected to challenge or too powerful to shoot down?!

In the absence of any evidence, we can only guess what happened and when, but somehow the Master Word has gone from its 'traditional' place in the First Degree, to the Third Degree. It is not unreasonable to assume that someone (Desaguliers?) took what was around in 1720-23, re-arranged it and then did much superb writing/re-writing and produced something that Prichard could build on, so the Third Degree **must have been almost complete before 1730**.

Whoever did the work must have felt that the old catechisms and history were just a bit too crude for the up-and-coming Speculative Masons. In fact, an item called *Antediluvian Masonry 1726* was published as a newspaper advertisement. It tells about a forthcoming meeting of antediluvian Masons (whoever they were supposed to be!). The second and third paragraphs are:

There will be several Lectures on Ancient Masonry, particularly on the Signification of the Letter G and how and after what manner the Antediluvian Masons form'd their own Lodges, **shewing what Innovations have lately been introduced by the Doctor and some other of the Moderns** with their Tape, Jacks, Movable Letters, Blazing stars &c, to the great Indignity of the Mop and Pail.

There will likewise be a Lecture giving a particular description of the Temple of Solomon, shewing which way the Fellow Crafts got into the Middle Chamber ... with the whole History **of the Widow's Son killed by the Blow of Beetle, afterwards found three Foot East, three Foot West and three foot perpendicular**, and the necessity there is for a Master to well understand **the Rule of Three**.

KJH2 is fairly certain that the date is right and if so, we have almost unbreakable evidence of the existence both of unhappiness with the Moderns (the cynical reference to the fancy floor cloth) and references to HAB and the Murder (Beetle is an old term for a heavy maul.)

In 1725 came *The Whole Institutions of Free-Masons Opened.* Nothing special, except an extended (and not very enlightening) description of the FPOF. It then gives 'an explanation of our secrets':

J..n and B..z, two Pillars made by *Heirom Jachin,* signifies
Strength, and B..z Beautiful, M and B signifies **Marrow in the
Bone** so is our Secret to be Concealed.

(We will come back to 'marrow' later in this Chapter.)

Then:

Yet for all this I want the primitive Word, I answer it was God in
six Terminations, to wit I am, and Jehova is the answer to it and
Grip at the Rein of the back.

In 1730, some unknown person (probably a Mason, from the apparent inside knowledge) published *The Mystery of Freemasonry 1730.* It gives the two pillar words in full and introduces the five noble orders of architecture among other items, but there is a tantalising reference to a 'master's part', which shows that there were three Degrees, although the third allegedly not being so popular. There is no mention of anything relating to our Third Degree.

The first Degree was the 'Apprentice' and the second the 'Master'. It then says:

Q. How old are you.
A. Under 5, or under 7, which you will. N.B When you are first
made a Mason, you are only entered Apprentice; and till you are
made a Master, or as they call it, pass'd to Master's Part, you are
only an enter'd Apprentice and consequently must answer under 7;
for if you say above, they will expect the Master's Word and
Signs. Note, there is not one Mason in an Hundred that will
be at the Expence to pass the master's part, except it be for
interest.

The implication is that there was a third Degree, but qualified Freemasons of the time (Fellowcrafts!) did not feel it necessary to pay for yet another Degree which might not be of any value to them.

Pause for thought
I wonder if there is the slightest chance that this *'master's part is*

too expensive' actually was an early Royal Arch degree? I don't recall any evidence for this but worth thinking about!

What seems to have happened is that a Third Degree is rapidly crystallising, but the questions and answers are still a hotch-potch of the old ones, plus some that look like our modern ritual. But, was there more to it?

This might be a time to introduce a piece of Latin history which may have helped someone to construct the wording of the Third Degree legend. The body of Master Hiram found after his death may allude to a passage in the sixth book of Virgil:

Anchises had been dead for some time, and Eneas, his son, professed so much duty to his departed father, that he consulted with the Cumaean sybil whether it were possible for him to descend into the shades below, in order to speak with him. The prophetess encouraged him to go; but told him he could not succeed, unless he went into a certain place, and **plucked a golden bough or shrub**, which he should carry in his hand, and by that means obtain directions where he should find his father. Anchises, the great preserver of the Trojan name, could not have been discovered but by the help of a bough, which was plucked with great ease from the tree. The person that was murdered and buried was Misenus, *monte sub aerio*, under a high hill like HAB (also his grave was found by the direction of a shrub, which came up easily). The principal cause of Eneas's descent into the shades was to inquire of his **father the secrets of the fates which should some time be fulfilled among his posterity.** *The Fellowcrafts searched diligently for their master to receive from him the secret Word of Masonry to be delivered down, as a test, to their fraternity of after ages.*

This remarkable verse follows : *Praeterea jacet exanimum tibi corpus amici, Heu nescis!* - The body of your friend lies near you dead, Alas, you know not how!

Also, remember from Chapter 4, where the *Graham MS* talked about Noah's grave and finding secrets.

It seems quite possible that Desaguliers looked at the operative workings in existence, made major revisions, and restructured them into a work which was much closer to our Speculative ritual. Some sources claim that he produced a three-degree system as early as Payne's second term, but it was not until Prichard that the three Degrees appeared in print. We assume that many lodges stuck to the 'old' workings because they were familiar with them and did not want to get involved with the new-fangled changes.

Samuel Prichard and *Masonry Dissected* (MD)

Some person (or persons, in my view) did a very great service to the Craft in creating MD. If you look at the catechisms that were probably in use in the early 1700s and at the various OCs and early exposures, you can see that they are a rag-bag of questions, answers, comments, signs, etc.

Our someone(s) must have spent ages - reading, sorting, collating and re-writing - in order to get as far as MD (if indeed, this was the final 'new ritual'). Between Prichard and the Lodge of Reconciliation (Chapter 9), others must have carried on reading, digging, etc. to get to where we are today.

In 1730, the Craft was given something that **we must celebrate and treasure for ever** - Prichard published his exposure, called *Masonry Dissected*. We don't know why he published, although there is some 'aggro' against the Craft in it. There has never been any real proof that he was a Mason but at the end of his exposure, he produces 'the author's vindication of himself from the prejudiced part of mankind'.

It starts off by saying:

Of all the Impositions that have appear'd amongst Mankind, none are so ridiculous as the Mystery of Masonry which has amus'd the World and caused various Constructions and these Pretences of Secrecy, invalid, has (tho' not perfectly) been revealed, and the grand Article viz. the Obligation, has several Times been printed in publick Papers ...

He finishes with:

I was induced to publish this mighty Secret for the publick Good, at the Request of several Masons, and it will, I hope, give entire Satisfaction and have its desired Effect **in preventing so many credulous Persons being drawn into so pernicious a Society**.

Well, I never!

He claims on the front page that the book is:

... a description of all its Branches from the Original to the

MASONRY

DISSECTED:

BEING

A Univerſal and Genuine

DESCRIPTION

OF

All its BRANCHES from the Ori_
ginal to this Preſent Time.

As it is deliver'd in the

Conſtituted Regular Lodges

Both in CITY and COUNTRY,

According to the

Several Degrees of ADMISSION.

Giving an Impartial ACCOUNT of their Regular Proceeding in Initiating their New Members
in the whole Three Degrees of MASONRY.

VIZ.

I. ENTER'D 'PREN- ⎰ II. FELLOW CRAFT.
TICE,   ⎱ III. MASTER.

To which is added,

The Author's VINDICATION of himſelf.

By SAMUEL PRICHARD, late Member of a
CONSTITUTED LODGE.

LONDON:

Printed for J. WILFORD, at the Three Flower-d. Luces behind
the Chapter houſe near St. Paul's. 1730. (Price 6d)

Fig 5.5: *Masonry Dissected* cover page.

Present Time as it is deliver'd in the Constituted Regular Lodges both in City and Country according to the Several Degrees of Admission.

Whoever he was and for whatever reason he published, we really don't know where the material came from. It seems to represent a very convenient transition from the old, ie. 17th century, to the new, ie.18th century and it seems extremely unlikely that Prichard was not a Mason and was not involved with working current, well-developed ceremonies such as those he published.

The book starts with some of the old history babble, but then gives complete, detailed wording for three Degrees. The 'Master's Degree' contains much of our Third Degree, including 'ruffians', 'slips' and 'porch, dormer and pavement'. At the end, he lists 67 regular lodges in numerical order.

It is important to look at extracts from MD in more detail. As we have said, it provides a bridge between, on the one hand, the basic question and answer (catechetical) ritual of the late 17th and early 18th centuries and, on the other hand, what must have eventually developed, by the early 19th century, into what we do today.

It has to be regarded as one of the most important exposures ever, in publishing the ritual for **all** three Degrees for the first time and for the next 30-40 years it was probably used as the main training aid (blue book!) in many UK and overseas lodges. It presents the three Degrees as earlier works do, with catechisms, but there is quite a lot of ceremonial work as well.

Let us look at the Entered Apprentice Degree. After an introduction, it goes on:

Q. Are you a Mason?

A. I am so taken and accepted to be amongst Brothers and Fellows

Q. How shall I know that you're a Mason?

A. By signs and tokens and perfect points of my entrance

Q. What are signs?

A. All squares angles and perpendiculars

Q. What are tokens?

A. Certain regular and brotherly grips.

Note that he says **Brothers and Fellows**. He makes no mention of **Masters**!

The EA takes up ten of his pages. The FC takes five pages and the Master's Part five pages too. Obviously the First Degree is very detailed because it reflects what was until fairly recently (say 1670-80), almost the whole of what was worked. *HC1* in the Appendix gives the whole of the three Degrees. So does the restricted area of the Pietre-Stones website (Chapter 11).

Then a bit more, then:

Q. What makes a Just and Perfect Lodge

A. Seven or more

Q. What do they consist on

A. One Master two Wardens two Fellowcrafts and one Enter'd 'Prentice.

Then the questions start to reflect ceremonial:

Q. How gained you Admittance

A. By three great Knocks

Q. Who received you

A. A junior Warden

Q. How did he dispose of you

A. He carried me up to the North-East part of the Lodge and brought me back again to the West and deliver'd me to the Senior Warden

Q. What did the Senior Warden do with you

A. He presented me and showed me how to walk up (by three steps) to the Master

Q. What did the Master do to you?

A. He made me a Mason

Q. How did he make you a Mason?

A. With my bare-bended knee and body within the square, the compass extended to my naked LB, my naked right hand on the H B *[sic]* there I took the Obligation (or oath) of a Mason.

Q. Can you repeat the obligation.

A. I'll do my Endeavour (*Which is as follows*).

There then follows an obligation:

... that I will 'Hail', 'conceal' ... 'write', 'carve' ... 'sands of the sea' ... 'no more remembrance.'...

Sound familiar? It seems that now we really are forming-up some full workings. The questions then go on to discuss the form of the **conceptual** lodge, lodge furniture and furnishing and then ask:

Q. Have you any jewels in the lodge?

A. Yes

Q How many?

A. Six. Three Movable and three Immovable.

Q. What are the moveable jewels?

A. Square, Level, and Plumb-rule

Q. What are their uses?

They are then explained. Throughout the Degree, there are traces of what we could call Speculation, not seen before (in any publication).

Q. What is the other Furniture of a lodge?

A. Bible to God, Compass to the Master and Square to the Fellow-Craft.

Q. What Q. do you learn by being a Gentleman-Mason

A. Secrecy, Morality and Goodfellowship.

Further on, the EA Sign and Token are given and both pillar words with their explanation. One of the last questions is a little curious, with both words being given:

Q. Give me the word

A. I'll letter it with You

Exam. B - - Z *[NB. ..... B..z and J..n were two Pillars in Solomon's Porch. I Kings, chap. vii. ver 21].*

We have already seen that *The Mystery of Free-Masonry 1730* showed both words in full.

The 'Fellow-Craft's Degree' has a discourse on the letter G and then some ceremonial:

Q. Did you ever work?

A. Yes, in the building of the temple

Q. Where did you receive your wages?

A. In the middle chamber

Q. How came you to the middle chamber?

A. Through the Porch

Q. When you came through the Porch, what did you see?

A. Two great Pillars.

Q. What are they called?

A. J.B. *[i.e J..n and B..z]*

Pause for thought

Note the order of these. The question above in the Entered Apprentice part shows 'B' **and** 'J'. Firstly, why 'J' as well as 'B'? Secondly why is this order different from the FC degree?

There then follows some material which was definitely used later in the Second Degree Tracing Board – 'winding staircase' … 'seven or more' … 'coming to the door of the middle chamber' and so on. It then gives the full FC Sign and Token. It finishes with a further repetition of the letter G 'which stands in the middle of Solomon's Temple'.

The Master's degree is definitely the most exciting. The first page is so important, it is quoted almost in full. (If you look carefully, you will see tit-bits that go into various parts of our present ritual, notably in our Openings):

Q. Are you a Master-Mason?
A. I am; try me. Prove me, disprove me if you can
Q. Where was you pass'd Master?
A. In a Perfect Lodge of Masters
Q. What makes a Perfect Lodge of Masters?
A. Three
Q. How came you to be a pass'd Master?
A. By the help of God, the Square and my own Industry
Q. How was you pass'd Master?
A. From the Square to the Compass.

Now we go to Ex(amination) and R(eply)

Ex. An Enter'd 'Prentice I presume you have been
R. **J** and **B** I have seen
…
Ex. If a Master-Mason you would be, You must rightly understand
The Rule of Three And **M.B** (sic) shall make you free.

After a bit more:

R. To seek for that which was lost **and is now found**.
Pause for thought
Companions of the Royal Arch will certainly query the 'found' in this reply. Remember, we are only in 1730, the Second and Third Degrees are only just starting to be finalised and Royal Arch ritual, whatever its form, was a long way from maturity and probably had a decade or two to wait for 'Sojourners', 'vault', 'being lowered down', etc. Hence, in this context, at this time, 'what is found', is almost certainly the master word 'M .. B…'.

Not for this book, but it raises the whole question of 'things' being lost in Craft and being discovered in RA.

Ex. What was that which was lost and is now found

R. The Master-Mason's Word

Ex. How was it lost

R. By Three Great Knocks, or the Death of our Master *Hiram*

Ex. How came he by his Death

There then follows a pretty good and detailed description of 'the murder', 'our traditional history' and the FPOF with the word signifying 'the b...der is s...tten.' Interestingly, the murder weapons are the Setting Maul, Setting Tool and Setting Beadle (different-sized mauls).

Finally, **and tantalisingly**, it says that the 'master word' is whispered in his ear – **and doesn't tell us what it is!** It is not M...B because:

Ex. Give me the Master's word

R. **Whispers him in the Ear**, and supported by the Five Points of Fellowship before-mentioned, **says M...nah**, which signifies **The Builder is smitten**.

This is a bit strange because Prichard should have had access to some of the documents or at least known the kind of detail being published. We saw in Chapter 4 that in *The Whole Institution of Free-Masons Opened 1725*, there is a pretty fair description of the FPOF with 'M' and 'B'.

Pause for thought

Am I being a bit thick here? 'Whispers in his ear' and 'says', to me implies that there was a Master Word in addition to that given within the FPOF. This doesn't appear anywhere else?

What we do know is that Prichard's incredible work caused such a storm at Grand Lodge that they decided to do something about it – starting off major ramifications.

In response to *The whole Institution*, on 28th August 1730, Desaguliers recommended 'several things to the Consideration of the Grand Lodge ... for preventing any false Brethren being admitted into regular Lodges and such as call themselves Honorary Masons.'

A couple of months later there was a reference to MD, characterized as 'a foolish thing not to be regarded' (an early case of 'head in the sand').

The PrGL at the same time, 'to prevent cowans and impostors being Made Masons', told its constituent lodges to make certain variations in the ritual and lodge procedure:

Any visitor had to be vouched for by a brother and his name recorded in the visitors' book

Anyone making a Mason irregularly (ie. by reference to Prichard's work rather than in a proper ceremony) to be subject to strict laws.

The biggest change was that **the two pillar words were changed around** (ie. J for the First and B for the Second).

The two 'builder' words

So where are we in 1730? We have quite a lot of material giving pointers to signs, tokens, words, questions and answers, and some ceremonial matters. We have the new raising legend.

From what we have looked at in this Chapter, we can be sure that by then there were three separate ceremonies, even if not necessarily being practised by all that many lodges!

We have seen the FPOF introduced and explained many times. We have seen the basis of the raising via Noah and the *Wilkinson MS 1727* which has a brief reference to 'our Great Master Hiram's grave'. **But,** no real evidence of complete ceremonies apart from Prichard (whose book sold for the next 40 years or so).

While looking at the Degrees and secrets, this could be a good time to discuss the Third Degree Word. (Yes! There are two words, but that came much later, after the Union.)

The 'M' word has been referred to in the manuscripts as 'matchpin', 'Magbin', 'Maughbin' and 'Mag and Boe'. Traditionally, we are told that this has something to do with the Hebrew for 'the builder is dead' or something like it. A Hebrew scholar will tell you that this is nonsense – there is no way what we say can be correctly translated into Hebrew.

It has always been my theory that the word *marrow* is significant in this context. Either the Noah legend was more widespread than we know, with the word marrow (or a derivative of it) being in common use, especially when the Third Degree and the Hiram legend were finally established, or (and in my opinion), there is a much simpler explanation.

Until relatively recently, it was still possible to detect some touch of old Nordic in the language of people from the North East of England (Geordies) and a tiny bit in East Anglian. The word 'marrow' or something very like it ('marrer' perhaps), means 'mate' or 'buddy'. In addition, I think the FPOF, until the late 1600s, were barely mentioned in our manuscripts, because, in a throwback to the heady days of the medieval building boom, if you fell off a ladder or platform, you might have been picked up using the Masonic version of a fireman's lift, with the words 'oop ya coom me **marrer** (or matey)'.

This may seem trivial, but I think it is much better than trying to murder a piece of quasi-Hebrew to force it to have some sense. (Older Royal Arch Companions will remember how a particular Word, which was supposed to have lots of meanings, was finally scrapped as nonsense over 30 years ago.)

A word of warning

This is a quotation from *KJH1*:

> … taking everything into account, there would seem fairly good grounds for thinking that the early Masonic catechisms, written or printed before 1731, however reliable they may be in some respects, **do not accurately reflect** the character of the ceremonies practised by accepted Masons in the first three decades of the eighteenth century…

We are looking at the words of probably the world's greatest authorities on the development of the ritual from the end of the 17th century to after the formation of PrGL. One would hope that 'do not accurately reflect' really means '**may** not accurately reflect', otherwise a lot of us have spent a lot of time chasing rainbows.

If so, it has still been fun.

6
Craft history 1731-1750

1731!

We have PrGL, a sort of Grand Lodge, at least for London, with its influence slowly spreading to the whole metropolitan area around London. Masonic 'discipline' was rather vague and we believe that being 'made a Mason', ie. being initiated into the Craft, did not necessarily mean that you were 'admitted to' (joined) the lodge that brought you in. Grand Lodge records later on in the century actually listed members under these two separate categories – 'made' and 'joined'.

We saw from Chapter 4 that quite a lot of the wording of a ritual had been identified, but even after Prichard, we are still not really sure how many Degrees (two or three?) are being practiced regularly, nor the ceremonial in detail. However, things are coming along rather quickly.

In several exposures produced in the period, there is clear evidence of the FPOF, in various forms, even if they are not quite the same as ours (see *Trinity College MS 1711*, *A Mason's examination 1723* and *Grand Mystery 1724*, all in Chapter 4). We also saw reference to three ceremonies (if not actually Degrees yet). *A Mason's confession* of 1727 showed definite ceremonial for an Initiation.

Premier Grand Lodge had only been in existence for 13 years by this time. We can be sure that outside London, not many took too much notice for a further number of years and in other parts of the country, **who knows what those old boys did**?

The 1738 Constitutions

We have discussed the general feelings about the 1723 Constitutions and the general unreliability of Anderson's memory of things. The following extracts are from the actual Minutes of Grand Lodge relating to his 1738 edition, and presumably are his attempts to 'clear things up'.

1735, Feb. 24. Dr Anderson reported to Grand Lodge 'that he had spent some Thoughts upon some Alterations and Additions' to his First Edition of 1723 - then 'all sold off' - and GL 'appointed a Committee to revise and compare the same &c.'

1738, Jan. 25. 'Bro. Anderson informed the Lodge that he had sometime since Prepared a New Edition of the Book of Constitutions with several Additions and Amendmts which having been perused & (after some alterations made therein) Approved off by several Grand Officers was now ready for the Press and he therefore desired the Grand Master's Commands & the approbation of this Lodge for printing the same, which request was granted him.'

Thus, these Minutes indicate Anderson's work, after modifications being made, was approved by Grand Lodge. In the absence of any other evidence, we know no more about the formation of the PrGL from the four founding lodges, however unsatisfactory this is.

Life, it is a-changing

KJH1 gives a number of publications after Prichard's *MD*. The following are important in showing things evolving after Prichard.

Dialogue between Simon and Peter 1740

A bit more description of proceedings, especially some alternative wordings; a description of various words and their alternatives, some of which have not come down to us. Items in brackets are explanations given at the end of the dialogue, but dropped in where they are actually referenced.

Simon	Are you a Mason
Philip	I am (so taken to be by all Fellows and Brothers) (This is the way that Old Masons answer this question. But the New Masons **under J.T. Desaguliers Regulation** answer only **I am**) …

Pause for thought

This is quite exciting. Note that it refers to Desaguliers **not** Anderson.

Sim	And whats the Word of a Mason?
Phil	The word is Right (This answer is Subtle enough. The word of a Mason is B..Z. But they answer the word if Right and they'l Letter the Word with you &c) …
Phil	And what are the points of your Entrance?
Sim	To Heal and Conceal the Secrets (To Heal and Conceal this part of the Old Oath, but the New Masons do

it By pointing to their left breast with their Finger) of a Mason.

Pause for thought

Could this be the origin of 'and recover to the centre'?

There are obvious developments from Prichard, but it is intriguing to note that there is no reference to the Third Degree at all and certainly no FPOF or 'M' or 'B'.

There is a fairly detailed description of the floor cloth (future Tracing Board) which is 'commonly made, with white tape nailed to the floor …'.

The diagram is interesting for two particular reasons. Its caption again refers to Desaguliers and the position of both Wardens is shown in the West. This was their original siting – they were said to represent the two pillars through which you had to pass to gain entry.

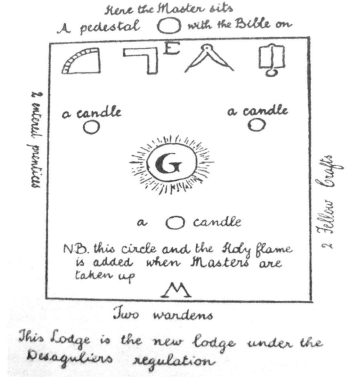

Fig 6.1: Layout of a lodge 1740.

Essex Ms 1750

In this, we see increasing Speculation in the alleged ritual.

Q What was your first step towards your entring
A a willing desire to know the Scret
Q How came you into the lodge
A In ignorance and came out in knowledge
Q What did you see thire
A I saw truth the World & Justice
Q What was behind you
A Perjury & exclamation of our fraternity.

The Perjur'd Free Mason Detected

This appeared in 1730. It starts by going through the old history. It disputes Hiram as the 'Head Mason' saying that his main work was 'the casting of the two vast Brazen Pillars'. It also explains why Hiram was not buried in the Temple.

In part II, it then **seriously tears Prichard to pieces** for breaking his oath (fortunately for Prichard, it made no difference to sales of his book):

Q. Pray, Sir, is your name *Samuel Prichard*?

A. Yes, sir

Q. Are you the same Man who has publish'd that wonderful Book call'd the *Free Mason* dissected?

A. Yes, I am Sir, what have you to say to it?

Q. Nothing at all Sir, only I wonder you did not give it a better Title.

A. What title cou'd have been more to the Purpose and to the Design of the Book?

Q. O, a great many; but one in particular.

A. What is that pray, what wou'd you have had it call'd?

Q. Why, I wou'd have had you call'd it Mr *Samuel Prichard* dissected, or Mr *Samuel Prichard* who calls himself a *Free Mason* dissected.

Q. Ay, but once a Renegade, and always a Turk; once a Traytor and always a Renegade …

The author then goes on with his 'destruction Derby' for another 13 pages.

France

We have said that ritual development from 1696 (*Edinburgh Register House* MS) to Prichard, and then from Prichard to *TDK/J&B* (Chapter 7) in 1760/62, is largely undocumented, hence largely conjecture (guesswork?). We have some French material for the period which gives some clues, so we should now look at how and why Masonry 'went to France', what happened there and whether anything was re-imported to England. It is thought that in 1725 (perhaps even earlier), Speculative or rather non-operative Masonry went to France. Freemasonry as practiced under the English (1717), Irish (1725) and Scottish (1737) Grand Lodges began to spread to Europe. Many believe that the main impetus for the establishment and early development of Masonry in France was expatriate, ie. exiled, Jacobites - some from the 1715 rebellion, when James VIII (the Old Pretender) had to flee to France; and later, after the 1745 rebellion, when James' son (the Young Pretender, Bonnie Prince Charlie) was defeated and his troops massacred by 'Butcher Cumberland'.

There were a few lodges in the 1730s consisting of French Masons living in England. Presumably some of these would have returned home taking something from English Craft with them.

There does not seem to have been the same basis of traditions of the mason trade in France as there was in England and Scotland, and when French Freemasonry started, it would have been very unlikely to have involved any who were purely operative masons (in the English sense). Meetings would probably have been held in the homes of the well-to-do (and even the ennobled), with membership consisting of the gentry, who might have been attracted by some of the high-born Jacobites, members of the military and the clergy.

Also, bear in mind that with a history of war and disagreement, the French would have a high degree of sympathy with people from any nation **who were giving grief to the English**.

There is no real evidence of any organisation until 1738 when a Grand Lodge was formed (there is a reference to this in Anderson's 1738 Constitutions, presumably prepared a year or so earlier).

As the Craft was becoming established in France, there would have been a lot of conflict and backbiting - what with a different culture from England, no long tradition behind it and hence far less pressure to prevent change and innovation, plus various other degrees being formed - it is not surprising that any kind of unity was a long time in coming. Not many years later, there were almost riots when excluded Brethren tried to break into a Grand Lodge meeting!

Over the period 1738-1745, various publications in French appeared. To start with, they were little more than material pinched from *MD*, but over time, they started to include descriptions of what was done in France, plus various extensions reflecting additional practices, together with pure fantasy gathered from who knows where.

We must be very careful when looking at any documents which give details of Masonic procedures. If they do not bear any resemblance to what we do now, either they have been dropped, for whatever reason, or they were just someone raving away, perhaps to make a publication more saleable!

> Pause for thought
> I am indebted to Harry Carr for *The Early French Exposures 1737-1751* (*HC2* in Chapter 11). The book reviews the development of French exposures and offers many complete texts. It also offers many examples of floor cloths in use. Also *CB1* (Chapter 11) pages 125-130, will give you a bit more.

We have seen in some of the documents covered in Chapters 4 and 5 that Masonic and non-Masonic writers of 'authentic' material, 'clearly describing' ritual and ceremonial, were often stating total rubbish and this may well have applied to French writings. Certainly, some of what is described was not the practice in England and did not get imported back to England.

At the end of the English *Whole Institutions of Free-Masons Opened*, 1725, there is a description including signs of two words, J and B and then M and B. OK so far, but then we have a third word 'Gibboram' which is answered by 'Esimberel'. There is no other reference to these two words in any of the other documents, nor in the writer's experience anywhere else in Craft Masonry. Why should the writer have invented the words?

If you look at some of the French ceremonial, you will see that it is very detailed, but many parts bear no resemblance to anything English.

Reception d'un Frey-Macon 1737

This was the first exposure in French. It is primarily a detailed description of the ceremonial associated with an Initiation ceremony. After publication, it was translated into English, German and Dutch. Harry Carr expresses surprise at this because by this time *MD* had already run to five or more editions. After the detailed description of how the Candidate is initially received and prepared, Brother Orator (presumably a lodge officer) says:

… You are about to embrace a respectable order, which is more serious than you imagine; there is nothing in it which is against the Law, against Religion, against the King nor against Manners; The Worshipful Master will tell you the rest.

There is then more description of how the Obligation is taken and the disclosure of J and B and their respective signs.

This is followed by a description of 'at table', of drinking the health of the new Brother. They called the wine 'powder' and the master says 'charge' then 'lay your hands to you guns'. They then drink with an elaborate kind of 'Masonic fire'.

La Reception Mysterieuse 1738

This is supposed to be a 'general and true account' of Prichard's work, but comparing it with *MD* and other works, the author seems to have had little understanding of what really went on, with lots of mistakes and misunderstandings.

Le Secret de Francs-Macons 1742

This goes on and on about recent Masonic history. It says more about the elaborate firing and then gives a very detailed view of Initiation, including some of the ritual used.

Le Parfait Macon 1744

This has:

Q. What is the word of a Fellow?

Q. There are two

Q. What are they?

Q. Manhu, Magdal or Magdala

Q. What is their meaning?

A. *Manhu* means *what is this*; *Magdala* means *the Tower*.

The explanation seems to refer to the destruction of the tower of Babel, from which speculative   explanations follow. Again, they do not appear anywhere else.

The Grand Mystery Laid Open 1726

This has 'Gibboam', 'Gibberum', 'Thimbulum' and 'Timbulum' as 'temporal signs' of a Mason!

Le Sceau Rompu 1745

This is an interesting piece of work. It finishes with catechisms for all three

Degrees, which are pretty similar to other material, French and English. He book starts however, with seven short chapters:

General impression of Masonry - a short history.

The Objects of Masonry – various moral views.

The Ranks and Offices – this is interesting in mentioning the names of the lodge officers and referring to other French exposures. Note that there is a reference to being 'undressed in a dark room'. French Masonry had a tradition of the Candidate being placed in a 'chamber of contemplation' and when he emerged, the 'Frère Terrible' used a sword to test his steadfastness on entry.

Reception of Apprentices and Fellows – in which he corrects the wording of other texts, and gives the proper wording for the oath.

Reception of Masters – a major criticism of the master's part given in other texts.

Signs of the Masons – some waffle about specified and extraneous signs

Masonic characters – a short item on Masonic cipher.

L'ordre des Francs-Macons Trahi 1745

This would seem to be the most important document of the period. The name is often shortened to *Le Trahi*. Harry Carr felt it as important to European Masonry as *MD* was to England and as the summit of the French exposures, some of it must have been re-imported to the UK, thereby affecting some of our practices and ritual development.

The work is very detailed and starts with three pages or so of 'philosophy'. It then describes floor layout for apprentice and master ceremonies, with full details of the ceremonies and two very interesting floor plans. Next there is a very detailed Third Degree traditional history, followed by a long catechism, more detailed than we have seen in English exposures. There is a curious bit in the middle:

Q. What is the name of a Mason?

A. Gabaon

Q. And that of his son?

A. Lufton.

'Lufton' could be a corruption of a French term for the equivalent of our Lewis, but there seems to be no explanation for 'gabaon'!

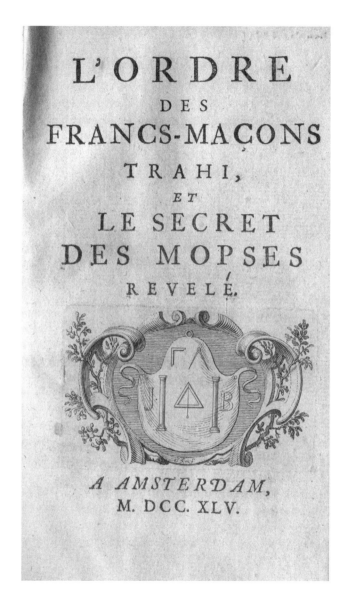

Fig 6.2: *Le Trahi* 1745.

Much of the content is similar to *Le Sceau Rompu* from which it may have been copied.

Over the next few years, a number of other exposures appeared. In the relatively short time since we believe that Masonry started in France, a lot of people must have been very busy to produce a dozen or so pieces of work. They seem to have been quite keen to show workings, not just words. For example, in the *Trahi,* in the specification for the reception of a Candidate for the Third Degree, the actual raising is described 'finger by finger', such as 'four fingers separated and bent claw-fashion at the joint of the wrist'.

Rumblings

Between 1730 and 1740 we perceive indications of the beginning of what turned out to be an event almost as important as the formation of PrGL - the emergence of what became the Grand Lodge of the Antients. We can be sure that there were in existence lodges which would have nothing to do with the PrGL and because of their refusal to agree to a proper Constitution, would be considered to be irregular.

London at this time was taking in from Ireland what we now call economic migrants, some of whom would be Masons (the Irish Grand Lodge was formed in 1725). Many were artisans, ie. workers, who would have had little in common with the fancy new lodges of the PrGL and would have joined or formed lodges dissociated from 'the authority', especially since they saw changes which they could not accept. Over the next ten or so years, they would have encouraged their friends and relatives to join their 'irregular' lodges.

Anderson in the 1723 Constitutions had said that:

Several Noblemen and Gentlemen of the best Rank with
Clergymen and learned Scholars of most Professions and
Denominations … frankly joined and submitted to take the
Charges, and to wear the Badges of a Free and Accepted Mason,
under our present worthy Grand Master, the most noble Prince,
John, Duke of Montagu.

Irish 'artisans' would not exactly be delighted by this!

Pause for thought
They don't become the Antients until Chapter 7, but it is more
convenient a term than 'the dissident Irish Masons'

The PrGL Minutes for the meeting of December 1735 show this:
Notice being given to the Grand Lodge that the Master and
Wardens of a Lodge from Ireland attended without, desiring to be
admitted, by virtue of a Deputation from the Lord Kingston present
G. Master of Ireland. But it appearing there was no particular
Recommendation from his Lord'p in this affair their Request could
not be comply'd with, **unless they would accept of a new
Constitution here**.
In other words, **become regular or stay out!**
The Minutes also show that representatives of some 57 lodges were at
the meeting, including Payne and Anderson, who was probably still fed up
with the Irish because the Irish Grand Lodge had ripped off his
Constitutions for their own. (This may explain partly why the Irish were
kept out.)

Something to note, though. The offer to admit lodges, provided they
accepted the Constitution, shows that they were being treated as a serious
threat and it is possible that the Irish lodge which was refused may have
become a focus for the discontent with the PrGL procedures, and
perhaps the driving force in the eventual emergence of the Antient Grand
Lodge.

There were many Masons belonging to lodges not in any way associated
with the PrGL. They had no reason to show any allegiance - their workings
could claim the 'time immemorial' excuse. Another force towards the
weakening of the PrGL, or the floodgate towards the eventual formation of
the Antients, was the probable influx of thoughts and ideas coming in from
French working and the Grand Lodges of Scotland and Ireland.

The 'floodgate'

We can now examine reasons for the floodgate of change and the increasing
pressure for something to offer as an alternative to the PrGL. Many books
of reference refer to these sore points, but some authors believe that they
were to an extent just cooked up to cause trouble. Remember that the prime
reasons for discontent among the non-Moderns were the general feeling
that the PrGL had gone sloppy in its operation. With pompous
'pronouncements' had undoubtedly introduced innovations almost
indiscriminately, whether changes, or just dropping off what others
considered cherished items. There is no clear evidence that the Antients
slowly built up resentment until the switching of the pillar words was the

last straw. It seems far more likely that some sore points were really objectionable, while others were a mild nuisance and just a cause for trouble. Current thinking seems very much against the idea that the Antients Grand Lodge was formed **as a schism** within the PrGL.

> Pause for thought
>
> It would not just be the Antients who might show disgust at the goings-on of the PrGL. It appointed Lord Byron, a relative of the poet Byron, as Grand Master. He attended three meetings within five years of office, the Grand Lodge itself only meeting nine times in the whole period.
>
> BJ1 says that between 1745 and 1755, over 50 London lodges were closed (or perhaps became unaffiliated and hence, independent lodges) and therefore lost to the PrGL

The Antients almost certainly had some legitimate grievances, feeling that PrGL was in many respects trying to destroy their Masonry, and they could complain about many things:

De-Christianisation

The Anderson Constitutions clearly pointed the way for the eventual dropping of Christian references in the ritual and hence the admission of non-Christians.

Saints' days

It had always been almost a sacred thing to hold assemblies on the two Saints' days. The Moderns didn't seem to care and were happy to hold assemblies when convenient.

For both of these, we can be fairly sure that many of the Irish Masons, brought up as Catholics, would feel very strongly about the need to maintain the Trinitarian aspect of the ritual. They also were not happy about the shortening of prayers by the Moderns.

Catechisms

Whether from sheer laziness or because they thought them 'old hat', the Moderns tended to shorten procedures and the catechisms (coming from the OCs) would again be considered as part of ancient usage and dropping them was beneath the pale for the Antients.

Preparing Candidates

Many Modern lodges cut out some (or all) of the preparation of the Candidate (not bared nor slipshod, etc.). Antients did it properly (in the traditional manner).

Prayers

There is evidence that the Moderns only had a prayer at the beginning and end of the First Degree. Antient Masons again would have felt this another blow to their religious beliefs.

Deacons

These were in use by the Antients from 1727. The Moderns did not adopt the office of Deacon until nearly 1810, the work being done by the Wardens.

Installation

The Moderns had a very basic ceremony, where the new Master was virtually just acclaimed. The Antients' ceremony contained an 'esoteric' element, with the passing of Chair secrets.

Lodge layout

The Moderns changed the position of the three Great Lights. The Wardens had always both been in the west (representing the two pillars), but the Junior Warden was now placed in the south.

Floor cloths

Tradition indicated that there was always the need to lay out the floor of the lodge for a ceremony, originally with chalk marks (or pins and tapes) and later drawn on a floor cloth for re-use. The Moderns 'sophisticated' their floor cloths by (horror!) actually using metal images of symbolic items such as Mason's tools – yet another modernisation!

Pillar words

In response to MD and other exposures, the PrGL changed the pillar words from 'B and J' to 'J and B' – a major attack on the ancient Landmarks!

Position of Royal Arch

Until 1756, the Moderns officially ignored it, even though many of their members belonged to Royal Arch lodges. To the Antients, it was the 'root, heart and marrow' of Masonry and treated virtually as a Fourth Degree.

This is a difficult area. It was at one time suggested that the Antients felt the Third Degree was not complete and needed an extra bit (a Fourth Degree?). The Moderns would have regarded this as an un-necessary and anti-Landmark addition. Nevertheless, although not recognised officially by the PrGL until 1767, many of them practised the Royal Arch. At the time, it remained a sore point and was just one of many items adding to the bubbling up.

And therefore?

One must have sympathy for the Antients – they saw the alleged 'official' Grand Lodge of the country scrapping much of what they held dear, often for no proper reason, and with a fairly extreme reaction to those who could not or would not conform to PrGL regulations. Many either formed their own lodges or joined those not affiliated to the PrGL.

> Pause for thought
> The general idea of making changes in response to various exposures, so that the 'profane' would not find it so easy to pass themselves off and illegally join in the work of the lodge, is just a little pathetic and was felt excessive at the time. In a lodge of sincere but knowledgeable Masons, an impostor would surely not be that difficult to spot!

Even some of the regular lodges (such as the Goose and Gridiron lodge) were loath to accept all the revisions and the net result was to make the Antients feel even more detached from the PrGL. Something had to happen, and in 1751 the Antients 'arrived'.

The Obligation evolving

Finally for this chapter, before the Antients actually arrive, just a quick look at how the Obligation of the Initiate was forming up. Perhaps these exerpts will convince you that a considerable amount of our ritual was largely in existence long before the end of the 18th century.

Chetwode Crawley Ms 1700
Neither by word or write, nor put it into write at any time nor draw with the point of a sword or any instrument upon the snow or sand nor shall you speak of it but with an entered Mason ....

Mason's confession 1727
As I shall answer before God at the great day, and this company, I shall heal and conceal, or not divulge any or make known the secrets of the Mason-word, (here one is taken bound, not to write them on paper, parchment, timber, stone, sand, snow etc.) under the pain of having my tongue taken out from beneath my chowks and my heart out from beneath my left oxter and my body buried within the sea-mark where it ebbs and flows twice in the 24 hours.

Mystery of Free-Masonry 1730
I solemnly protest and swear, in the presence of Almighty God and

this society and I will not by word of mouth or signs, discover any secrets which shall be communicated to me this night or any time hereafter; that I will not write, carve, engrave, or cause to be written, carved or engraven the same, either upon paper, copper, brass, wood or stone, or any movable or immovable, or any other way discover the same, to any but a brother or fellowcraft, under no less penalty than having my heart plucked through the pap of my left breast, my tongue torn by the roots from the roof of my mouth, my body to be burnt and my ashes to be scattered abroad in the wind where I may be lost to the remembrance of a brother.

Masonry Dissected 1730

I hereby solemnly Vow and Swear in the presence of Almighty God and this Right Worshipful Assembly, that I will Hail and Conceal, and never reveal the Secrets or Secresy of Masons or Masonry, that shall be Revealed unto me; unless to a True and Lawful Brother, after due Examination, or in Just and Worshipful Lodge of Brothers and Fellows will met.

I further Promise and Vow, and I will not Write them, Print them, Mark them, Carve them or Engrave them, or cause them to be Written, Printed, Marked, Carved or Engraved on Wood or Stone, so as the Visible Character or Impression of a Letter may appear, whereby it may be unlawfully obtain'd.

All this under no less Penalty than to have my Throat cut, my Tongue taken from the Roof of my Mouth, my Heart pluck'd from under my Left Breast, them to be buried in the Sands of the Sea, the Length of a Cable-rope from Shore, where the Tide ebbs and flows twice in 24 Hours, my Body to be burnt to Ashes, my Ashes to be scatter'd upon the Face of the Earth, so that there shall be no more Remembrance of me amongst Masons.

Look in your ritual book as see how close it was getting nearly 200 years ago!

7
Craft history 1751-1801

The Antients 'arrive'

At the beginning of this period we see, very clearly, the three separate Degrees and as we will see with the two exposures of the 1760s, some of the ceremonial/floorwork that went with them. What we don't see yet are complete Tracing Boards, Working Tools, Openings and Closings, Charges and other items that make up our current working. Almost all these were to come somehow between the 1760s and 1813.

In Chapter 6 we looked in a fair amount of detail at why a large number of Masons were becoming very unhappy with the way that the PrGL was practising and controlling the Craft, while their ancient practices remained 'pure and unsullied'. In mid-July 1751, a group of the largely 'unhappy Irish' Masons got together and decided to set up a rival Grand Lodge, even though there were only six of their lodges in existence. Five of the lodges were typically unaffiliated to the PrGL and it has been suggested that the sixth was set up shortly before the meeting.

> Pause for thought
> There has been talk for a long time about a schism that is supposed to have occurred, but the Antients were never under or part of the PrGL so a schism or split has no real meaning here.
> Later on, Brethren were often members of both Antient and Modern lodges and at a higher level, eg. the Lion and the Lamb Lodge No. 192 not long afterwards held Antient and Modern Warrants.

The five lodges involved were by (meeting place):
    The Turk's Head, Soho
    The Cripple, Little Britain
    The Cannon, Fleet Street
    The Plaister's Arms, Grays Inn Lane
    The Globe, Covent Garden.

They agreed to form the 'Most Ancient and Honourable Society of Free and Accepted Masons according to the Old Constitutions' (we will call it the **AGL**). Its first Grand Secretary, John Morgan, issued a set of regulations for the new Order, then resigned soon after taking office. They contain 18 rules and orders, headed:

> Rules and Orders to be Observed by the Most Ancient and Honorable Society of Free and Accepted Masons. As agreed and Settled by a Committee appointed by a General Assembly held at the Turk's Head in Greek Street, on Wednesday the 17th day of July 1751 …

Morgan's successor in February 1752 was Laurence Dermott. This man, who was almost entirely responsible for starting and then making the Antients very powerful indeed, was Irish and apparently Master of a lodge there about 1746. He came to England in 1748 and joined an affiliated (PrGL) lodge, but soon after joined one of the 'rebel' lodges.

His records show that he was Secretary for some 20 years and Deputy Grand Master several times. He is generally recognised as having an extremely powerful personality (remember Anderson a few years before?); was a great organiser, a 'people-inspirer' and did more for the Antients Grand Lodge than anyone else.

Whatever else he did, he is known for two things:

He described the PrGL as the 'Moderns', an insulting term, meaning that they had not maintained the 'antient' traditions (which is why the new AGL was referred to as the 'Antients').

He overrode Morgan's Constitutions with a new set, a private venture which he called *Ahiman Rezon (AR),* allegedly the Hebrew for 'help to a brother', although no-one is exactly sure where the title came from.

> Pause for thought
> *AQC* 23:162-166 has an interesting paper by Rosenbaum on its origin; Vol. 46:239-296 by Adams is an extremely detailed analysis of the work and there is a more recent one in Vol. 105:49-68 by Sharman.

Ahiman Rezon

It was published in 1756. The regulations start with:

> AHIMAN REZON OR A help to a Brother Shewing the EXELLENCE OF SECRECY And the first Cause or Motive of the

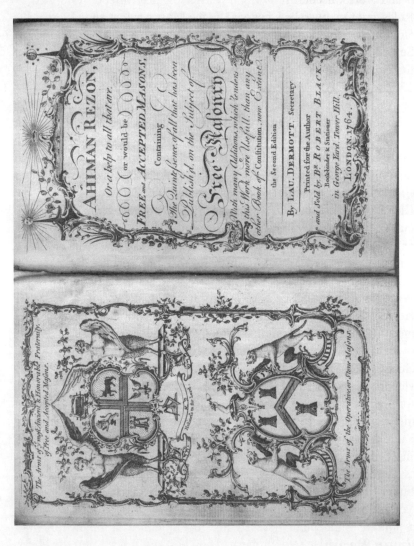

Fig 7.1: *Ahiman Rezon* frontispiece.

Institution of FREE MASONRY; THE PRINCIPLES of the
CRAFT and the Benefits arising from a strict Observance thereof;
What sort of MEN ought to be initiated into the MYSTERY...

Robert Turner was the first Grand Master of the Antients, followed by Edward Vaughan, but it was not until 1756 that a 'noble' Grand Master, the Earl of Blessington, took over and this may be why *AR* was not published earlier. The dedication starts:

MY LORD, AT the Request of several Worthy FREE-Masons, I undertook to publish the following SHEETS, wherein I have endeavoured to let the young Brethren know how they ought to conduct their Actions with Uprightness, Integrity, Morality, and Brotherly Love, still keeping the ancient Land-Marks in View. On the Perusal, Your LORDSHIP will find that the Whole is designed not only for the Good of Fraternity, but also to shew that the true Principles of FREE-MASONRY are to love Mercy, do Justice, and walk humbly before GOD.

Dermott must have used Anderson's Constitutions as a basis, and possibly the Irish Constitutions which he might have been used to in his Irish Masonic career - Spratt, the General Secretary of the Irish Grand Lodge, published his Constitutions (based on Anderson) in 1751.

At the beginning, instead of Anderson's history, is an extended introduction attacking the original Grand Lodge, now calling itself the Grand Lodge of England, but saddled by Dermott with 'the Moderns' in contrast to the 'Antient' usages of the new Grand Lodge.

He then pours deep scorn on *Masonry Dissected*, including an incredibly non-PC piece of anti-Jewish material about a Jew called Balthazar Amraphel – how about '... Dat iss de vay moy boy dat aur peoples ...' - with a long and weird description of the author of MD, followed by more strange history (it seems that the main qualification for producing a working Constitution was the ability to generate 'history'). He continues with an account of how, while writing a history, he fell asleep. He dreamt of a conversation with Ahiman about Masonic history, after which an Ancient in a shining breastplate perused his first attempt at the history and pronounced an old Hebrew proverb 'Thou hast div'd deep into the water, and hast brought up a potsherd'. This implied that the history was rubbish, but that with time and learning he would 'write many other things of great service to the community'.

He was woken from the dream by his neighbour's puppy 'which had eaten his manuscript'. Full of sorrow and grief, he rushed to the dog's owner who said 'he would hang the cur, but at the same time he imagined I should be under more obligation to him for so doing than he was to me for what happened'. As a result of all this, he says that after feeling chastened by the experience, he then re-thought how to present the history (what a truly humble man!).

He then goes into a mixture of Masonic philosophy and recommendations. Then he rips into the Moderns, making very sarcastic claims:

> About the year 1717 some joyous companions who had passed the degree of a Craft, (though very rusty) resolved to form a lodge for themselves, in order (**by conversation**) to recollect what had been formerly dictated to them, or **if that should be found impracticable**, to substitute something new which might for the future **pass for Masonry** amongst themselves.
>
> Did anyone know the master's part? Answer No!. Resolved, that the deficiency should be made up with **a new composition and what fragments of the old order found amongst them** should be immediately reformed and made more pliable to the humours of the people.

In other words, he says that they had a chat and what they couldn't remember or didn't like, they cooked up something to get by on!

There then follows another burst of sarcasm on the Moderns' 'unconstitutional fopperies', relating to dining, the wearing of aprons, etc.!

Next, more history and more morals and behaviour, with strong statements of belief in the Craft and its precepts.

Then follow seven 'old charges', similar to those in Anderson; the manner of constituting a new lodge and various prayers; and after more history, he goes into the administration side of running lodges with 'THE GENERAL REGULATIONS OF THE Free and Accepted MASONS' and, finally, a whole string of songs!

Pause for thought

A very interesting paper, *The Moderns & The Antients*, by A. Heiron, says much more about the activities of Dermott, including a quote from *Ahiman Rezon*:

A Mason should not only perform his Duty to his great Creator, but also to his Neighbour and himself: For to walk humbly in the sight of God, to do Justice and love mercy are the certain Characteristics of a Real, Free and Accepted Ancient Mason.

AGL Progress

Dermott and the rest of the AGL must have worked very hard to promote the lodge and its degrees. They gave a kind of 'authorised respectability' to their lodges by issuing Warrants from 1752 (which the Moderns did not do until later). In 1753 there were listed 10 or more AGL lodges, and by 1766, more than 80 were added. The success of the Antients, now presenting a major challenge as a rival to the PrGL, was probably due to the number of Masons who really wanted to be part of a lodge that claimed to all and sundry that it was ancient, had a basis way back in time, and was not interested in time-saving and other innovations.

The AGL got ahead of the PrGL by issuing Warrants to military lodges, which led to the spread of the Antient Craft throughout the world where the flag of the English army flew. When a regiment settled for a time, it would have attracted local candidates, who would no doubt seek to form their own lodge when the regiment went on to further glories.

Pause for thought

America! Both before and after the War of Independence, there would have been many opportunities for the spread of the Craft there and this may help to explain why a fair amount of US working is more 'Archaic' than English, perhaps deriving from early Irish working. Some State Grand Lodges still use Dermott's title for their Constitutions. In 1868, Daniel Sickles published in the USA *The General Ahiman Rezon and Freemason's Guide*, containing much ceremonial and symbolic information (but no ceremonies as such!)

At this time, we have two Grand Lodges operating quite independently. The existence of these two 'Grand' Lodges led to competition and bitter rivalry. They were each laying down the law about wording, ceremonies and procedures, much of which was totally ignored by 'those old boys', ie. old-established lodges with years of tradition and who were probably a long way from London (news travelled slowly in those days!). We start to see the gradual rise of a culture of 'we've always done it that way (even if it is not strictly correct)'. This might have been part of the driving force behind the later variations in ritual, both printed and word-of-mouth.

Perhaps for nationalistic (anti-English) reasons, the AGL had good relations with the Grand Lodges of Scotland and Ireland - perhaps the loftiness of the PrGL as 'the very first Grand Lodge' was another factor. Within 50 years of its inception, the AGL was probably as powerful as the PrGL, which had major consequences when the two Grand Lodges finally combined (Chapter 10).

Early Antient Grand Masters

1753	Robert Turner
1754-56	Edward Vaughan
1756-59	Earl of Blessington
1760-66	Earl of Kelly
1766-70	Hon. Thomas Mathew
1771-74	John, third Duke of Atholl
1775-81	John, fourth Duke of Atholl
1783-91	Earl of Antrim
1791-1813	John, fourth Duke of Atholl
1813	Duke of Kent.

The fact that a Duke of Atholl was Grand Master for a total of nearly 30 years led to AGL lodges being referred to as 'Atholl' lodges, a name that continues today.

The Moderns

After the formation of the AGL, the PrGL went through a doldrum period, mainly because it and its Grand Masters just didn't bother - refer back to Chapter 6 for the undistinguished career of Lord Byron.

> Pause for thought
> BJ1 (p.208) says that in 1764 Cadwaller, the 9th Lord Blayney, became Grand Master of the PrGL, aged 44, even though he was actually an Antient Mason (from a military lodge) and after some years of difficulty, he managed to re-establish and extend the power of the PrGL and its lodges.

Over the years, Blayney made suggestions about the ritual and, in some cases, recommended that Antient working might be introduced. He had joined the Royal Arch and was the first of the PrGL Grand Masters to sponsor it. He was responsible for the issue of the 'Charter of Compact' in

1766, which formally launched the 'Supreme Grand Royal Arch Chapter of England', thereby removing one of the major objections of the AGL to PrGL working.

In 1760, he appointed Thomas Dunckerley as Provincial Grand Master of Hampshire. Dunckerley was said to have been a bastard son of King George II. He had spent a long time in the navy but was eventually pensioned off. While in the navy, he was involved with the setting up of various naval lodges. He served as Grand Master for a number of Provinces, had much to do with raising funds for the new Freemasons' Hall and managed to re-open Masonry in places where it had ceased to operate. His other hat was to do PR work for the PrGL and 'recruit' AGL Masons.

Battle between the two Grand Lodges was apparently fierce. There was much made of 're-making', ie. a PrGL Mason would have to be re-initiated (ie. re-obligated) into an AGL lodge and vice versa.

J&B/TDK

As far as the ritual was concerned, we now come to one of the more exciting, but probably most frustrating, elements of Masonic history. We have looked at the situation regarding the Third Degree after Prichard (1730) and we know that there were certain developments occurring in France. Nevertheless, the material presented in the next set of exposures - *Three Distinct Knocks* (*TDK*) in 1760 and *Jachin and Boaz* (*J&B)* in 1762 - is very much more detailed and richer both in the ritual wording and in the descriptions of the ceremonial. We will look later at the work of people such as Preston and others, and how they would have further enriched the ritual, but the material in *TDK* and *J&B* is not too far from what to what we do today.

> Pause for thought
> This is exciting! But it is also frustrating. There appears to be very little information available explaining, or even guessing, at how and from where, between 1730 and 1760, all this extra richness came from. There have been other occasions mentioned in the book where lack of evidence leads to supposition and guesswork. In this case, I think we are unable to suppose or guess anything. _

The two pieces of work are quite similar, although allegedly written by quite different people. *AJ* (Chapter 11) gives a complete reproduction of both.

TDK was written by a German who claimed, in the introduction, to have read Prichard and other publications and, after travelling in France and England, was completely accepted in English lodges. He says in the rambling introduction that he was invited to an 'Irish lodge that call'd themselves the most antient Masons'. He also says '… but the other I don't meddle with because there is a book already published called Masonry Dissected which …'. In other words, he implies that *MD* is for the Moderns and his super new book is for the Antients. This is reinforced in the title page of the work, which says:

> Three distinct Knocks or the Door of the most ANTIENT FREE-
> MASONRY, Opening to all Men, Neither Naked nor Cloathed,
> Bare-foot nor Shod, &c …

J&B, which looks like a major rip-off of *TDK*, was written by a self-confessed 'intruder' into the Craft. He says in the introduction that he became interested, read some papers, and quickly conned his way into lodges. He wrote *TDK* apparently both to get the Craft a good reputation among people and to encourage others to consider joining (with a very brief explanation of what he does in the book).

The title page of *J&B* says:

> JACHIN AND BOAZ; OR, AN AUTHENTIC KEY To the DOOR of
> FREE-MASONRY…

It is difficult to say whether *J&B* and *TDK* actually contain 'Speculative' material. They are textually more complex and appear more symbolical than *MD*, but this could just reflect 30-odd years of development.

TDK main Details

There is a detailed description of the preparation of the floor and mention of the mop and bucket to clear it up afterwards. The rest is as follows:

Opening the lodge – very similar to today except that:

- … This Lodge is open in the name of God **and holy St John** …

There is no specific ritual for Closing the lodge (see Calling On and Off)

- Entered Apprentice lecture (catechism) and prayer followed by
  the Obligation
- Further catechism, including Working Tools and the giving of
  Signs, Tokens and Words

There is an interesting answer to a question:

- I was order'd to be taken back, and invested with what I had been
  divested of; and to be brought back to return Thanks, and to
  receive the benefit of a Lecture **if Time would permit**.

THE

THREE DISTINCT KNOCKS

OR,

The Door of the most Ancient

Free-Masonry,

OPENING TO ALL MEN,

*Neither Naked nor Clothed, Bare-Footed
nor Shod, &c.*

BEING

AN UNIVERSAL DESCRIPTION OF ALL

ITS BRANCHES,

FROM

ITS FIRST RISE TO THIS PRESENT TIME,

As it is delivered in all Lodges

Giving an exact Account of all their Proceedings in the making a
Brother, with the Three Obligations or Oaths belonging to the
First, Second, and Third Degrees of Masonry, viz. The Entered
Apprentice, Fellow-Craft, and Master-Mason; with the Obligation
belonging to the Chair, and the

Gripe and Word.

Also, full Descriptions of the Drawing upon the Floor of the
Lodge, with the Three Steps, and a Prayer used at the making of a
Brother; with Songs to be sung after grave business is done; and
the Examination of a Brother, whereby they may get Admittance in to
a Lodge, without going through the Obligations.

By W***O***V***N.

Member of a Lodge in England at this time.

London:

PRINTED AND PUBLISHED BY J. BAILEY,
CHANCERY LANE.

One Shilling.

FRONTISPIECE.

The interior of a Masonic Lodge, with the Ceremony of
making a Mason.

Published by J. Bailey, Chancery Lane, London.

It sounds as if they often could not be bothered to go through all the details of the lengthy explanation and questions (reasons) still to come.

• Calling On and Off – similar to today with a couple of twists. After Calling Off, '**If Time does not permit for the Craft's lecture** … then they close the lodge ... the **Senior Warden** declares it …'.

It seems from this that our current Closing procedure, where the Master gives the SW permission to close, probably stems from this.

• Fellow-Craft's Part – a detailed description similar to today with Signs, Words, etc. There is no specific Tracing Board. The wording we know is included in the Fellowcraft's part and we hear about 'brass pillars', 'wages in the middle chamber', 'clay ground', etc.

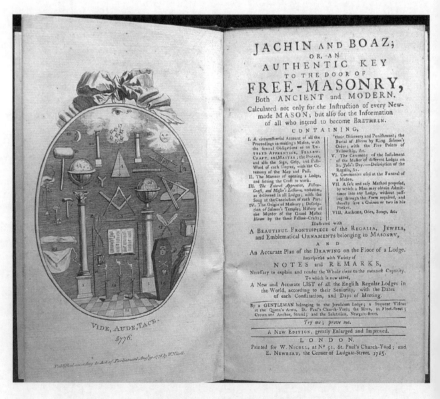

Fig 7.3: *Jachin and Boaz* 1762.

- The Master's part – the description is similar to today, with all Signs and Words, a very detailed 'traditional history', with a mention of the blood-stained cloth thrown over the Candidate during the lowering (from the French exposures?), and full details of the FPOF.

Note that near the end is a description of the position of the Bible, Square and Compasses - how they should be laid out (corresponding very closely to what we do today).

J&B main details

- Opening the lodge – as for *TDK*
- A very detailed description of the preparation of a Candidate (not done in *TDK*).

Two aspects that may have come from France - in the Old Charges, the Candidate is taken outside and terrified before the ceremony. *J&B* say that he is left to reflect on things in a Chamber of Reflection before being brought in. After light is restored to the Candidate, he sees that he is within the circle of swords.

- The Oath and further specification of the ceremony
- The Entered Apprentice Lecture and prayer and more questions – very similar to *TDK*, but referring to the oath that was specified earlier!
- More questions, Signs etc. – similar to *TDK*
- Calling On and Off – very similar to *TDK*
- The Fellow Craft's lecture and the Master's part – as *TDK*
- The Installation and investment of Officers and a description of some officer's collar jewels (not in *TDK*).

There are various bits and pieces within the works which don't tell us much about ritual or ceremonial. Whether either exposure was specifically geared to one particular Grand Lodge, it seems clear that, with the popularity of the two, we can be fairly sure that we have identified much of Antient and Modern practices of the time. Some time later the two were published together, ie. both in the same book.

Pause for thought

Far and away the most significant difference between the two is as follows:

In the 'Fellow-Craft's part', in response to the question 'what were the two brass pillars called', *TDK* (alleged Antients) says 'B..

and J..' while *J&B* (Moderns) says 'J.. and B..' This is clear evidence that the pillar words were different for the two Grand Lodges.

The state of the Degrees and the ritual

Ceremonies vs. Lectures

An important point, which may not have been made so far. If we look at the OCs, from the *Regius* right up the 18th century derivatives, they all have questions and answers. It seems very likely, as we have already said, that the ceremonial part was probably quite short – not a lot more than a prayer, an oath (obligation) and the giving of various secrets.

One might wonder why, both in the later OCs, in *TDK*, *J&B*, etc, the authors could not have realised that the obvious way to lay out the details was similar to our current Blue Books, with clear distinction between 'black' and 'red', ie. ritual in black, procedural notes in red and other comments, either as footnotes or in an appendix – too much to ask for, unfortunately!

This was not done, probably because the ceremony as such was quite short, so we cannot be sure if it was actually done during a ceremony or as one of a series of lectures, at a later stage. (For example, after our present Second Degree, we might these days, if time is short, say that the Tracing Board 'will be done on a future occasion'.)

Fig 7.4: … hele, conceal and never..

We refer to the above series of lectures as 'the lectures' - other aspects of the working, such as Opening and Closing, Obligations, Working Tools, Tracing Boards, etc, are the ceremony itself. The separation of the two fairly obviously is a nod to the traditions of the early practices as detailed in the manuscripts. As we will see shortly, the ceremonial aspects were largely specified (although not necessarily followed) after the Union, but the lectures did not stabilise until later. (Chapter 10 looks at the work of Richard Carlile, whose lectures of 1832 are very similar to our modern version.)

Degrees

The diagrams of an Initiation and a Raising that follow are taken from prints produced by Thomas Palser in 1809.

Examination of the Old Charges would indicate that there was at first just one degree, that of the Entered Apprentice, which many Masonic experts would say was to enter a trained mason, rather than a young, untrained initiate.

By the end of the 17th century, we know that there were two Degrees, one for the acceptance of the Entered Apprentice and one for the Fellow of the Craft and Master (the two not being separated as far as the ceremony was concerned).

Pause for thought
Remember from Chapter 4, the *Edinburgh Register House* MS and

Fig 7.5: '…and laid him lifeless …'.

others have reference to Fellowcrafts and then Masters and from say 1720 until Prichard (1730) the degree ceremonies were 're-organised' and the material for a Third Degree started to evolve (murder, raising ...), even though not specifically worked as a Third Degree.

By the way, we need to be clear about the term 'master'. In the early days of operative masonry, **the** master mason was actually a master builder in charge of all the operative masons, who elected him with no specific ceremony (other than some form of obligation?). But as we have seen from later Old Charges and from Prichard, the term 'master's part' began to be used to describe the 'murder, raising..' ceremony and once this came into more common use, the practice started of calling the mason who had been through the ceremony as a 'pass'd master' or 'passed master'. The term 'chairing' was also used for the ceremony. The term 'installation' probably came in after the formation of the PrGL.

Until the Third Degree became fully established, there were a number of 'masters lodges' in existence (we would call them 'Installed Masters' lodges today).

A slightly different use of the word 'chair' is of importance. As the Royal Arch started to mature, some time in the 1730-40s, it became obvious that there was no Degree for a Master associated with the Chair. There was an Installation ceremony and presumably some form of Obligation, etc. which defined the Master. It is not the place of this book to offer views on the development of Royal Arch ritual and whether it was partly derived from Craft ceremonies, but it became the practice to insist that passing this Chair ceremony was a pre-requisite for Exaltation. You will perhaps recall from Chapter 5:

Note, there is not one Mason in an Hundred that will be at the

Expence to pass the master's part, except it be for interest.

Since the 'Chair Degree' was not that popular, and most Masons not going through their Chair anyway, the Royal Arch degree might never have got off the ground. A device was invented whereby a Master Mason could in effect be 'chaired' in a ceremony which **temporarily** put them into the Master's Chair, thereby allowing the transfer of 'certain secrets'.

We will meet a certain John Knight in Chapter 9. Of the material I have access to, part is the Exaltation ceremony. The following is a short extract:

- ... Open the Masters Lodge in the usual form.
- The Candidate is prepared to enter the Masters Lodge by **the usual Knocks & Questions**, brought up to the Pedestal by election. Exhorted to Kneel. Administer the following Ob.

    I, ..., ..., In the presence of Almighty God and this Right Worshipful Lodge, Do most Solemnly and Sincerely Swear that I will not reveal the Chair Word that shall now be given to me to any person in the World...
- Raised by the Master's Grip. Give the Grip and Chair Word...
- After Candidates **passing the Chair**, the RW Master **resumes the chair**, and proceeds to deliver this Charge ...

    Pause for thought

    Much material has been offered about why and how the Third Degree evolved from the First and Second (probably) and the evolution of the Royal Arch ceremony and ritual. It is a very complex subject and, with regret, we have barely scratched the surface in this book.

In *TDK* and *J&B* there seem to be many questions, reasons, lectures, etc., and it is difficult to accept that in the 18th century the Brethren in a lodge, still probably held at an inn, with the festive board (or at least the next glass of punch) coming up soon, would have been happy to sit right through everything in one hit. I think it makes more sense for some of the material to be used as lectures, perhaps when there was no Candidate. This may be where and why such material as our Questions before the Second and Third Degrees come from – at least their creators had some history to fall back on!

It does seem likely that the ceremony of Initiation or Passing would have been done in a room aside, while catechisms or lectures given at the festive board or when there was no Candidate. They do not help us to work out what exactly was done during a typical ceremony, but we can clearly see how *TDK/J&B* ritual could be 'cleaned up' a bit more into the form which was eventually suggested after the Union in 1813.

The more I look at our Degree ceremonies and how they evolved, the more perplexed I become. We know there were definitely two Degrees in 1696. (The *Edinburgh Register House MS 1696* – Chapter 4). It says that the prentices are to be removed and only masters to stay before the Second Degree. Unfortunately there is almost no detail about how the Degree is worked, apart from a mention of the Master's sign and a brief FPOF, and there is no separate catechism.

At the time of the formation of the PrGL, the manuscripts say 'entered apprentice' and 'master and fellow Craft', ie. two Degrees.

The *Kevan MS (1714)* says a little more about the Second Degree ceremony but no murder yet!

The *Dumfries No. 4 MS (1710)* has a long and detailed 'history', in the middle of which is a reference to Solomon, a king called Hiram who gave timber to Solomon, and an artist 'in whom was the spirit if wisdom…a man of Tyre his name was Hiram…'.

> Pause for thought
>
> To avoid even more confusion at this stage, as stated above, I propose to skate over whether there was a working-over of the Second Degree, part going into the First and part going towards a Third Degree (about which process little is known); and the sources of material about Hiram King of Tyre and the other Hiram, their origins and families, which are very confused.

The ritual by *TDK/J&B* had not yet become as rich and detailed as today and without going into the minute details, the later wording contains material, sometimes very obscure, from an incredible range of sources including numbers (Kabbala?), esoteric aspects of old religions, some Enlightenment-like science and the OCs (and contemporary documents). In all, the ritual is a strange mixture of practical working, moral philosophy and near-religious invocations, much overlaid with a touch of the mystic!

It has been suggested that Dr Desaguliers, possibly helped by the Revd Anderson (Chapter 5) spent a lot of their time re-writing and expanding the ritual and changing the workings and, in the absence of any evidence, it seems reasonable to assume that this is what they did. However, there does not appear to be any indication that either were mystics in any sense and one wonders **just who else was involved**.

As we go from (say) 1696 to *TDK/J&B*, we see the original catechisms being expanded (lots more questions), but items such as charges, addresses and prayers were still to come, although there is just a little evidence that some did exist.

> Pause for thought
>
> In the 1723 Anderson Constitutions there is a bit that says:
>
> … and after each of them the Grand Master or his Deputy shall

rehearse the short and pithy charge **that is suitable to the thing presented**.

At some point, someone would have documented these Charges and eventually expanded them to include some of our present ritual – 'your place is ... your duty is...'.

Much of the extra padding would come from the works of the people described shortly.

It does seem likely that the details of 'the drama' were known for some time. The *Graham* MS 1725, as we saw in Chapter 4, has the lifting-up of Noah's body by his sons. It also has a bit about:

'…Here lies the heart all secrets could conceal Here lies the tongue that never did reveal…'.

The *Wilkinson* MS (probably 1730) has a reference to 'our Great Master Hiram's grave' and then *MD* with the new 'Hiramic legend' and a murder, etc.

The 'whoevers' who developed the ritual must have realised that they had material for a Third Degree which would characterise the Master, as opposed to the old Second Degree for 'master and fellowcraft', but as we have said before, what directed Desaguliers (possibly!) to take a fairly simple murder and a burial/raising and turn them into a remarkable piece of 'history' and 'traditional history' will never be known – **we just have to thank him (or them) for doing it.**

Pause for thought

One point worth making! As we have said before, the previous two to three centuries had been full of strife, suspicion, battle and hatred, especially in relation to religious differences. There have been suggestions that the Raising is a thinly-covered reference to the Resurrection. But HA **does not come back to life** – his poor, mouldy old corpse is dragged out of the grave and any secrets he held are dissolved in his own corruption! Eminent scholars have said that the Third Degree is complete, in that although three persons could share the secrets, one had died and therefore because of the 'rule of three', they could no longer be communicated. It is possibly stretching things a bit to say that they were **lost** by the murder but would be recovered later on

Nevertheless, sincere Royal Arch Masons will claim that the

> earlier Christian character of the Degree is fundamental and both the Third Degree and the Exaltation ceremony clearly represent the steps to the Resurrection and man's search for Salvation. 'In the beginning was…' is both Old **and** New Testament.

From then, until 1762, some material could have come from Irish or Scottish working, from Masons 'in the outback' and from France, but there does not appear to be any clear evidence of how we got from *MD* to *TDK/J&B* and this 30-year gap in our Masonic knowledge has been a constant source of irritation to many Masonic scholars!

More ideas, from where

The Prestonian Lecture for 1928, *Masonic Teachers of the 18th Century* by John Stokes, reviews the work of many, including some covered below.

We are more fortunate in our knowledge of the period from 1768 to the Union in 1813. In this period we have the appearance of what Harry Carr calls the 'moralists'. These were people who were concerned as much with **what the Craft was about,** as to **its ritual and practices.** Perhaps they were the first who might be called 'deep Speculatives'. Five names stand out in both classes – Wellins Calcott, William Preston, William Hutchinson, John Browne and William Finch. Not all have a good reputation, but all must have contributed in some way to what we now do.

Calcott and Hutchinson were motivated **to explain the meaning/purpose of the Craft**. By contrast, Preston and others were looking for material that could be used to refine and extend the catechisms and lectures, add prayers, charges etc, **to assist in lodge ceremonies**.

Preston and others must have decided that the basic 'old-fashioned' operative ritual, even after *TDK/J&B*, was not well-enough structured, nor grand nor serious enough, so they worked on it, drawing on the language of the Bible and some of its content, together with words of their own from sources known and unknown to us.

Wellins Calcott

https://babel.hathitrust.org/cgi/pt?id=dul1.ark:/13960/t2s47p15n;view=1up; seq=242 will get you there.

In 1768, Wellins Calcott produced a defence of the Craft containing addresses, lectures, charges, etc. Harry Carr says it was a new approach – a search for some satisfactory explanation of what the Craft was about. The title page of his 1769 edition says:

A candid disquisition of the principles and practice of the most
Ancient and Honourable Society of Free and Accepted Masons
together with some strictures on the origin, nature and design of the
institution.

It starts with a long introduction containing wise and sensible notes on
Masonic history, behaviour and other matters, all with a strong basis in
Christianity. Then comes a 'disquisition', another long, detailed and very
verbose piece that contains much like the introduction. There are some very
interesting parts though. There is a detailed description of the Tabernacle
and Ark of the Covenant (which I think likely to have been incorporated
into the Royal Master Degree of the *Order of Royal and Select Masters*).

There is also a detailed breakdown of who was employed in the building
of the Temple (300 Harodim, etc.).This could well have found its way into
the Mark Master Masons' history.

Next comes a strange section. This is a letter relating to what looks like
an updated Old Charges manuscript. It claims to represent (in modern
English):

Certain questions, with answers to the same, concerning the
Mystery of Masonry, written by the hand of King Henry VI and
faithfully copied by me by command of his Highness.

It seems to be yet another history of the Craft, mixed with some philosophy,
backed up with a glossary of some of the words used. Just one question in
the original:

Are maçonnes gudder men then odhers?

Some maçonnes are not fo virtuous as fome odher menne; but yn
the moft part, they be more gude then thay woulde be yf they ware
not maçonnes. Goddit?

The letter dates it to about 1530 and says it is a copy of one 100 years
earlier!

Then comes a list of GMs and Deputy GMs from 1721 to 1767. Next
we have a list of Grand Masters, and Masters of a long list of what we now
call Provinces and Districts.

Next comes 'an account of the establishment of the Present Grand Lodge
of Scotland' from 1430 and includes the declaration by William St Clair on
being made Grand Master. The section includes a list of Scottish Grand and
Deputy Masters up to 1769.

Then a charge generally given to newly admitted Brethren:

You are now admitted by the unanimous consent of our Lodge

fellow of our most ancient and honourable society; ancient as
having been established from time immemorial and honourable as
tending in every particular to render a man so ... The greatest
monarchs ... have been encouragers of the art ... not thinking it
any diminution of their imperial dignities to level themselves with
their brethren in Masonry.

To God, in never mentioning his name ... To our neighbours in
acting on the square. To ourselves in avoiding all intemperances
and excesses.

Another Initiate charge follows, which covers different aspects, but between
them, you could almost make up today's. (You can now see how the ritual
is really starting to bubble up on the back burner!)

Then come a couple more Charges and finally 'The Postscript'. This
contains a pro-forma set of 10 bylaws for a lodge, including meeting nights,
election of officers, the payment of dues and so on. This is followed by a
set of rules that could be adopted by a lodge.

In the book there is nothing of a ritual nature, that is, no material that
changes the basic wording or ceremonial of the Degree ceremonies, but
even with the few examples given, you can see how it would have some
effect on Charges, Addresses, etc. Much of the philosophy and expression
of Masonic principles is so fine that it is amazing that the work is not widely
recognised. It contains perhaps the finest essay on charity to be found.

William Preston

It is well worth looking at a very nice review of Preston, given in
http://Freemasonry.bcy.ca/ritual/preston.pdf.

I am indebted to Colin Dyer for some ideas expressed in this section. His
book - *William Preston and His Work*, published by Lewis Masonic in 1987
- deserves more than just being on a reading list. The book covers the life
and work of Preston and has a massive Appendix, which is a complete set
of his Lectures. Just one particular quote: a certain Charles Bonnor, as part
of the Lodge of Promulgation (Chapter 10), was asked to say what
Landmarks needed to be restored. He said:

To an accurate description and recitation of the Ancient practice as
adhered to in the Lodge of which he is a member in the several
Ceremonies of Opening and Closing the lodge in the first, second
and third Degrees, and likewise in the mode prescribed and
practiced for the communicating and receiving the particular

Fig 7.6: Preston's *Illustrations of Masonry.*

secrets in those several Degrees which constitute the Ancient Land Marks in Question.

Dyer then goes on to say:

...This implies that not only was Preston's system ... different from the general practices under the premier Grand Lodge, but that Preston himself and his associates in the lodge believed it to be very close to the practices of the Antients Grand Lodge.

Preston was born in Edinburgh in 1742. He entered the London book publishing trade and in a few short years was established. He joined the Craft in 1763 in an Antients lodge. Later he joined a Moderns lodge and there are records of his being a member of a several lodges (not necessarily at the same time). He seems to have shot up rather quickly – by 1765/6 he was made Grand Steward (and was responsible for organising the Grand Festival). Over the early years of his membership of the Craft he became very interested in its history, ritual and symbolism. He devoted much of his early life to discussion with English and foreign Masons and did a vast amount of reading. He felt the need to expand on and enrich the earlier material and publish his ideas, He also wanted to 'train' and 'educate' other Masons and he developed a series of Lectures.

He was said to be extremely hard-working, had a terrific memory and was a great people-person – getting his peers to help with study, practice, etc. When he became Master of his lodge for the first time, he said:

When I first had the honour to be elected master of a lodge, I thought it proper to inform myself fully of the general rules of the society, that I might be able to fulfil my own duty and officially enforce obedience in others. The methods which I adopted with this view excited in some of superficial knowledge an absolute dislike of what they considered as innovations, and in others, who were better informed, a jealousy of pre-eminence which the principles of Masonry ought have checked. Notwithstanding these discouragements, however, I persevered in my intention.

Major sources at the time would have included Anderson's Constitutions and the two main exposures of the 1760s, *TDK* and *J&B*, as well as the earlier *MD* and the various French exposures. He certainly had access to Calcott (see Book 3 below).

The following is a quotation from *The Builder,* Vol. 1, No. 1 (1915). I make no apology for including such a large quote – it so clearly points out Prestons' value:

It was a bold but most timely step when this youthful master of a new lodge determined to rewrite or rather to write the lectures of Craft Masonry. The Old Charges had been read to the initiate originally, and from this there had grown up a practice of orally expounding their contents and commenting upon the important points. To turn this into a system of fixed lectures and give them a definite place in the ritual was a much-needed step in the development of the work. But it was so distinctly a step that the ease with which it was achieved is quite as striking as the result itself.

When Preston began the composition of his lectures, he organized a sort of club, composed of his friends, for the purpose of listening to him and criticising him. This club was wont to meet twice a week in order to pass on, criticise and learn the lecture as Preston conceived it. Finally in 1772, after seven years, he interested the grand officers in his work and delivered an oration, which appears in the first edition of his Illustrations of Masonry. After delivery of the oration, he expounded his system to the meeting. His hearers approved the lectures, and, though official sanction was not given immediately, the result was to give them a standing which insured their ultimate success. His disciples began now to go about from lodge to lodge delivering his lectures and to come back to the weekly meetings with criticisms and suggestions.

He collated much of this material (and expanded it with his own ideas). Eventually he put it all together as his 'system of lectures' for the First Degree in 1772 and the Second and Third in 1774. He taught each of them separately but never actually published them.

In 1772, Preston delivered to the Masonic world the first edition of his *Illustrations of Masonry*, a book that was to appear in many later editions, one being dedicated to the Earl of Moira, the acting Grand Master of the PrGL (who was to have so much to do with the eventual union of the two Grand Lodges). The book covered some of the Lectures for the First Degree with references to the other two, together with material on ceremonies other than the three Degrees (such as consecrating a lodge, funerals, etc.). In later editions (from 1775 and up to 12 in all), this was expanded to include all three Lectures.

To publicise the ideas that he had formulated (and perhaps to plug the book), he organised a great 'Gala', at his own expense. This was like a big, impressive lodge meeting. Grand Officers were present and the whole thing seems to have been almost as if Preston had taken over Freemasonry and was demonstrating 'his' new ritual, ceremonial and Lectures. Hopefully, he was being much more Masonic and was putting forward the equivalent of a proposal (or an 'Aunt Sally') for the Craft to accept, reject or modify.

The 1804 edition of *Illustrations*, the last edition produced by Preston before the Union, breaks down into four major elements.

Book 1: This contains 10 sections in which Preston philosophises, giving his views on friendship, the origin of the Craft, the difference between operative and Speculative Masonry, Masonic secrets, charity etc.

Book 2: Now we get into Preston's views on the ceremonies. The earlier sections do not give ritual details – they are more into offering philosophical comments on behaviour within and outside the lodge. Much of the material is quite detailed, such as the description of the five noble orders and the five senses. Looking through the work, you can spot elements that have come down into our 20th/21st century working, such as:

- Do you seriously declare upon your honour … that unbiased by friends against your own inclination and uninfluenced by mercenary motives …
- As a Mason, you are to study the moral law … to consider it as the unerring standard of truth and justice …

Section VI of this starts to explain ceremonies, beginning with the Consecration of a new lodge, including the Installation of the Master and appointment of his Officers. This ends with an address, starting:

Such is the nature of our constitution, that as some must of necessity rule and teach, so others …

Then come miscellaneous ceremonies including a Masonic funeral.

Book 3: This starts with **exactly the same material contained in Calcott** – the letter and Old Charges. It ends with an explanation of some of the questions and answers, and more history!

Book 4: Has an interesting and wide-ranging set of 14 historical sections containing Preston's views on the history of the Craft, starting before the Middle Ages and ending right up to the date of publication of the edition. The final part contains odes and songs.

> Pause for thought
> Masons of the time must have been very vocal. Preston has 34 songs. Calcott had 10 and only 3 songs are common to both lists!

Preston was expelled in 1779 by the PrGL for the material published and allegedly being involved in a public procession, and was out of things for the next seven years or so. He came back with a society he organised called 'the Order of Harodim', containing many of his distinguished colleagues, using it to teach his new Lectures. His revised sets of Lectures were published as 'pocket books'. They appeared later in 1796 as 'syllabus books', particularly for use in rehearsals.

These are very detailed indeed and although primarily concerned with Lectures, which cover all aspects of the Degrees, they contain much of a 'spiritual' nature. We said earlier that Preston was more concerned with the practicalities of the working, but a lot of the material in the pocket books is purely Speculative. The Lectures in each Degree are divided into Sections which further subdivide into Clauses. The 1st Clause in the First Degree starts with:

What is the Groundplan of Masonry?

Instruction

Why?

Because no man living is too wise to learn

What will the wise man do?

He will diligently seek knowledge

What will the Mason do?

He will do more, he will travel to find it.

The 4th Clause contains:

Whence do Masons principally come?

From the holy Lodge of brethren and fellows

What recommendation do you bring?

A double salute to the Master of the work

What other recommendation?

Hearty good wishes to all brethren assembled under his direction

What is the purpose of your visit?

To rule and direct the passions, and make a progress in the art of Masonry

How do you hope to do that?

By the aid of Heaven, the instructions of the Master and by my own industry

What he had achieved must have been impressive, because the *Illustrations* were clearly supported by the Grand Officers of the time. Over the next few years his respect and popularity grew. His system gained acceptance after he had extended his demonstrations and books to include all three Degrees and rather more material of a symbolic and speculative nature as well as Craft governance. Presumably as the whole of his system was coming into acceptance, he felt sufficiently confident to advertise his teaching arrangements (a sort of paid-for LOI of the three Degrees).

Just a small section of the Degree rituals, showing part of his Opening in the Second Degree:

What is the first care of a FC?

To have the Lodge close tyled to all under the degree

Let that duty be done

What us the second care?

To order as Masons

Are you a FC?

Try me and prove me

By what instruments can I try you?

By the square

He was obviously advancing the ritual by leaps and bounds. We should bear in mind that Preston's work up to this date was not quite the same as the two main exposures (*TDK/J&B*). He was a regular Mason and was therefore bound by his oaths of secrecy. The Lectures even now provide a good basis for ritual, ceremonial and Constitutions, but of course do not contain details of Signs, Tokens and Words (which would be essential if a cowan was to read up and then try to get in illegally!).

Preston died in 1818 and left £300 in order to fund the continuance of his system of Lectures:

To the right Hon the Earl of Moira acting as Grand Master of Free Masons in England for the time being I bequeath three hundred pounds per cent consolidated Bank annuities the interest of which shall be applied by him to some well-informed Mason to deliver annually as Lecture on the First second or third degrees of the order of Masonry according to the system practiced in the Lodge of Antiquity during my Mastership.

Before leaving Preston, this is a quotation from his 1796 edition:

Masonry passes under two denominations, **operative** and **speculative**. By the former, we allude to a proper application of the useful rules of architecture, whence a structure derives figure, strength, and beauty, and whence result a due proportion and a just correspondence in all its parts. By the latter we learn to subdue patterns, act upon the square, keep a tongue of good report, maintain secrecy, and practise charity. Speculative Masonry is so far interwoven with religion, as to lay us under the strongest obligations to pay that rational homage to the Deity, which at once constitutes our duty and our happiness. It leads to the contemplative to view with reverence and admiration the glorious works of creation, and inspires them with the most exalted ideas of the perfection of the divine Creator. Operative Masonry furnishes us with dwellings, and convenient shelters from the inclemencies of seasons; and while it displays the effects of human wisdom, as well in the choice as in the arrangement of the materials of which an edifice is composed, it demonstrates what a fund of science and industry is implanted in man for the best, most salutary, and beneficent purposes.

In later Chapters we will look at ritual after the Union and it becomes obvious that quite a lot of Preston's ritual was never used, but the basic structure and the sense of the words certainly was.

William Hutchinson

It is worth looking at http://www.phoenixMasonry.org/spirit_of_ Masonry.htm for more background.

In 1775 William Hutchinson produced, initially from a set of lectures delivered in his lodge, his publication *The Spirit of Masonry in Moral and Elucidatory Lectures*. The work is very Christian in character and is clearly the kind of speculation we **are** familiar with. In the introduction, he says:

- These lectures it is hoped may serve to detect the wretched artifices used by wicked men to impose upon the world: and may also excite in you the due exercise of those moral works which our *profession* enjoins.
- From the nature of our Society and its laws, it is difficult to write on the subject of Masonry. We are not allowed that explicit language any other topic would admit of. The moral intention of the work must plead for what is couched in allegory, or comprehended in that peculiarity of language our mysteries prescribe.

He then dedicates the book:

To Benevolence that Great Attribute of the Divinity the emulation of which dignifies the human race. This work is mostly devoutly dedicated with supplications to the Supreme that the heavenly influence of that excellent virtue may prevail with Masons unpolluted with the corruptions of the earth throughout all nations and in all ages to the end of time.

There is then the note of a sanction approving its publication by the Moderns Grand Master and other Grand Officers.The book has 14 of what he calls lectures, covering in a highly philosophical and deeply religious way a range of subjects including the nature of the lodge, lodge furniture, geometry, charity and brotherly love.

It then has 20 or more addresses and charges. From the following extracts taken from several of them, you can spot where some of our present-day wording might have come from.

There are many appropriate examples and these are selected to show you that well before the Union in 1813, we had a basis for today:

- It directs us to be peaceable subjects, to give no umbrage to the civil powers, and never to be concerned in plots and conspiracies against the wellbeing of the nation …
- It instructs us in our duty to our neighbour; teaches us not to injure him in any of his connections, and, in all our dealings with him, to act with justice and impartiality. It discourages defamation; it bids us not to circulate any whisper of infamy, improve any hint of suspicion, or publish any failure of conduct …
- It teaches inviolable secrecy; bids us never to discover our mystic rites to the unenlightened, nor betray the confidence a brother has placed in us. It warms our hearts with true philanthropy, which directs us never to permit a wretched fellow creature to pass unnoticed …
- Such is the nature of our constitution, that as some must of necessity rule and teach, so others must of course learn to obey; humility therefore, in both, becomes an essential duty; for pride and ambition, like a worm at the root of a tree, will prey on the vitals of our peace, harmony, and brotherly love.
- You have been of too long standing, and are too good a member of our community, to require now any information in the duty of your office. What you have seen praiseworthy in others, we doubt

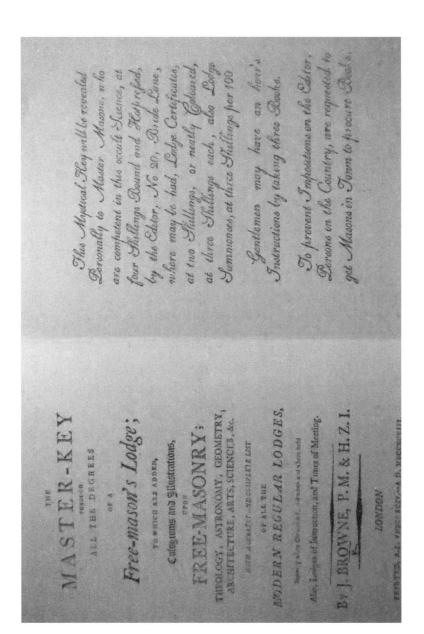

Fig 7.7: Browne's *Master-Key*.

not you will imitate; and what you have seen defective, you will in yourself amend …

- We have therefore the greatest reason to expect you will be constant and regular in your attendance on the lodge, faithful and diligent in the discharge of your duty ...

- For a pattern of imitation, consider the great luminary of nature, which, rising in the east, regularly diffuses light and lustre to all within its circle. In like manner it is your province, with due decorum, to spread and communicate light and instruction to the brethren in the lodge.

John Browne

A horrible link but the only one I can find is:

https://books.google.co.uk/books?id=lkNfAAAAcAAJ&pg=PA68&lpg=PA68&dq=master+key+di+john+browne&source=bl&ots=lHhZt30XfQ&sig=ocmm2p2TQ-PnkyULaWe4gPwrn0&hl=en&sa=X&ved=0ahUKEwjJmvr_wInOAhVKL8AKHZPSCLkQ6AEIIjAB#v=onepage&q=master%20key%20di%20john%20browne&f=false

(To access the link, you need to set it up as a single line of unformatted text in your browser.)

In 1798, John Browne produced his *Master-Key through all the degrees of a Free-Mason's Lodge,* allegedly following the Moderns. It was updated in 1802.

> Pause for thought
>
> This book is mind-blowingly frustrating. The first part is in a letter-substitution code. Apparently he substitutes each vowel 'a e i o u y' with 'b r o w n e' (a become b, etc.) and 'k c o l n u' for 'a e i o u y' (k become a, etc.). There are further complications, such as putting in padding letters, splitting up words, etc. Decoding is largely up to the creative intelligence of the trier!
>
> A reprint of the book (without decoding) is available via *Eighteenth Century Collections Online*

After the title page, there is a 'letter to the reader', in which the very generous Mr Browne offers a full book at four shillings, with an introduction containing:

This book being the first book of the kind ever presented to the

Public, the Editor is well aware that at its first appearance, it will cause much altercation in the different lodges with respect to its contents … By those who are not Masons, the author is well convinced no information can be obtained (because the ritual is encoded) …

Then follow the encoded rituals of the three Degrees:

First page heading – Sit Lux et Lux Fuit (let there be light and light will be).

Splrbsrtwbs Sostmronwprnongthrlwdgr – Brwthr Rirn owrwbrdrn ….

I think we can stop here.

Next are a set of 'Eulogiums and Illustrations' on Theology, Astronomy, Geometry, Freemasonry, Architecture, Arts, Sciences etc. These consist of a series of what seem to be randomly-selected, essay-like sections, including the Creation, the four Cardinal Virtues, the Exodus from Egypt, Faith, Hope and Charity, secrecy, the seven Liberal Arts and Sciences and the FPOF.

Two items are worth mentioning which clearly show that if Browne is to be believed, his work represented true working of the time for **Speculative Masons**. In his 'Origin of Hieroglyphical figures' we find an almost lyrical piece of prose:

… Chalk, Charcoal and clay to show that we as Free-Masons serve with Freedom, Fervency and Zeal, for there is nothing so **Free** for the use of Man as chalk, as it seldom touches but it leaves its trace, there is nothing so **Fervent** as Charcoal for when lighted, no metal is enabled to resist its force, and there is nothing so **Zealous** as Clay our Mother-earth, which is always labouring for our welfare; from whence we came. And to what we must return, as it will kindly receive us, when all our friends have forsaken us; ...

The other item is 'Jepthah's Decisive Battle over the Ephraimites', which is very much like a summary of the Second Degree Tracing Board:

… the Ephraimites crossed the River Jordan in order to pick a quarrel with Jephtha …

… gave them battle and defeated them with great slaughter …

… to pronounce the word Shibboleth …

and so on.

Next, he offers a list of lodges in the order in which they were consecrated up to 1796, a table of London lodges, a table of country lodges, the Grand Officers for the year, the Red Apron Lodges (Stewards) and then, very interestingly, a list of LOIs for each day of the week showing where and when they meet. The book ends with a list of RA Chapter meetings, showing annual calendars.

> Pause for Thought
> It seems very likely that that his ritual notes, in combination with Preston's works, were used by Brethren and were of great significance to the Lodge of Reconciliation (after the Union in 1813).

A detailed review of Browne's work is given in *AQC* 105:1 in a paper by D.S. Vieler - **God bless him!** On pages 10-13, he gives a decoded ritual. Just a brief excerpt from the Initiation ceremony:

- The lodge is opened in due form in the first degree …
- He is admitted on the point of a sharp instrument
- The Master orders him to kneel and receive the benefit of prayer (the same as ours today).
- The Master asks him in whom he puts his trust. He answers: In God …
- The Master asks him what he desires most. He answers: the light
- The Master on counting three, the Senior Warden takes the bandage from his eyes, the Brethren standing around each gives a clap on his badge …

The Passing and Raising ceremonies are similarly detailed and by the time that Finch (coming up next) had done his work and with Preston hacking around until his death in 1818, the ritual is really starting to look familiar. (We look at how things progressed after the Union of the PrGL and AGL in Chapter 10).

William Finch

See *http://Freemasonry.bcy.ca/ritual/finch.pdf*.

Finch was a tailor. He was initiated in 1794. In 1801 (revised in 1802), he produced *A Masonic key*, the later and more complete edition being called a *MASONIC TREATISE with an ELUCIDATION on the RELIGIOUS AND*

MORAL BEAUTIES of FREEMASONRY. It is in code but much less difficult to decipher than that of Browne. Although the book has lots of detail, he is very careful not to disclose any secrets of the Craft.

Finch was treated as a crook by his contemporary ritual developers. Unlike Preston, who made changes and improvements, Finch seems to have been mainly concerned with collating material in use, however varied and variable, partly to rationalise it and partly to ensure that the better parts were preserved from what was available. After publication, he was in deep trouble with Grand Lodge for the breach of his Obligation and for the rest of his life he seemed always to have been in some kind of trouble. This may be why he and his work had a bad reputation. (Carlile, who comes up in Chapter 10, referred to it as 'Brother Pick's pickpocket rubbish'!)

It is essentially a ritual book, with some material taken from Preston and Browne. The material is similar to that of earlier compilers but there is often much more 'explanation'. For example, in the first section of the EA Degree:

Q. Who are you that want instruction,

A. Free and Accepted Mason,

Q. What kind of man ought Free and Accepted Masons to be,

A. A free Man born of a free Woman, brother to a King, and companion to a beggar if a Mason,

Q. Why free,

A. That the habits of slavery might not contaminate the true principles on which Masonry is founded,

Q. Why born of free woman,

A. Because the Masons who were chosen by KS to work at the Temple, were declared free, and exempt from all imposts, duties, and taxes for them and their descendants; they had also the previlidge to bear arms. Since the destruction of the Temple by Nebuchadnezzar, they were carried into captivity with the ancient Jews, but the good will of Cyrus gave them permission to erect a Second Temple, having set them at liberty for that purpose. It is since this epoch that we bear the name of Free-Masons,

Q. Why brother to Kings or companion to beggars if Masons,

A. A King is here reminded that that although a crown may adorn his head, and a sceptre his hand, yet the blood in his veins is derived from the common parent, and no better than that of his meanest subject; the wisest Senator, or the most skilful Artist, is taught, that equally with others he is exposed by nature to infirmity, sickness, and disease, that unforeseen misfortunes may impair his faculties, and level him with the meanest of his species: men of inferior talents are here reminded (who are not placed by fortune in such exalted stations) to regard their superiors with peculiar esteem, when they behold them divested of pride, vanity, and external grandeur, condescending in **a badge of innocence and bond of friendship,** to trace wisdom and follow virtue, assisted by those who are of a rank beneath them; virtue is true nobility; wisdom is the channel by which virtue only can distinguish us as Masons.

Some of the material seems to be new. From the same section (with a few little changes!):

Q. By this I presume you are a Mason,

A. So taken

Q. How am I to know that, (I approve of you),

A. By being often approved (in sundry lodges)

Q. These brothers having given me convinceing proofs, they are Masons, how do you know yourself to be such

A. By Ss., Ts., and perfect points,

Q. What are s . . . s,

A. All Ss., Ls., and Ps., are true and proper s . . . s, to know Masons by,

Q. What are Ts.,

A. Certain regular and friendly Gs., whereby we know Masons in the dark as well as in the light,

Q. Will you give me the p . . . of your en . . . . ,

A. Of, At, and On,

Q. Of, At, and On what,

A. Of my own free will, At the door of the Lodge, and On the P. of a . . . . . or some s . . . . l .

Q. When was you made a Mason,

A. When the Sun was in its due meridian,

Q. This seems a paradox, how do you reconcile it,

A. The earth being globular (!), the Sun is always in its meridian on some part thereof,

Sound familiar?

Another set of questions is interesting, considering that Anderson's statement about religion was nearly 60 years earlier – we seem to have a writer who wants to ensure that Christianity stays in:

Q. Our Ls. being thus finished, furnished, and decorated, to whom were they dedicated,

A. To K. S.,

Q. He being a Hebrew, and dying long before the Christian era, to whom do we, as Christians, dedicate them,

A. To St. John the Baptist,

Q. Why to him,

A. He being the forerunner of our Saviour, preached repentance, and drew the first line of the gospel,

Q. Had St. John the Baptist any equal,

A. He had; St. John the Evangelist,

Q. Why is he equal to the Baptist,

A. He coming after the former, finished by his learning what the other began by his zeal, and drew a line parallel…

Yet another interesting question is the basis of the Third Degree Traditional History:

… two of the brethren then descended the g . . . e and attempted to raise him by supporting his back, but the flesh being putrid their fingers penetrated to the bone, and on smelling to them said M B, **which proves the initials of the first casual W.** they then attempted to raise him by the EA grip, which proving a slip.

Pause for thought

We saw in an earlier chapter that the MB word(s) is supposed to be the Hebrew for 'something' and I offered a thesis about 'marrow'.

'which proves the initials …' to me indicates a definite connection between 'bone' and MB – remember the *Graham manuscript* of 1726 which had Noah's sons saying 'there is marrow in the bone' and 'it stinketh'. Perhaps a bit obscure, but I hope you will give it some consideration.

Just a little more to show that the wording is nearly with us:

Q. Name the Movable Jewels,

A. The S., L., and P.R.

Q. Their uses,

A. The S. is to try and adjust all irregular corners of buildings, and
to assist in bringing rude matter into due form;
the L. is to lay Levels and prove horizontals;
the P.R. is to try and adjust all uprights while fixing them on
their proper basis.

Q. These seem to be mere emblems of labour, for why are they
called Jewels,

A. Because they have **a moral tendency**, which render them
Jewels of an inestimable value.

Q Please to give their moral tendency,

A. The S. teaches us morality and justice; the L., equality, the P.R.
integrity.

Q. By whom worn in a Mason's L.,

A. The Master and Wardens.

Q. What is the Master distinguished by,

A By the S.

Q. Why so,

A. As it is by the S., that all rude matter is brought into due form,
so it is by the same, that all animosities are made to subside,
should any there be, that order and good fellowship might be
rendered perfect and complete.

Q. What is the SW distinguished by,

A. By the L.

Q. For what reason,

A. That being an emblem of equality, points out the equal measures
that officer is bound to pursue, in conjunction with the Master,
in well ruling and governing the Brethren of the L.

Q. What is the JW known by,

A. By the P.R.

Q. Why so,

A. That being an emblem of uprightness, points out that upright
conduct, he is bound to pursue, in conjunction with the Master,
and his Brother Warden, in the well-ruling and governing the
Brethren of the L.; but more particularly, in a due examination
of strange Visitors, lest by his neglect any unqualified person
should be enabled to impose on the L., and the Brethren

innocently led to violate their O.

For each Degree there are many questions, not all of which have wording that was taken up as such, but you can recognise quite a lot, such as the Second Degree Tracing Board history, the five noble orders, etc. Near the end, he has a very detailed account of the holy vessels, etc. which made up the Tabernacle of Moses, and later, Solomon's Temple.

Whatever we have said about developments in the ritual and how it is being enriched to what we now practise, if you compare *MD* with *TDK/J&B* and then with Browne and Finch, it is surprising just how much of the 'older' ritual is still in there. Tradition has died very hard, and, even now, we can see some traces.

A comprehensive paper that covers Finch, Preston and Browne is by Douglas Vieler (who was referred to above in a paper on Browne) entitled *William Finch – the Positive View, AQC* 102: 61-97.

Remember that here, at the end of this Chapter, we are still only in 1801, just 70 years after *MD*. Things really have moved on!

A bit of excitement

Just before Finch's publication, with the profusion of clubs, societies and lodges meeting in relative secret, the government, seeing how 'secret discussions and plottings' might have helped to foster the French Revolution and desperate to prevent this Gallic disease spreading to England, put forward the *Unlawful Societies Act* in 1799. This made illegal **the administration of a secret oath.** However, through the intervention of the Earl of Moira (Acting Grand Master of the Moderns) and the Duke of Atholl (Grand Master of the Ancients), a special exempting clause was inserted in the Act so that Masonic lodges were excepted, provided they had met before the Act and they registered a list of members with the local Justice of the Peace.

In Chapter 8, we look as some theories of the origins of the Craft, some sensible, some not. We can then deal with the steps that led to the eventual Union of the PrGL and the AGL.

8
Lots of 'origins' theories

Before looking at where the Craft would go towards Union, perhaps this Chapter will be a welcome break. We examine some of the many theories that have been advanced to try and explain where the Craft came from and how it developed. Some make sense; others are nonsense but because they relate to 'time immemorial', we still don't throw them in the bin!

Early 'systems'

There has always been an element in our Craft that looked into the distant past to find esoteric beliefs, symbols and ceremonies and there is a sort of fascination with material which could have come from (in chronological order) ancient Egypt, ancient Greece and Rome, Hebrew pre-Christian cults and Mithraic mysteries. We could say that this is a serious attempt to determine the original basis of Freemasonry, but if you accept the ideas offered throughout the book, you may agree that our broad origins are fairly well established and have no need for 'mumbo-jumbo' support!

> Pause for thought
>
> Mithraism was probably practiced by 1st-4th century AD Persians and then by Romans but spread throughout Europe for a while. Mithras was said to have been born from a rock. The religion had a strong association with the planets and stars and some of the history and beliefs are said to be similar to those of Christianity.

If you are acquainted with any of these early ideas, you will find it quite easy to see something in Craft symbols, furniture, ceremonies, etc. that reminds you of them. However, seeing a square and compasses on a sculptured stone just proves that Egyptians and Greeks, as builders, must have made use of them. It is a great leap to say that this means they were early Freemasons!

Perhaps the most respected Masonic author of the 19th century was R.F. Gould, especially for his major publication *The History of Freemasonry*. This often appears as a five volume set. I am lucky enough to have a two-volume set published in 1883. You may be surprised to know that some 250 (large) pages are devoted to 'the ancient mysteries', 'the Old Charges', 'the Steinmetzen' and the French Compagnonnage.

Pause for thought
It is sometimes difficult to understand why Gould said some things. He claims for example that the Steinmetzen had a set of 73 ordinances relating to the 'Fraternity of Stonemasons'. Many of them look very much like those of the Old Charges regulations.

Notwithstanding all the work done on this by Gould, none of my text sources of information repeat this. However, as I was finishing the book, I came on a reference to *the formation of the first Grand Lodge of Freemasons, Germany 1250* on the Pietre-Stones site.

Could be worth investigating.*(http://www.freeMasons-Freemas onry.com/freeMasons_history_germany.html)*

Also, look at *http://freimaurer-wiki.de/index.php/ Steinmetz-Bruderschaften*, for an article on the Steinmetzen (an English translation is made available)

Roman Colleges

The Romans created 'Colleges' for various crafts. Something like the English guilds, some were just social, others were religious. Colleges existed, amongst others, for chair-makers, actors, brothel-keepers and wine sellers. The Colleges seemed to have a welfare aspect with a communal pool to provide for helping the poor and for funerals. There is some evidence that they brought building Colleges to England as part of the Conquest and it is very tempting to see Craft working and organisation as a derivative. It seems unlikely however that these traditions could have lasted (in secret!) from 400 AD, when the Romans left until the Gothic building period started.

Comacines

A body of masons formed near Lake Como in Italy and legitimised by Papal Bull, the Comacines were supposed to have secrets, symbols, etc, which could have come down to the Craft. Another theory that sounds nice, but has little to back it up.

Steinmetzen

Another body, apparently created after a Papal Bull, with lodges of stonemasons travelling around and involved with the building of cathedrals and other ecclesiastical buildings, with trade ordinances, apprentices, marks and feasts. Again, no real evidence that our Craft relies on it.

Compagnonnage

An alleged guild-like group of French journeying workers existing from the Middle Ages. They travelled around seeking training and experience. Allegedly, their initiation ceremony had some similarity with that of the Craft.

> Pause for thought
>
> This piece quoted from Gould is very appropriate to what we have just been saying.
>
> ... the modern Craft is like a mighty river produced by the confluence of two separate streams. The source of one is found in the Roman Colleges of Artisans (Collegia Artificum) established by Numa, King of Rome from 715 to 673 BC. They had several grades of membership, and various officers not unlike our Master and Wardens ... when barbarian invasions shattered the Empire in the fifth century of our era, the mystic art lingered on in the Lombard community of Como, Italy, where it was nursed through the Dark Ages by the famous Comacine masters ... ventured forth from Como with the Pope's blessing as 'travelling masons', and proceeded to fill Europe with majestic Gothic cathedrals. In 1410, they implanted Masonry in England and engendered the Craft guilds, the eventual parents of Freemasonry. At some stage in its long career the builders' Craft absorbed the tenets and methods of the ancient mystery religions ... certain moral and philosophical truths which they communicated to their initiates by means of symbols. At the centre of their ritual was often a legend recounting how some hero or divinity was raised from the dead.

With a pinch of salt!

The Old Charges 'history'

We have referred to the OCs or manuscripts throughout the book and it is interesting, if not enlightening, to overview the 'history' as offered from the *Regius poem* right up to the later Constitutions. Since there is so much 'Masonry' in this history, you should read it for yourself to see how quaint it is. You will see how it is possible to get time completely muddled up, but at the same time there are delightful echoes of modern Craft practice.

Here is a rather quaint but nice piece (in modern English) from the *Cooke manuscript of 1410*:

The worthy clerk Euclid was the first to give it the name of Geometry; although it was practiced before his time, it had not acquired the name of Geometry ... Euclid was one of the first founders of Geometry and gave it that name.

For in his time the river of Egypt, which is called the Nile, so overflowed the land that no one could live there. Then the worthy clerk Euclid taught them to make great walls and ditches to keep back the water and by Geometry he measured the land and divided it out into sections ... in order to provide for themselves and their children, because they had so many. Among them at the council was this worthy Clerk Euclid.

When he saw that none of them could devise a remedy in the matter, he said to them 'Lay your orders upon your sons and I will teach them a Science by which they may live as gentlemen, under the condition that they shall be sworn to me to uphold the regulations that I shall lay upon both them and you'.

The classic sources for the Regius and Cooke manuscripts are *The two Earliest Masonic MS* by Jones and Hamer published in 1938 and *KJH1* (already referenced).

Recent theories

AQC from about 1980 until about 2000 was extraordinarily rich in papers offering theories of Craft origin and it is important to review some of them. Note that for most of them, a short summary is not enough. If you are serious, you need to read them for yourself!

C. Batham, 'The Origin of Freemasonry' (*AQC* 106:16-50)

The approach is based on the secrecy resulting from several centuries of religious, political and social strife, which we looked at in earlier Chapters. There is quite a lot of persuasive evidence that monks or other members of the Church were involved with the building and the early masons. There is no doubt that the wording of later versions of the OCs and probably the wording of ritual prior to the major exposures (see Gandoff theory below) are not only Christian in nature, but quite formally Christian, as if written by and perhaps intended for enlightened Christians.

As suspicion, spying and denouncement increased, religious and other 'esoteric' bodies went underground and maintained their traditions and rites in secret. As the general environment started to improve and as the Age of Enlightenment dawned, these secret societies slowly started to emerge and eventually came out under the guise of Freemasonry.

Perhaps the major objection (voiced at the end by Bro. Richard Sandbach) is that he finds it inconceivable that such a society could have remained underground, and in secret, for such a long time, considering how powerful the authorities were and how skilled in 'rooting out opposition'. Bro. Bob Gilbert comments that he sees no evidence and no reason why ceremonies practised in secret by these societies have been in any way Masonic.

M. Brodsky, 'The religious sources of Freemasonry' (111:45-78)

This reviews the situation around the formation of the PrGL and extends this to review the possible religious influence on the development of the Craft.

H. Carr. '600 years of Craft ritual' (81:153-205)

We have met his **transition theory** before. In summary, it started with the old stonemasons. Gradually as the trade diminished it became less for actual working masons and increasingly, as a gradual, smooth transition, more for men who wanted to use the history and symbolism of the operative masons as the basis for philosophy and morality. The transition process results in our Craft - almost entirely Speculative, but which still uses ritual very close to that used when most Brethren were operative masons.

Dissenters object to the evidence and point to the opposite of a smooth transition. They say there is almost no evidence of lodges starting as purely operative, gradually expanding to non-operative and finally becoming purely Speculative. Khambatta (see below) is not happy with the theory that our present 'accepted Mason' has a link with the Accepcon (Chapter 4).

Bro. Eric Ward, in reply to Harry Carr's paper, said:

The customs regulating the trade of freestone masons, the original freemasons, were instituted and maintained for the sole purpose of protecting the interests of those who earned their living by fashioning stone. The enforcement of these regulations which these days, would not merit the term 'ritual', were themselves developed over the centuries to meet the changing circumstances of the building trade and indeed the ordinances of mason companies still in being by the time free and accepted Masonry was taking shape are quite well known.

They bear not the slightest to a beautiful system of morality etc, nor did they veer that way before 1717, although real Freemasons still operated as indeed they do today.

C. Dyer, 'Some thoughts on the origins of speculative Masonry' (95:120-169)

This very important paper, by one of the most respected Masonic historians of the 20th century, covers a vast amount of ground and contains ideas, some of which have been freely adapted throughout this present book. He firmly rejects the transition theory. There are about 24 pages of text, followed by 16 pages of discussion by many equally famous historians. A lot of work, but you need to read this for yourself!

J. Hamill, 'The Jacobite conspiracy' (113:97-113)

This paper looks at the theory that speculative Freemasonry came, during the first half of the 18th century, from the Jacobites (the supporters of Charles Stuart, the young pretender to the Scottish throne). The author is at great pains to point out that his paper presents the facts and that from them he, in effect, kills off the theory. It rests on the Jacobites forming early lodges and having great influence. It claims that Bonnie Prince Charlie was the Grand Master and could transfer authority to whomsoever he wished. It is also supposed to be the case that GL in 1717 was formed as a reaction to the Jacobite revolution of 1715.

The author states that there is no evidence at all that any of the early Grand Masters of the post-1717 Grand Lodge had any Jacobite connections, nor that the Prince was in fact a Mason. During the 20 years or so after 1717, much Masonic activity occurred in France, with active Jacobites possibly driving things, but no real evidence that French Masonry shows any Jacobite influence. (The paper and comments by learned Brethren seem to have killed it stone dead.)

J. Mandelberg, 'Secrets of the Craft' (113:14-38)

Not a theory as such. This is a very heavy paper, which covers much ground, starting by adding more persuasive comment against the transition theory; at the same time reviewing much of the history of the 13th-15th centuries.

The rest of the paper looks at the philosophy and esoteric traditions associated with building over the millennia.

His conclusion is a very nice summary of why we need to be very careful about origins theories, based upon what we **know**, rather than what we **believe**. (Another paper that the serious reader must become familiar with.)

R. Sandbach, 'The Origin of the Species - The Freemason' (108:48-80) Various comments on the development of Speculative Masonry. He starts with 'what' – the difference between non-operative and Speculative. Then 'when' – at what point did speculation appear. 'Who', a review of some of the people concerned. 'How' – what mechanisms and documents assisted in the development. 'Where' – which parts of the country – London, Scotland, elsewhere? 'Why' – some review of history, with the idea that one source of development could have been the need, in the violent and troubled times of the 16th-17th centuries, for people to have access to groups, via secrets, for protection as much as for meetings to discuss philosophical questions in a convivial atmosphere

.

A.T. Stewart. 'English Speculative Freemasonry: Some possible Origins, Themes and Developments' (117:116-182) This is a long and complex paper, which, for readers of this Chapter, will reinforce and considerably extend this author's ideas. The paper's main thesis, that whatever happened in the centuries before the 18th century, whatever were the 'doings' and 'thinkings' of building trade guilds, secretive religious societies, operative lodges etc, the basis of our Freemasonry owes it structure and much of its content to thinkers in the 18th century (often called the 'Age of Enlightenment'). He defines clearly a 'Stage I' when things were fairly primitive and for which there is little documentary evidence and a 'Stage II' which starts to look more like today and for which there is plenty of evidence.

The paper shows how some of the content of the OCs was employed by people, such as Preston. There is much more and any reader who has enjoyed this book so far must refer to this important paper (even though tough to handle!).

R. Khambatta, 'Ars Quatuor Coronatorum of the Twentieth Century' (114:1-9) Finally, for AQC papers, W. Bro. R.B Khambatta, in his inaugural paper in

2001 as Master of QC Lodge, provides a summary of a wide range of origins theories.

Bernard Jones - You should read *BJ1* pp. 97-8 for questions raised by him on the emergence of Speculative Masonry.

Freemasonry Today – the Best of Ten Years, published in 2007, has an article by the Revd N. Barker Cryer on the significance of guild mystery plays in the development of our ritual. He shows how some of the histories acted out and have a remarkable 'overlap' with what we do.

The Gandoff 'Knock-up' theory

Being cynical but also realistic, with such a lack of evidence available to us, **I suggest** there is the distinct possibility that the 18th century ritual (say up to 1730) could have been largely produced by a Mason who had done some research and thought it was a good idea to develop and promote another 'other degree' for Masons. Suppose Prichard and a couple of educated and classics-oriented colleagues (such as Desaguliers) got together a while before 1730 and agreed that what they thought was a relatively unsophisticated, operative ritual needed beefing-up and made a little more esoteric and more to the liking of the 'gentry' rather than the 'common mason'. It was also an opportunity to look at the two Degrees and re-arrange and add parts to form, nominally, what would be a degree for Masters, not just with the Fellowcraft's and Master's combined.

Taking what they thought was current practice, with a number of recent manuscripts to go on, perhaps they added a whole lot of new stuff and Prichard then published his book, claiming that the ceremonies represented what was being done **all over London!**. In the absence of any other widely available, written sources of ritual, it is hardly surprising that it was so successful and that lodges adopted the well-defined 'extra practices'. Eventually everyone (!) would be likely to believe that they were 'since time immemorial' – a common Masonic excuse for doing something without always having a good reason!

If this was indeed the case, **what a superb piece of marketing**! You want to introduce a major change (in effect a whole new ritual), but instead of trying to do it by pussy-footing it within lodges, with a good chance of hitting the brick wall of stuffy and reactionary 'old Masons' at every stage, you slam-dunk the Craft with a sure-fire scandal:

**You are a bunch of crooks: I am going to expose you as such
and tell the world all about your ridiculous ceremonies.**

Some person or persons, in this author's view, did a very great service to
the Craft. If you look at the catechisms that were probably in use in the
early 1700s in the various OC manuscripts and early exposures, you can
see that they are a rag-bag of questions, answers, comments, signs, etc.

Our someone(s) must have spent ages, reading, sorting, collating and
re-writing, in order to get as far as *MD* (if indeed, this was the final 'new
ritual'). After this (ie. from Prichard, via *TDK/J&B* and the Lodge of
Reconciliation) others like Preston must have carried on reading, digging,
etc. to get to where we are today. Refer back to the beginning of Chapter 5,
where when looking at Desaguliers, I offer the 'unique' view that he might
actually have been Prichard!

My idea certainly cannot be proved, but no-one can say that it is total
nonsense. In fact, although this section appears to be scornful, perhaps the
'writers' of the ritual and those they associated with, genuinely thought that
they were developing the earlier wording, bringing in more of the **building**
aspects. Their thinking and philosophy led them to believe that the whole
basis was that of **building a better world**. While this was almost certainly
not entirely new thinking for Masons, coming after the Age of Reason, it
may at least offer a partial explanation as to why:

**all our basic Craft traditions are related to the building of
King Solomon's Temple, to the greater glory of the GAOTU!**

9
Moving on – 1802-1817

Attempts at reconciliation

For this period, we have Masons considering themselves up-to-date with regulations and workings, the PrGL in existence for 90+ years and AGL for 50+. Both Grand Lodges realised that they could not compete profitably for ever and many members and probably the management, would have looked for items and whole areas where some kind of fraternal rationalisation might be effected.

The cooperation between the two Grand Lodges over the *Unlawful Societies Act* showed that there could be some coexistence between them. There is quite a lot of evidence of non-hostility, if not actual cooperation, especially with many Masons being in both PrGL and AGL lodges and PrGL Masons having long before been exalted into Royal Arch, directly against the rulings of the PrGL. In 1797, a motion was put forward by the AGL, to set up a Committee to examine if there was any way that a union with the PrGL could be organised. (It didn't succeed at the time, but nice try!)

In 1804 attempts were made through the Earl of Moira (who served as Acting Grand Master of the PrGL until the Union) to look at a way to a union but again, nothing happened. Then in 1808, Moira did something earth-shattering – he negotiated a complete acceptance of the Moderns by the Grand Lodge of Ireland, thereby matching what the Antients had negotiated earlier and probably broke their monopoly (hence more pressure on them to 'think union').

On 12th April 1809, after switching the pillar words back to their original significance (B then J), the PrGL very generously (!) issued a resolution:

That it is not necessary any longer to continue those measures which were resorted to, in or about the year 1739, respecting irregular Masons, and do therefore enjoin the several lodges to revert to the Ancient Land Marks of the Society.

As well as reinstating the pillar words, the PrGL surely must have looked at all workings to see what changes they would need to achieve in order to provide a basis for a union, especially the Installation ceremony, which they had neglected. They admitted that it was a true Landmark and must be preserved (an attempt to provide a graceful but hidden offer to the Antients?).

The Lodge of Promulgation

The next earthquake was when the Earl of Moira issued a resolution on 12th April 1809, as to the formation of the 'Lodge of Promulgation', a vital 'lodge' within the PrGL, which would make recommendations as to the Landmarks, differences in ritual and procedures, etc. The Resolution was:

That this Grand Lodge do agree in opinion with the Committee of Charity that it is not necessary any longer to continue those measures which were resorted to in or about the year 1739 respecting Irregular Masons, and do therefore enjoin the several Lodges to revert to the ancient Land Marks of the Society.

The Warrant was issued on 26th October:

We therefore for the better carrying into effect the intention of the said Grand Lodge do hereby constitute [the brethren who are named] into a Lodge of Free and Accepted Masons to be opened at Freemasons Hall for the purpose of Promulgating the Ancient Land Marks of the Society and instructing the Craft in all such matters and forms as may be necessary to be known by them in Consequence of and Obedience to the said Resolution and Order … And we do hereby will and require you the said Brethren to appoint days of meeting when you will give such instruction … in order that all Masters of Regular Lodges and such other Brethren as you may think proper may have an Opportunity of attending the same And we do further require the Master to take special care that all and every the said Brethren do perform and keep all the Rules and Orders contained in the Book of Constitutions.

The Warrant was originally for one year but was extended to 31st March 1811. The Lodge commenced its deliberations on November 21st, 1809. The members held it to be their duty first to ascertain what were the Ancient Landmarks and the Ancient practice, and then to communicate them to the Craft at large.

At its second meeting it invited:

a Special attention in the first instance to the ascertaining what
were the Ancient Landmarks which they were required to restore.

The Secretary then asked for a detailed review of the difference between
Antient and Modern working, which was given by a former member of an
Antients lodge. The full workings of the three Degrees and Installation
ceremonies were examined in detail, with a clear intention to assist union
with the Antients (even if they had to bend over backwards!). It made
several Resolutions including:

the Ceremony of the Installation of Masters of Lodges is one of the
two Landmarks of the Craft and ought to be preserved. (The word
'two' is thought to be a misprint for 'true'!)
Deacons (being proved on due investigation to be not only Ancient
but useful and necessary Officers) be recommended.

Other matters included the situation of the Wardens, Opening and Closing,
the forms of preparation and the Initiation of Candidates.

In spite of their frustrations, the Antients were not very good at making
decisions without reporting back to a quarterly meeting of their own Grand
Lodge, but in October 1812 they finally gave their representatives full
power to negotiate personally. The AGL must have seen the writing on the
wall and just before the end of the work of the Lodge of Promulgation, it
grudgingly (!) resolved:

that a Masonic Union on principles equal and honourable to both
Grand Lodges, and preserving inviolate the Land Marks of the
Ancient Crafts, would, in the opinion of this Grand Lodge be
expedient and advantageous to both.

In other words 'let's resolve our differences and return to the Ancient
Landmarks once we have ascertained what those ancient Landmarks and
obligations were.'

As soon as this was presented to the PrGL (who, by now, were almost
gagging for union, in order to ensure that the Antients could never supersede
them in the future), within one month they leapt in with:

That this Grand Lodge welcomes with unfeigned cordiality the
desire expressed by the Grand Lodge under his Grace the Duke of
Atholl for a Union.

Pause for thought

AQC 23:37-71 (1910) has a long paper by W. Hextall entitled *The Special Lodge of Promulgation, 1809-1811*. It contains detailed notes on meetings and has a wealth of information about the work of the Lodge. A comment on the paper made by W. Wonnacott (a very respected Masonic scholar of the period (page 60) is worth quoting:

… the Grand Lodge of the Moderns did not suddenly assume a benevolent attitude towards its opponents in order to pass this resolution of April 1809, on the Landmarks of the Order, but that it was practically forced to this conclusion by the pressure of the rank and file after some years of negotiation, official and semi-official, all of which had resulted in failure, **largely due to the attitude of the Moderns themselves.**

Finally - Union

At the end of 1813 the PrGL authorised the members of the Lodge of Promulgation to act as a Committee to negotiate the 'desirable arrangement' with the Committee from the Antients. The time was ripe for *The Articles of Union between The Two Grand Lodges of Freemasons of England,* which were developed and signed on the 1st December 1813 by the two Grand Masters.

On 27th December, St John the Evangelist's Day, the two Grand Lodges opened themselves separately (the Duke of Sussex, son of King George III, Grand Master of the Moderns and the Duke of Kent as Grand Master of the Antients) and the Royal Brethren moved quickly to accomplish the reconciliation. They then processed into the main Freemasons' Hall and the *Act of Union* amalgamating the two Lodges (to form the United Grand Lodge) was confirmed.

The Articles proclaimed:

Be it known to all men, That the Act of Union between the two Grand Lodges of Free and Accepted Masons of England, is solemnly signed, sealed, ratified, and confirmed, and the two Fraternities are at one, to be from henceforth known and acknowledged by the style and title of **THE UNITED GRAND LODGE OF ANCIENT FREEMASONS OF ENGLAND**; and may the Great Architect of the Universe make their Union eternal.

Fig 9.1: The Moderns Arms on an
enamel jewel

Fig 9.2: Ancients Arms on a
ceramic jewel

Fig 9.3: The Arms of United
Grand Lodge

The first three Articles are as follows:

I. There shall be, from and after the day of the Festival of Saint John the Evangelist next ensuing, a full, perfect, and perpetual union of and between the two Fraternities of Free and Accepted Masons of England above described; so as that in all time hereafter they shall form and constitute but one Brotherhood, and that the said community shall be represented in one Grand Lodge, to be solemnly formed, constituted, and held, on the said day of the Festival of Saint John the Evangelist next ensuing, and from thenceforward forever.

II. It is declared and pronounced, that pure Ancient Masonry consists of three degrees, and no more; viz: **those of the Entered Apprentice, the Fellowcraft, and the Master Mason, including the Supreme Order of the Holy Royal Arch**. But this article is not intended to prevent any lodge or chapter from holding a meeting in any of the degrees of the Orders of Chivalry, according to the constitutions of the said Orders.

III. There shall be the most perfect **unity of obligation, of discipline, of working the lodges, of making, passing and raising, instructing and clothing Brothers**; so that **but one pure unsullied system**, according to the genuine landmarks, laws, and traditions of the Craft, shall be maintained, upheld and practised, throughout the Masonic World, from the day and date of the said union until time shall be no more.

Article IX (in summary) dealt with creating a new seal for UGL based on the seals of the PrGL and AGL.

Article XV is rather important:

XV. After the day of the Re-union, as aforesaid, and when it shall be ascertained what are the obligations, forms, regulations, working, and instruction, to be universally established, speedy and **effectual steps shall be taken to obligate all the Members of each Lodge in all the degrees**, according to the form taken and recognized by the Grand Master, Past Grand Masters, Grand Officers, and Representatives of Lodges, on the day of Re-union; and for this purpose the worthy and expert Master Masons appointed, as aforesaid, shall visit and attend the several Lodges, within the Bills of Mortality, in rotation, dividing themselves into quorums of not less than three each, for the greater expedition, and they shall assist the Master and Wardens to promulgate and enjoin the pure and unsullied system, that perfect reconciliation, unity of obligation, law, working, language, and dress, may be happily restored to the English Craft.

Immediately after the Act of Union was signed, the Duke of Kent proposed that his brother the Duke of Sussex should become Grand Master of the newly united Grand Lodge. Thus Augustus Frederick, Duke of Sussex, became the new Grand Master, which office he held until 1843.

Lodge of Reconciliation

Pause for thought

The Lodge of Promulgation certainly provided the basis for union, but as far as this book is concerned, the Lodge of Reconciliation is more important, in that its eventual product was at least a notional 'standard' form of working (ritual working such as Opening and Closing, the ceremonies, etc., and associated ceremonial). Perhaps the first lodge should have been about **reconciling** the two Grand Lodges and the second about **promulgating** new procedures.

The Articles of Union established a number of items, including the re-numbering of lodges, but in particular, from Article XV, it was agreed that the effectual steps involved a lot of new management and a wide range of discussion between members of the once-rival Lodges. An early duty of the new UGL was to warrant a *Lodge of Reconciliation* to sort out common ritual and ceremonial matters and to assist in the healing process (one of the Secretaries was a former Secretary of the PrGL).

Pause for thought

As with the Hextall paper on the Lodge of Promulgation, there is a superb paper in *AQC* 23: 215-307 (1910) by W. Wonnacott on The Lodge of Reconciliation. A long, unbelievably important work with much detail, especially about who attended for tutoring and where they went to spread the word of the new ritual.

According to Brother Wonnacott, the nine members selected by each of the previous Grand Masters had either been part of the Lodge of Promulgation, or were part of the Union process or had served in senior positions, such as District or Provincial Grand Masters.

The Lodge worked during the next three years, demonstrating workings at Craft meetings as they developed them. In February 1816, an Installation ceremony was demonstrated (for future approval) and in May, the 'final' set of Workings (Opening, Closing and three Degree ceremonies) was demonstrated to UGL, together with First and Second Degree Obligations, to which it gave formal approval.

The Lodge existed for about three years, during which time the former Antients managed to get the former Moderns to back down on many matters and agree a common form of ceremonies, largely based on the Antients' old claim to pure and ancient practices. The re-adoption of the Antients' Installation ceremony was a major success for them (the Moderns' Installation had been little more than an Obligation).

It examined the differences between Antient and Modern practices, making firm suggestions for Opening and Closing, the layout of the lodge, the communication of secrets and the Deacon as a lodge officer. It also regularised the giving of Words and Pass Words, in and between Degrees. (I think the use of two alternative words in the Third Degree dates from this time – it being one of the few points on which the Moderns would not give way entirely.)

The Antients particularly got their way over the Royal Arch. They felt that **as a Craft degree,** it was the **root, heart and marrow** of Masonry. When, years before, an Antient applied for charity, the Moderns Grand Secretary said 'Our society is neither Arch, Royal Arch not Ancient, so you have no right to partake of our charity'. To emphasise the importance of the Royal Arch and its alleged link with Craft, it was eventually agreed that a Chapter had to be attached to a Craft lodge and inherit its number.

It is difficult to understand today, notwithstanding the importance and current popularity of the Royal Arch, why the Antients should have been adamant about maintaining it as the absolute pinnacle of Masonry. We know that all overtly Christian aspects of Craft ritual had been removed, the same eventually applying to Royal Arch ritual. The Antients, like it or lump it, had to accept this but managed to keep some of their earlier traditions alive.

Pause for thought

We will soon be looking briefly at the work of John Knight. I have a copy of some 1810 Royal Arch material. In the opening, a reading of St. John 1:1-5 is called for, and in the ceremony Thessalonians 3. There are other terms that have a distinctly Christian air.

My research for this book has not covered the development of Royal Arch ritual, but in view of what is in Knight in 1810, it would seem not unlikely that both from the time of the formation of the AGL and perhaps well before, it had a very Christian content. The Antients' insistence on keeping it going after Union must reflect its earlier history.

The Lodge of Reconciliation was very concerned that the large number of illicit publications, still in wide circulation, could jeopardize any standardisation that might result from the Union. They asked for all available copies of such publications to be collected and placed in their custody. In spite of this, manuscript and printed rituals soon began to appear in even greater numbers for general consumption, though many lodges continued to teach their ritual by word-of-mouth only.

The Lodge of Reconciliation demonstrated a preferred ritual but never actually published one. The new specification, as well as the actual wording of the ceremonies, particularly included Opening and Closing, Obligations and perambulation details. It also seems to have removed completely all Christian references. Notwithstanding the brief it was given, it would appear that the lodge members seem to have felt that they had almost a free hand in specifying what was to be in the new ritual and workings.

A standard ritual never did come out of the Union – presumably the powers-that-be resigned themselves to the fact that any attempt to enforce a ritual on groups of Masons, many claiming to have 'old-established' ritual, was doomed to failure (you know very well, it would have no more success today – some of us can still remember the long arguments when the Obligations were changed in the 1980s – '…I would rather have…' to '...at one time included…'). What did happen was that Brethren from many lodges were summoned to observe new workings so that they could propagate them in their own lodges.

One very clear requirement was that no written notes could be made of the procedures of the Lodge of Reconciliation, especially relating to ritual and ceremonial, so we cannot really know what was demonstrated to all the people who came to the demonstrations).

It should also be made clear that the Lodge only approved the parts of the ceremonies relating to Openings, Closings, Degree prayers, Obligations and entrustings. The remainder, such as the Tracing Boards, Working Tools, Charges, etc, were excluded from approval.

Some of the earlier records of the Lodge indicate that the Antients and Moderns opened their own lodges and then merged together for business. There are notes such as 'proceeded to re-obligate 78 Brothers'. Presumably, to get everything on an even footing, every Brother was re-obligated in the 'other' lodge.

The UGL realised that having no official printed record of the approval would be bound to result in, at least, minor differences being taken back home. The poor old DC or Secretary representative who had attended may have taken surreptitious notes on his shirt-cuffs or on the odd scrap of paper, but with misunderstandings, memory lapses and with the desire to maintain old traditions, the chances of 'the' ritual taking on universal adoption were slim!

This was a recommendation offered early in 1814:

It is earnestly recommended to the Provincial Grand Masters, and Masters of Lodges at a distance from London, to take the earliest opportunity of deputing, by written authority, some **one or more of the most qualified Members of their respective Lodges, to attend the Lodge of Reconciliation** which will be convened weekly at Freemasons Hall (the precise days of its Meeting may be hereafter learned upon application to the Grand Secretaries) that **the acknowledged forms, to be universally used, may be made known to them for the information of their Brothers**. In the meantime the Members of the two Fraternities are hereby empowered and directed to give and receive, in open Lodge, the respective obligations of each Fraternity; in order that they may cordially meet together **and be placed all on the same level, and the better to receive the recognized forms, which are alone to be practised in the future.**

Work continued regularly, re-obligating Brethren and demonstrating ceremonies. In September, an interim report was issued to the Grand Master:

To His Royal Highness Augustus Frederick Duke of Sussex Grand Master of Masons.

The Lodge of Reconciliation respectfully beg leave to report to the

Most Worshipful Grand Master that they have proceeded so far in performance of the duties entrusted to them, as to have thrice exhibited to the Lodges in the London District **the newly arranged modes of Masonic instruction, as far as relates to the opening and closing of a Lodge in the three degrees, the several obligations therein required and the ceremonies of making passing and raising, together with a brief test or examination in each degree**, and that they are also prepared to proceed in their system of elucidation, by such means as may be considered the best adapted to their purpose.

The Lodge continued into mid-1816. Detailed records were kept of which members from which lodges attended meetings, including Moderns and Antients lodges for London, Country and foreign.

One interesting result of the new regime was the declarations of the 'traditioners' or 'memorialists'. These were Masons who would not accept the new regime on the grounds that it departed from ancient usages and had made far too many changes. The Lodge of Reconciliation was obviously not amused and spent quite a time treading all over them, including a questionnaire in which they were asked specific questions about their objections.

Since the work of the Lodge of Reconciliation, Grand Lodge has kept clear of involvement in ritual (apart from the change regarding the traditional penalties) and has never officially recognised any particular working and, subject to Regulation 155 (current Book of Constitutions), which is very open to interpretation, lodges are in theory, free to teach and practice whatever ritual they wish, **provided the Landmarks of the Craft are not breached**!

Pause for thought
In fact, part of the wording of the Regulation is worth seeing because it adds to the confusion in some ways:

The members present at any Lodge duly summoned have an undoubted right to regulate their own proceedings, provide they are consistent with the **general laws and regulations** of the Craft but … contrary to the **laws and usages** of the Craft …

So does this mean we can do what we like? I suspect that your lodge Visiting Grand Officer might take exception to this! (Note that the

Appendix to the book says more about Landmarks.)

This all seems to have resulted in the situation whereby lodges do have variations, but they are of a non-essential nature and usually relate to specific aspects of the workings, rather than changes in wording (or worse, in the order of presentation).

In 1819, the Grand Master (the Duke of Sussex) said:

It was his opinion that so long as the Master of any Lodge observed exactly the Land Marks of the Craft he was at liberty to give the Lectures in the language best suited to the character of the Lodge over which he presided …

Not strictly a ritual matter, but Grand Lodge have recently made it mandatory for a Master Mason Candidate to have seen the Third Degree Traditional History in order to receive a Grand Lodge Certificate.

Pause for thought

Regarding variations, at least one lodge includes much of the Second Degree Tracing Board material within the text of the Second Degree ceremony. Another misses out most of the wording altogether. These seem to be OK in that the Grand Lodge Liaison Officer and visiting Grand Officers are happy. In other words, they do not regard the Second Degree Tracing Board as a landmark!

Suppose I tried something like:

'Let's save time and have all three sets of Working Tools and Tracing Boards out together from the start'.

'Does the Candidate really need a Pass Word to get back in after the Opening?'

Both entirely out of the question of course. In fact, this leads on to the 'Landmarks' of the Order. In Chapter 10, we will look at some ritual variations and, in particular, you will see just how much (or little) of the Second Degree TB is done. I always felt that the Tracing Board was in effect a Landmark and failure to do it not in accordance with our tradition. It seems that a Landmark to one may be a permitted variation to another.

Having seen and read about many different rituals, it is clear that Grand Lodge could never allow major deviations from the ritual - but why should it? The ritual (and there really is only one major ritual) has now been in use for a long time (with its variations) and most of the Craft are happy with the situation. To make major changes would require a very powerful reason!

The work of the Lodge of Reconciliation was entirely dependent on finding bases for compromise and it is really gratifying to note that after more than 60 years of competition, a high degree of agreement was eventually reached.

Many papers delivered at QC meetings are followed by discussions and follow-ups. One of the replies to the Wonnacott paper above, was by Brother Sidney Klein and included the following about the Antients, which is very enlightening:

… they had a good deal of right on their side; for over 75 years, *circa* 1735-1813, the premier Grand Lodge ... expunged from its Ritual … the Mystical or R.A. Degree, … action which caused the war between them and the Ancients … No compromise could have been accepted in 1813 by those Ancients, which did not restore once more to the Ritual that Royal Degree ... **It would appear, therefore, that the Moderns had succeeded in retaining at least a considerable part of their ritual, and against this the Ancients re-established the Royal Arch Degree** … to this day many Lodges jealously preserve special variations of their own, and rightly so because … **some of the most interesting differences in working, if pruned away, would be lost to us as valuable historical evidences of former Customs** …

We are very fortunate that in spite of all the vested interests of previous Antient and Modern Brethren, we now work a general ritual which satisfies most Masons and very few see the need for change, in spite of grammatical and historical weaknesses in some cases and the strange use of words (not always because they were originally used like that).

Pause for thought
We will see in Chapter 10, the *Revised Ritual*, where the compiler has made, with his justifications, many changes to the grammar and use of words. The final result does look different from what many expect, but, nonetheless, its content is principally the same as any other ritual. It is practiced in several lodges in the UK. We

will also look at Humber Lodge No. 57, where the ritual book clearly defends the 'strange' use of words!

John Knight

Knight was a very prominent Mason in Cornwall, especially in his work for the Royal Arch. In 1815 he published *Sketches in Craft Masonry*.

Pause for thought

I am indebted to Worshipful Brother John Mandelberg, with whom I had many happy contacts before his death. Knight's book was on the shelf of the *John Coombe Masonic Library* at Hayle in Cornwall. The book was in a fairly basic code which John translated and he provided me with a complete set of the work.

There is too much for the full details to be shown, but the material is broken down as follows. The ceremonies are very much abbreviated (parts just skipped over) and nowhere does Knight give any secrets in full:

First Degree
1. Opening in the First Degree
2. Short First Degree ceremony
3. Lectures - 202 questions in 6 sections
4. Closing

Second Degree
1. Opening and very short skip-over ceremony
2. Lectures – 158 questions in 4 sections
3. Closing

Third Degree
1. Opening
2. Raising ceremony – very stripped down
3. Remarks to the MM
4. Lecture – 161 questions in 6 sections.

The Lectures are quite interesting – they are something like those of Preston, in a different order. Some of the explanations are based on OC questions that Preston did not use. Also, there are many answers to questions that are much more detailed than Preston.

Pause for thought

The 49th question in the MM Lectures is very interesting. You may recall remarks made in Chapter 7 about the answer to one of Finch's questions regarding the origin of the M..B words. Knight's answer is 'he is rot to the bone'.

Looking at the details of the Lectures, you can see much material that is used elsewhere in the current ritual, such as for the Opening and Closing and Second Degree Tracing Board. I find it difficult to understand why a man so connected with Masons and Masonry should take all the time needed to produce this major chunk of material. Brother Mandelberg says that Finch was heavily involved with the Royal Arch, but he presumably was acquainted with *TDK/J&B* and their lectures (reasons!) as well as Preston's Lectures. The work was out before the Lodge of Reconciliation had finished its work and Knight does not appear to have been a member. One can only wonder if members of the Lodge of Reconciliation had access to it and took some of its 'gems' into their recommendations.

Stability and Emulation Lodges of Improvement

Pause for thought

We now come to a slightly touchy subject. To be sure which is the more fundamental would require visits to a number of Stability and Emulation lodges and to examine closely the differences within each working and within the lodges that use each working (perhaps another book). It is my observation that most of the rituals I have seen appear to lean towards Emulation, which in 1825 possibly came out of Stability anyway, maybe because of the forceful nature of Peter Gilkes' approach (Chapter 10). I am reliably informed, by an experienced Stability brother, that the wording of the two is almost identical and the working pretty similar.

This Chapter heading says 'ending in 1817'. The date was selected to be that for the formation of the Stability Lodge of Improvement (with the Emulation Lodge of Improvement later in 1825). Most Masons would probably agree that the bulk of present-day rituals owe their details either to Stability or Emulation. Both claim to represent the recommendations of the Lodge of Reconciliation, but comments made by both have become quite heated in the past. (Although Emulation should really be in Chapter 10, we need to deal with both LOIs now.)

The article *Stability Lodge of Instruction* by F.W. Golby, (originally published in *The Freemason* of May 1915 and reprinted in *AQC* 113: 201-209) says it was founded under the sanction of the Lodge of Stability (Antient number 381 at the time) by seventeen Brethren, eight consisting of three members of the Lodge of Reconciliation, and five others who had learnt the new form of working in the Lodge, together with a further nine Brethren. The first two Preceptors were from the group of eight and practiced the working **together** for the next 34 years (until their deaths).

The next Preceptor, who joined Stability LOI in 1839, remained in charge until 1885 and the next until 1900. The claim therefore is that for 83 years, the LOI had an unbroken continuity of Preceptors, sticking strictly to what had gone before and hence, a continuing ritual.

The Emulation LOI first met on the 2nd October 1823 under the sanction of the Lodge of Hope (Antient No. 7 at the time), initially to work the Lectures. It was not until some years later that the LOI started working the ceremonies as well.

Supporters of Emulation have said that their claim to authenticity in adhering to the Lodge of Reconciliation is as strong as that of Stability, and the delay in starting to teach the approved ritual (1825 rather than 1817) was because Peter Gilkes (Chapter 10) was so fussy about the details that he held back until it had matured to an extent where it could be considered stable.

This fussiness of Gilkes in fact prepared the way for Emulation to claim that it has always strictly conformed to the letter and spirit of the ritual. Gilkes was masonically very active at the turn of the century and may have helped with the conceptual getting-together of PrGL and AGL. He was expelled by the PrGL for being too close (they said) to the Antients, but was re-admitted later.

Records show that he had some involvement with the Lodge of Promulgation. He attended several demonstrations of the Lodge of Reconciliation and was beginning to realise that the approved forms were not being picked up as quickly as he would have liked, but over the period he was always happy to carry out demonstrations to his pupils. At the same time, he fought hard to prevent any further new material being considered. Gilkes died in 1833. The Emulation Lodge of Improvement owes much to the work and influence of Gilkes.

We could go on (but won't) about the rivalry between the two contenders for the 'first ritual based on Reconciliation'.

Stability ritual was first published in 1902 (latest revision 1992).

Emulation ritual was not officially published until 1969 although well before then several publishers produced works such as *The Complete Workings of Craft Freemasonry* in 1975, which don't actually refer to Emulation, but seem to be almost identical (the Lectures are included and they are extremely similar to the Emulation Lectures). (This title will occur again under the name of George Claret in Chapter 10).

A number of tiny 'waistcoat-pocket sized' ritual books were produced, especially in the 1940s, and they have claimed to be '… according to Emulation working'.

Pause for thought

I have in my possession a 1960 edition of Nigerian Ritual, first published in 1939 and in quite common use in the 1950-80s. It is virtually the same as Emulation. (Chapter 10 says more about it.)

The next chapter looks at some of these so-called 'wide' variations.

10
Nearer to today – 1818 onwards

Richard Carlile

Carlile wrote what we could say was the last of the 'great' exposures (after Hutchinson and Finch).

He was a well-known political agitator especially concerned to reform and promote ideas of freedom and universal suffrage and spent a fair time in jail. He formed a publishing company for the release of various anti-establishment texts. He created a journal called *Sherwin's Political Register,* which, after a period of unrest, was banned by the government. He then in effect re-started it with a new name - *The Republican.* After putting various aspects of Masonry in the journal, including parts of rituals, in 1835 after

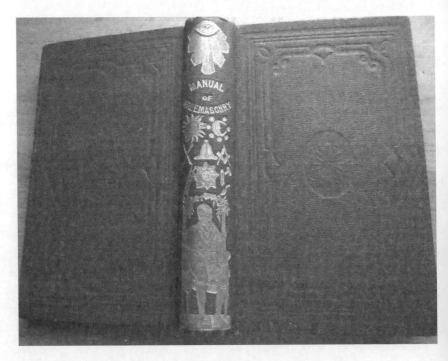

Fig 10.1: Carlile's *Manual of Freemasonry*

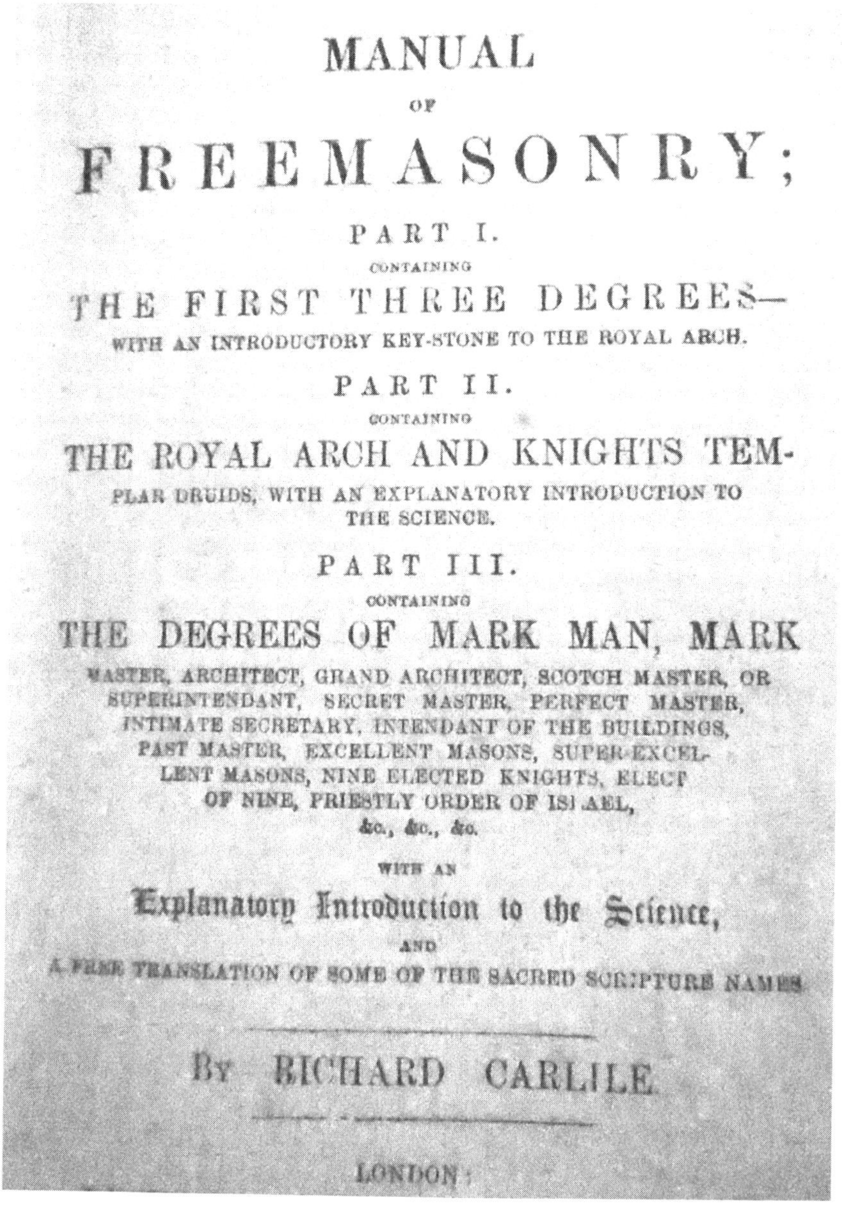

MANUAL

OF

FREEMASONRY;

PART I.

CONTAINING

THE FIRST THREE DEGREES—

WITH AN INTRODUCTORY KEY-STONE TO THE ROYAL ARCH.

PART II.

CONTAINING

THE ROYAL ARCH AND KNIGHTS TEM-

PLAR DRUIDS, WITH AN EXPLANATORY INTRODUCTION TO
THE SCIENCE.

PART III.

CONTAINING

THE DEGREES OF MARK MAN, MARK

MASTER, ARCHITECT, GRAND ARCHITECT, SCOTCH MASTER, OR
SUPERINTENDANT, SECRET MASTER, PERFECT MASTER,
INTIMATE SECRETARY, INTENDANT OF THE BUILDINGS,
PAST MASTER, EXCELLENT MASONS, SUPER-EXCEL-
LENT MASONS, NINE ELECTED KNIGHTS, ELECT
OF NINE, PRIESTLY ORDER OF ISRAEL,
&c., &c., &c.

WITH AN

Explanatory Introduction to the Science,

AND

A FREE TRANSLATION OF SOME OF THE SACRED SCRIPTURE NAMES.

_____

By RICHARD CARLILE.

_____

LONDON:

Fig 10.2: Frontispiece of Carlile's *Manual*

major updating, he re-issued this *Republican* material as *An Exposure of Freemasonry*. Eventually, in 1845, it became *The Manual of Freemasonry*.

The overall structure of the book is as follows:
- Three Degree ceremonies
- A long (27 pages) introduction, covering a range of aspects of Masonic behaviour and practice and some history. Interestingly, there are several pages which contain Christian tenets, some of which are applied to Masonry
- The ceremony of the Past Master's Degree

> Pause for thought
> I think this is unique – I have never seen this Degree in print before. Refer to Chapter 7 for details of the original need for this Chairing Degree as a preparation for Exaltation.

- A Royal Arch ceremony, including the 'Passing of the Veils' and five sections of Royal Arch lectures
- The ceremonies of about 15 other Orders, many of which no longer exist.

Just a few excerpts from the Craft ceremonies, which are very similar to today:

First Degree:
- Slightly longer Working Tools, otherwise almost identical, but followed by the First Degree lectures which are longer

Second Degree:
- Standard Tracing Board

Lectures – very much longer and containing 'earlier' Masonic material

It seems likely that with Carlile such a reformer and liberal thinker, his motives for producing his exposure (there is no apparent evidence of his ever joining the Craft) were his distaste for an apparently secret society with secrets and oaths, somehow protected from the Secret Societies Act and worse, and patronised by dukes and kings.

We do not know what material he relied on for the work, but he is said to have known Finch (Chapter 8). The book did fairly well, but it is doubtful to me whether it had any great impact on people like Claret, in that it does not add much new to the Degree ritual.

Pause for thought

Just one further point. With the Chair degree as essential for a non-Past Master to be exalted, in Carlile's section dealing with the Royal Arch, when the Candidate for Exaltation is brought in by the guiding officer, he tells the Chair that the Exaltee is a Master Mason who has also been '… entrusted with the Grip and Word … of a Past Master …'. The implication being that **even in 1845** the 'Past Master's' degree still existed for non-Past Masters.

Two important Brethren

Peter Gilkes

A man dedicated to the Craft for over 40 years, Gilkes (not a writer of ritual or exposures) by tireless energy and a terrific memory, did much to help in the standardisation of ritual after the two main LOIs were founded. During his career, he was Master both of 'old' Antients and Moderns lodges. He was involved with ritual and training after the Lodge of Promulgation and several years before and during the Lodge of Reconciliation, at which he made several appearances.

During his busy life, as a stickler for the correct wording of the ritual to be given, he forced through much of the acceptance of Emulation working.

Pause for thought

Peter Gilkes, 1765-1833 by A. Calvert, updated by C. Dyer, *AQC* 84:260-84, is a very detailed paper on the career of Gilkes.

George Claret and Claret working

We can now look at George Claret: a man whose Masonic career was similar to Peter Gilkes. Like Gilkes, he was Master of many lodges, got into trouble masonically and financially, but for our interest he had some presence at the Lodge of Reconciliation meetings.

Pause for thought

On pages 264-5 of the Wonnacott paper on the Lodge of Reconciliation (Chapter 9), there is a Minute of a rehearsal meeting of 20th September 1814. It says that someone went through the ceremonies of Initiation in the First Degree and then someone else went through the ceremonies of the Second Degree. It then says that George Claret **was raised** to the Sublime Degree of a MM. This could imply that he was actually raised,

Fig 10.3: Claret ritual facsimile

rather than acting as Candidate.

I nearly fell into the trap! Later in the Minute, it says 'Geo. Claret, the ritual-monger of later years, was the S.W. of Ionic and Prudence 16/18 Modern'. Hence, he must have been demonstrating the ceremony even if the wording indicates otherwise.

He must have been a busy man, because at the next meeting (22nd September), 'The Lodge was then opened in the third degree and Brother George Claret was after examination raised to the degree of M.M'.

In the section dealing with attendances, there is a record (p.290) that George Claret attended the lodge six times.

He was connected with many teaching bodies and eminent Preceptors and eventually (having changed occupations from greengrocer to engraver/printer), based on Gilkes' work, he published his *The Ceremonies* containing the three Degree ceremonies, Opening/Closing and Installation.

It was then issued in 1838 as *The Whole of Craft Free-Masonry*. This went to six or seven editions (later ones don't have a date!). The work is roughly contemporaneous with Richard Carlile and not many years after Knight and Finch (pre-Union material). His works on the new ritual and his obvious enthusiasm probably led to the success of his ritual book (compared to whatever else was available at the time). It was also clear to most contemporary Masons that his close links with Gilkes and their association with the Lodge of Reconciliation meant that the ritual could be relied on as being that which had been agreed as approved.

I have recently been very kindly supplied by the Secretary of Richard Gurney Lodge No. 8387 (one of two lodges in Norfolk which practise Claret working) with a copy of their ritual book. It is a facsimile of the 6th edition of the work and has some very interesting aspects:

Opening address by Claret, in which he plugs the book '… anxious to get genuine Masonic Information …' and states that its contents are warranted by UGL and are as taught by him at regular lodges and LOIs at the time. He goes on to say that, without the book, it might have been difficult to get lodges, especially in the country, to perform properly.

The Degree ceremonies, which apart from a very few words are identical to Emulation. Opening and Closing are almost identical. Calling On/Off are very slightly different – '… what is to be done at high time? ... Your Worship's pleasure …'!

The Installation and investiture of officers is almost identical to the basic Emulation ceremony.

The Lectures, which again are almost identical.

The Royal Arch ceremony with Addresses and Signs – no comment for this book of course.

Near the end of the book are 'a few general remarks', one of which says 'in working the Lectures …'

and goes on to explain how the questions and answers are delivered and what to do if a Brother does not know a particular answer.

> Pause for thought
> This seems to imply that even in 1875 or so, there were lodges that still did the Lectures as part of the ceremonial for the evening, otherwise why put them in the book?

What does seem strange is that with Claret ritual being around since 1837 and *The Perfect Ritual* now appearing in 1871, Stability did not publish its ritual until 1902 and Emulation theirs in 1969.

What also seems strange is that apart from some minor variations in wording, such as:

'Why are you so placed?' or 'Why are you placed there?'

'Let us invoke a blessing...' or 'Let us invoke the Assistance...',

the bulk of the ritual is almost identical and I am informed by knowledgeable Stability Brethren that the ceremonial is almost the same. Could this mean that Peter Gilkes and his followers in effect forced Stability to conform to Emulation, or more likely, was there just some sensible collaboration before Stability published in 1902?

I recently contacted the most senior member of my Mother Lodge, who was initiated in 1961. I asked him which ritual book he used and he said Emulation, but when I pressed him and said that this did not come out until 1969, he thought for a while and then said that it was the Nigerian ritual (see below). This is an excellent example of printed Emulation ritual even though not 'officially sanctioned' by the Emulation Lodge of Improvement.

Ritual variations in general

I started this Chapter with the intention of examining many different rituals and producing an analysis of some of the main differences. (I emphasise here that I have not looked for differences in ceremonial, only in the

Fig 10.4: Pick a ritual, any ritual.

wording, because they are so widely, but often quite trivially, different).

Before going on, just for interest, this is a fairly complete list of workings identified in the UK, some of which I have copies (marked c).

Bristol (c)	Bristol and Humber (c)
Brittania	Bury
Carver (c)	Castle
Claret (c)	Emulation (c)
English	Exeter
Humber (c)	Logic
Metropolitan	Merchant Navy
Montgomerie (c)	Nigerian (c)
Oxford	Perfect (c)
Plymouth	Revised (c)
Ritus Oxonienis	Stability (c)
Sussex	Taylor (c)
Unanimity	Universal
Veritas	West End (c)
York	

I am sure there are quite a few others!

I have included Montgomerie 1741 ritual. This is used in my Norfolk lodge and although the ritual is really quite similar to Emulation (they wouldn't agree), there are some interesting differences in wording. Everyone squares (or half-squares) and many say it's obviously Taylor (maybe!). Most interesting are the Second Degree Sign that has an extra part, and the Third Degree Sign, which appears to have a bit missing.

I would be very surprised if there are not many lodges whose basics are Stability/Emulation, but with variations much like Montgomerie.

Unanimity Lodge working

Because of my interest in Norfolk Masonry, after seeing their working several times I developed an interest in Lodge of Unanimity No. 102. I have compared their work with Humber Lodge No. 57, Bristol working and others.

H. Le Strange, who was Deputy GM of Norfolk, in *History of Freemasonry in Norfolk, 1724-1895,* published in 1896, in writing about Unanimity (which in those days met in Beccles under an older number), said:

This old-established lodge has preserved certain old-fashioned ways of working that give it a character of its own, which it would be a pity to disturb for the sake of an ideal and impossible uniformity. So long as the real landmarks of the Order are reserved, the retention of these little peculiarities is much to be commended as evidence of what the workings of our Craft was in days gone by.

I have found it is quite interesting to reflect on Unanimity. They call their working 'Bristol and Humber'. I have been in touch with Humber Lodge No. 57 and seen their Humber working which is not like Unanimity at all. Neither are either of them much like 'Bristol' working. Incidentally, like Montgomerie, the Unanimity Second Degree sign has an extra bit, but different from that of Montgomerie.

There have been theories that maritime trade may have brought French workings back to England and that trade between Bristol, the Humber and Norfolk ports may have caused ritual changes to spread to this relatively restricted group of lodges. My research shows that representatives of Unanimity were undoubtedly present at the Lodge of Reconciliation.

I have been given a copy of a 'revival' of the Unanimity *Ceremony of Initiation of 1758*, which was prepared for their 250th anniversary celebration. It purports to be a fairly accurate record of what might have gone on. The overall structure is similar to other sources for the time but some of the wording is a bit different. I am not entirely convinced that is as original as the date on it. The wording is much closer to *J&B/TDK* than *MD*. Unlike any of them though, it has a 'conclusion' which actually is a **Closing**.

It says that the ceremony and catechism (reasons) are done at a table and punch is served between Call-On and -Off! Then, when the Candidate comes back and has an apron presented, is given gloves and shown the Working Tools, they give fire, and drink. After the Charge to the Apprentice, they drink and there is a loyal toast too.

Although prepared as a presentation piece, I believe it may be quite representative of what was going on. The Lodge Secretary tells me that there is a quarto vellum book containing the 'old' ritual of Unanimity, in handwriting, dated probably about 1838. The lodge believes that its errors, etc. indicate that it was copied from something earlier. Other records prove that several Unanimity Brethren attended the Lodge of Reconciliation in 1714.

The oldest Bristol lodge (Beaufort No. 103) was constituted very soon after Unanimity and they may have shared a common source for their ritual.

The Perfect Ceremonies

The Perfect Ceremonies by John Hogg was published in 1871. The front page says:

The Perfect Ceremonies of Craft Masonry according to the most approved forms as taught in the Unions Emulation Lodge of Improvement for M.Ms, Freemasons' Hall, London. **With the most recent corrections.**

The pages of the book are illuminated on the left and right hand sides with what seem to be medieval engravings representing death, etc.

The text has the old feel – 'The brethren being affembled and clothed… ', '…affift me to open…'.

Perhaps this and the engraving give it an air of antiquity!

The text itself, in spite of the 'with corrections', seems almost the same as Claret. There have been suggestions that the Perfect working eventually superseded Claret working.

About this time, Oxford, Logic and West End rituals began to appear.

It has also been conjectured (*M. Barnes, 'Spoilt For Choice', MQ Magazine, Issue 10, July 2004*) that Taylor's working, although published in London by M.M. Taylor in 1908, was actually under the copyright of H. Hill, whose lodge had used Claret and then Perfect working. (Taylor's 4th reprint appeared in 2000.)

The Revised Ritual

After the work of the Lodge of Reconciliation, it was de rigeur not to print any ritual, and the first one to appear - not as an exposure - was published by George Claret in 1838, allegedly based on the ritual agreed by the Lodge of Reconciliation after the Union. As we have also said before, until most lodges used printed rituals, extensions to the ritual based on what people really wanted to do, coupled with Masons having to remember what they heard at demonstrations, meant that there were bound to be variations in lodges and a perpetuation of poor biblical history and use of English. With this in mind, it may be of interest to look briefly at the work of **Franklin Thomas**.

He was a very distinguished Mason, having held office in several Provincial Grand Lodges. In 1850 he and the Deputy Provincial Grand Master of Oxfordshire took George Claret's original ritual and sorted out what they considered grammatical and other errors. Several years later, Thomas then looked at the 'correction' of errors, illogicalities, misstatements and aspects of bad taste. The final version of his work was published in 1888 as the *Revised Ritual* (last updated in 1993).

The book is quite thick in comparison with other ritual books and has the following contents:

- The three Degree ceremonies with extended ceremonial instructions and **full** explanations of changes made (as footnotes)
- Two alternative and very long First Degree Tracing Board lectures
- A long and critically justified Second Degree Tracing Board
- The Lectures in all three Degrees, all revised to some extent
- The Installation ceremony, with an extended optional entrusting and Opening
- Extended addresses to Officers on being invested
- Two songs
- The Foundation Stone ceremony.

It is one thing to complain about mistakes, bad English, etc., even if we put up with them for traditional reasons. Thomas went much further – the printed ritual contains both footnotes and longer sections where he explains why he felt something was not right and why he changed it. Some of the changes will be called 'nit-picking' by many, but some make real sense. Just a few examples:

After being restored to light in the First Degree:

Rise duly obligated **novice** in the First Degree of Freemasonry.

Not '**brother among Masons**' – has is **not a full brother** until the Signs have been given and he has been fully invested.

After the Raising:

'and lift our eyes to that bright **Morning Star, whose rising brings peace and salvation ...**'

This is replaced by:

'and to lift our eyes to **Him in Whose hands alone ...**'

The change is because the term 'Morning Star' comes from the New Testament and refers to Christ. The ritual compiler makes the change because of the essential 'universal religion' aspect of the Craft.

In the First Degree Working Tools:

not all operative Masons but rather 'free and accepted or
speculative ...'
None of us are operative Masons any more. Since all lodges became
Speculative, it is now the case that if (eg.) a truly operative mason,
such as a stonemason, joined a lodge, he would be Speculative by
definition, so:
'but we, **not professing to be Operative**, but Free ...'

As you might imagine, such a 'drastically' changed ritual has not been
adopted in the UK except by a couple of lodges, but it is used extensively
in Africa and the Far East.

Humber working
The ritual book of Humber Lodge No. 57 (8th edition) says that the Warrant
of an earlier lodge was transferred to it and eventually it became No. 57.
There is a treatise at the beginning by F. De Velling (Honours in English,
University of London, 1886), which attempts to explain much of the 'old
fashioned' English in the ritual. This is very interesting because it is almost
the opposite approach to that of the *Revised Ritual.*

In particular, he shows that some of the 'strange' English was in common
use in the 18th century, thereby providing evidence of the antiquity of the
working. In particular, he shows how the subjunctive mood makes things
look quaint – '...except it **be** a higher degree...', '...that he **fail** not...'. He
also points out customs that have now disappeared, such as using the
adjective instead of the adverb – '...we are close [not closely] tiled...', '...
happy [not happily] have we met...'.

The ritual is very close to Emulation but has some small but nice
changes:
• a poor candidate ... humbly soliciting to participate with us in the
   mysteries and privileges of ...
• there was also a ... around your neck ... should you attempt to
   retreat your life is placed in equal hazard
• In such a state of impending danger as I have described you to be
   in, in whom do you put your trust? ...

Nigerian ritual
I have a **video** copy of the 1960 edition of this ritual. Someone did a real-
time copy, turning the pages at a fast rate. The frontispiece says:

NIGERIAN RITUAL
As taught in Emulation Lodge of Improvement
Complied by Bro. C. Browne Dep. DGM Nigeria.
WITH THE AUTHORITY OF THE
DISTRICT GRAND LODGE
OF NIGERIA.

It was first published in 1939. The preface says that the book was produced because Nigeria being a long way from where Masonry is usually practiced, it could mean that variations and other customs and expressions might come in.

The 'red' parts of the ritual are more detailed than you might expect – again because of the remoteness and the reduced chance of Emulation-aware Past Masters joining lodges.

The book starts with several very useful general instructions. There are also a couple of pages of useful instructions before each Degree ceremony. I found my old 1986 Emulation book and it is exactly the same as the Nigerian, but less informative. I wish I had been given it when I was a young Mason!

Scottish rituals

There seem to be a number of printed rituals, and I have been informed that many Scottish lodges still work only by word-of-mouth. Other Scottish Masons have told me that, not all that many years ago, a number of Scottish lodges had 'their own ritual' – word-of-mouth with very many differences. It would seem that some degree of standardisation might have been imposed eventually!

The William Harvey *Complete Manual of Freemasonry* is one of the popular printed rituals. It contains the three Degrees, the Mark Degree and 'the Masonic Catechisms' (very similar to the 'questions only' in the Emulation lectures).

The ritual is very similar to Emulation but has some extensions and slightly richer working in some cases. Just two examples worthy of note:
First Degree Obligation:

...I further solemnly promise that I will not be at the making of
the following persons as Freemasons:- A young man of nonage,
an old man of dotage, a madman, a fool, an atheist, a person
under the influence of liquor, and a woman under no pretence
whatever ...

Third Degree, after the 'third blow':
> An extra piece of drama – the Wardens go out by the gates and check out the grave, using their emblems of office, to ensure that it is HA's. Once done, the Candidate is 'slipped' and there follows a long prayer, after which he is raised.

Scottish Grand Lodge has made available a number of rituals including 'Modern', 'William Harvey', 'Complete', 'McBride' and 'Standard'.

More samples of ritual variation

Having said repeatedly that, apart from a very few exceptions, most rituals are very similar, I decided that it was just not productive to try and list all the variations. I began with Stability and Emulation but at the same time looked at a good range of others.

I will summarise briefly what I recorded. I have come to the conclusion that to do what I wanted would take a large book, so I have restricted my observations and comments.

I have also looked at the ceremonial differences and this is a problem. Most Brethren seem to guard jealously what they do in lodge. The ritual books sometimes have a lot of red as well as blue, but some don't. I have visited a fair number of lodges and most of the ceremonial 'little differences' **are** mainly little.

I now present to you just a few variations based on what I have examined. I know there are many more variations, but I believe that anything more than minor changes in wording would never have been allowed. The following is just a very small selection.

First Degree
> After restoring the Candidate to light, several lodges retain the old French 'circle of swords' procedure, designed to show that the Brethren of the lodge will protect the Candidate against enemies.
> *Lion Lodge No. 312 Opening*: Bro. SW. Your place - To observe the rising sun, for as the sun rises in the East to open and enlighten the day, so is the W.M. placed in the East, to open his Lodge, instruct his Brethren in Freemasonry or see or cause the same to be done with justice and equity, Worshipful Master.
> After the Opening in the three Degrees, the VSL is opened at a particular place and the Chaplain then reads from that place

(Psalms, Amos and Ecclesiastes respectively).

Bristol working: After being restored to light, Bristol has a long section on the Three Lights and a part of the ceremony which is almost unique to Bristol (which you need to see), which may have come from 18th century French workings. This is then followed by the Tools, which in most workings are done towards the end.

Working Tools: there are different long versions. The Stability version is different from Humber and Unanimity. Taylor has a standard short working but an optional extra bit. Bristol, Humber and William Harvey (Scottish) use 'mallet' rather than heavy maul.

Questions before Passing: Stability, Emulation, Humber and Taylor all very similar. Unanimity has a rather different set of questions, longer and including:

Why were you deprived of metallic substances? …

Why were you hoodwinked? ...

Why do you suppose that the ground of our Lodge is holy?

Closing the lodge: Taylor's working has an interesting 'Long Closing' address by the IPM just before the F … F … F.

Second Degree

Lion Lodge Prayer: Let us invoke a blessing from the GGOTU may the beneficent rays of his all seeing eye strengthen and enlighten us in these, our researches through the more hidden mysteries of nature and science.

Tracing Board: I can find no reference in the 1993 edition of Stability working. Unanimity, within the ceremony, has an abbreviated version done by the WM (no Jephtha and no steps). In Humber working, part is given when the Pass Word from the First to the Second is revealed, to explain the origin of the word (only the middle bit – about the battle with the Ephraimites).

In Bristol working it is given before the Working Tools and Signs (like Humber, only about the battle). The Harvey (Scottish) working refers to the battle as part of giving the Pass Word and does '3, 5 and 7 ...' after the Badge.

West End and Perfect have a very long version, including a history of Jephtha's military career before he became head of the Gileadites.

Calver working has an extremely long version with an insertion of

about 10 pages of Masonic symbolism and moralising, just before
'... had gained the summit ...'
Lion Lodge Second Degree: when the Candidate goes round to the
Wardens, there are some nicely extended answers:
- What is this?
- The Token or Grip of a Fellow Craft Freemason, or a Right
  Brotherly Grip, whereby one Fellow Craft may know another
  by night as well as by day ...
- Give me that word
- I was taught in this Degree, as in the former, to be cautious to
  whom I communicated this Word, but with you I will letter or
  halve it.
- I commend your caution, do which you please and begin.
  In the explanation of the WTs:
- The Level reminds us that in Freemasonry, all are on the level.
  However much the Prince, the Peer or the polished Statesman
  may pride himself on the superiority of his birth or intellectual
  attainments, yet in the grave, whither we are all hastening, all
  are on the level.

Unanimity Questions before Raising: a more complex set than other
lodges, including more questions about the two pillars.

Third Degree

After the Raising, Unanimity has a nice piece of wording and worth
repeating:
- You have this night represented H living and afterwards dead ...
  your days are numbered and the sands of your life may be
  nearly run out ...
- You will please to observe that the light even of a MM is
  darkness visible, serving only to distinguish that gloom which
  hands over the prospect of futurity.
- It is that mysterious veil which the eye of human reason cannot
  penetrate unless aided by that light which is from above.

One of the Bristol workings has a very different Third Degree. It does
not have a break for the Candidate to go out and come back for the
continuation and the ceremony around the discovery, and the actual
raising is quite dramatic.
Stability has a unique explanation of the PW, leading from the Second

to theThird:
- Who was T C
- The first A…r in metals. It was he who discovered the method of reducing o…s into l…s and l…s into s…s which with many improvements has been handed down to the present time.

Several rituals contain Charges after Passing and after Raising, which are not standard Emulation/Sability.

There was a working one used in Unanimity in which, when the Candidate for Raising was sent out for preparation, the most recent Master Mason had to do the questions after Raising. The questions are similar in structure to those before Passing and Raising. Just a small example:
- on being admitted to the lodge did you observe anything different in form from its usual character?
- I Did; all was d…ss save a gl…g l…t in the E.
- To what dos that d…ss elude?
- To the d…ss of d…h ….

Before leaving ritual variations, can I please apologise for the many workings not mentioned, especially from Yorkshire: I am sure there are many others.

Variations inside and outside the lodge

From the Union and subsequent developments we have a fairly stable basis for our workings, but many lodges have developed (or retained) a range of variations, both to the ritual and ceremonial. Having covered some of the ritual variations, it might be nice to look at other differences, how the various accoutrements (Working Tools, Tracing Boards etc.) vary and how they affect behaviour in and outside the lodge.

Festive Board

Like the working in lodge, the Festive Board is stylised, with minor differences:

Limit on the number of wine-takings

When to sing (or not) – during fire and the Master's and EA's songs

Fire – which of the many variations, and when – some lodges fire each toast, while others only fire if the is to be a reply.

Installation

After many years of aggravation, until the PrGL and AGL eventually forgave each other, the Installation ceremony had always been a problem. We believe that for the Moderns, it was not much more than an Obligation and a Chair word. The Antients treated it much more seriously.

The Inner Workings (Past Masters only) were finally defined and today, most Boards of Installed Masters carry out the essential elements. However (of course!), there are variations, some minor, other quite major. Obviously, the full details cannot be given in this book, but two examples:

The form in which the Past Masters stand for the ceremony of the Inner Working in some lodges is in a circle with the centre being 'used'. The details of the history lecture, which are an essential part of the ceremony, can vary and be extended.

A more important variation has the Master Elect being given a Passing Grip and Word and asked to leave the lodge. The Board is then opened and he has to prove himself with the Word, etc. before he is admitted.

Grand Lodge has made it very clear that this extension and any other words or additions to the history are definitely **not part of the essential ceremony**, but can be used **provided the Master Elect is made fully aware that they are not essential**. I think this is a throwback to the aggravation between Antients and Moderns. I wonder if the Antients got together and said something like:

'not only is the Installation ceremony vital, we have extended it to make it even more worthwhile!'

After the new Master has been put in the Chair, he is saluted by the Past Masters. There is only one Chair Word given to the Master, but the salutes can vary.

Knocks

Usually, when the WM gavels, the Wardens support and confirm him with the same knocks. When the JW addresses the WM, such as when there is a report, in some lodges he gives one knock, in others it is always those of the Degree.

Knocks by the Tyler also vary. In some lodges a report is always one knock and 'see who seeks …' will eventually work out who is there. More commonly, one knock is a visitor or late-comer, the Initiate is announced with the EA knocks and the Passing and Raising Candidates with the knocks of their current Degrees.

Lodges of Instruction

An LOI is officially a sub-set of the lodge itself and must conform to the same basic rules – VSL open, Open/Close, Minutes, etc. Most LOIs are really lodges of rehearsal, in which everyone practices the words and ceremonial of their role. A good idea is when officers all work 'one-up' and not in sync. with the lodge itself. It puts a little strain on the younger members but reduces the pure rehearsal aspect. Some lodges do devote some of the time to talks or Q-and-A sessions – not very many!

There seem to be three different levels of LOI:

1. Strictly by the book, with any mistake immediately being jumped on for correction and no books allowed at the LOI – 'learn the black at home, practice the red in LOI'.

2. Go with the flow – don't interrupt the flow at every small mistake if the words are coming. Tell him about them at the end of the passage. Revert to type 1 as the date of the actual ceremony approaches!

3. Similar but with the use of books. Pity, but you still hear so many people say 'come to LOI to learn your work' rather than 'practise it'.

Something that should be covered in the LOI is prompting. Too many Past Masters prompt, either because they are over-keen or just impatient. Practice is usually for the IPM to help the WM (quietly) and all other prompting in the hands of the Preceptor (usually the DC). Also prompting should usually be used only when stuck for words (after giving a suitable time to try and remember) and not for correcting. This is always arguable. Some would say that you should get it right to avoid bad habits, while others feel that word flow and sincerity of delivery are also important. There is nothing worse than seeing a potential Master having a go at a ceremony and, having paused to collect his thoughts or when making a slight mistake, to be jumped on immediately. It can often ruin the concentration.

Signs

There is much variety in the Signs and how they are given. We can't be too specific, but we can say something. The Sign of Fidelity is usually held during the Obligation in each Degree, but in some lodges, the **Penal sign of the Degree** is given instead. The Sign of Reverence (with the thumb completely concealed under the index finger) is used for prayers. Some lodges use the Sign of Reverence for **all** occasions, not using the Sign of

Fidelity at all.

In many lodges, whenever an officer is addressed by the WM, he always gives and holds the Sign of the Degree until instructed.

For the Degree signs, we can observe the following:

First Degree:

The Sign will normally be given with the hand going directly to the 'l o t w…'. In many lodges, the right arm is first stretched out straight ahead before the hand is moved.

I have seen the 'due guard' sign (holding the Bible) given, before the Penal Sign.

Second Degree:

A not uncommon variation is for the left hand to face the front, rather than sideways on. (It has been said that this is a Scottish variation, the open hand proving that there was no concealed dirk).

In one particular lodge, the completion of the second Sign is in two parts, 'that my b … be laid open …' and 'my h … torn …'.

Third Degree:

The First Casual Sign seems to have two different approaches. The more common is for the left hand to be held out to the left, with the right hand shielding the 'turned away h…d'. The alternative is to use the right hand as the shield with the left arm pointing behind.

The Second Casual Sign can be given with the fingers straight, tapping once, or bunched together, tapping three times.

The Penal Sign is pretty standard, except that many Brethren wrongly start it with the 't…b to the n…l', rather than straight to the lhs.

I have seen the sign of Grief and Distress given just before the Penal Sign.

An interesting note in the Unanimity ritual book: that in Bristol, Humber and Unanimity working the explanation of the three Signs is given in the continuation of the Traditional History, after the explanation of the FPOF.

Squaring the lodge

Whenever I ask what is different about Taylor working, many of my acquaintances say that is all about squaring. There is a rumour that this is because this working was heavily supported in military lodges.

I have seen many lodges where almost every movement on the square pavement is either full- or half-squaring and I think it has nothing to do with a military movement, but because by tradition and the words of the First Degree - '... all **squares**, levels ... are deemed...' - demand at least some squaring.

Tracing Boards

There are variations as to what they look like (another book!) and where they are placed during the ceremony. Most lodges have Tracing Boards that are placed usually against the JWs pedestal and turned round as the appropriate Degree is opened.

Some lodges have them in a wall cabinet, mounted on slides. This only becomes a problem for the Second Degree, where in most lodges the lecture on the Tracing Board is usually conducted with the Tracing Board on the floor and the Brethren and the new Fellowcraft gathered round to see the presentation. Not so easy if it is on the wall, because the wand used to indicate the various objects has to pass over (or through) the Brethren seated below it.

There is no reason in principle why all three Boards could not be open all the time, provided all present were not below the rank of MM. I don't know any lodge that does this, but I have visited a lodge where Tracing Boards are not used on Installation night.

Tyled

In many lodges, 'to see that the lodge is properly tyled' is done with the knocks of the Degree exchanged between the IG and the Tyler. Other lodges have the IG actually open the lodge door to **see** if the Tyler is there and doing his duty. During Closing, it seems always to be done with knocks.

Tyler's toast

Usually given right at the end of the Festive Board, after being summoned with a double-knock. The Tyler picks up the Master's gavel, knocks once and gives the toast. In some lodges, no-one touches the gavel except the Master, so the Tyler should ask the WM - 'will you please gavel for me'. In other lodges, there is no gavel for the toast.

Often the Tyler says 'by command of the WM, I ...'. I think it is the job of the Tyler to give the toast, by right of his position, and he does not need to be commanded. Sometimes the Tyler recites the 'Brethren of the Mystic Tie' piece before the toast and I have seen Tyler repeating it as he was walking up to the top table.

It is surprising how many variations are possible. I once gave a Russian toast to a Master who spent a lot of time in Russia.

Just one other: 'Happy have we met…' in Scottish and other lodges can be:

Happy have we met

Happy have we been

Happy may we part

And happy meet again.

Visiting

This is not usually a problem but there are two areas of note:

1. Although not all that common, since most visitors are invited by a member of the lodge who vouches for them, but a visitor should be prepared to be 'proved' by the JW or DC. This could be a basic question or two, but could involve an inspection of the Grand Lodge Certificate and showing a 'complete set' of Signs!

2. A visitor should be prepared to see different Signs. Which ones are given – the ones taught in the visitor's Mother Lodge or those of the guesting lodge? A visitor should check the protocol with the DC. I believe you were taught to use certain Signs and they are fundamental to you as a Mason. You should be allowed to retain them. I can't believe that the lodge you visit will be insulted.

Working Tools

The actual 'basic' wording of the First and Third Degree Tools seems to be fairly uniform. Some workings use 'mallet' rather than 'common gavel'. Bristol add the trowel as a fourth Tool for the Third Degree ('…for spreading the cement of Brotherhood and affection...' and incidentally, also used in the opening of the Royal and Select Degree ceremony). There are variations on the Second Degree tools, a 'long' version and a 'very long' one.

There are differences in how the Tools are presented. In Emulation lodges, they are pointed to and never touched. In some lodges, the presenter picks them up and shows them to the Candidate. In others, the individual Tools are demonstrated, eg. the Level is placed on the table to show it is level and the Plumb against the side, etc.

Pause for thought

I have always been very fussy about the wording. I believe that we should pronounce it as:

'…as we are **not** [slight pause] **all** operative Masons, but rather free [slight pause] and accepted or speculative…'.

Once many of us were operative but not any more. Why I

link 'accepted' and 'speculative' should be obvious if you have read Chapter 4.

Finally

The end of the history and development part of the book, but don't forget to look at Chapter 11.

I hope you now have a much better idea of where the ritual came from and hence what it means. I also hope you will find it easier to learn.

If you are interested in the history of the Craft and its workings, do some of the suggested reading, take out a subscription to *The Square*, join the Quatuor Coronati Correspondence Circle and see if you can find some of the 'older' members of your lodges who can help you with it.

Don't be frightened to approach foreign web sites for copies of papers and books. The e-world floats in the cloud but absolutely massive.

The very best of luck whichever way you decide to go.
Don't forget to look at Chapter 11!

11
Recap and further study

Reading

There are many books available (the list follows shortly) which cover particular aspects of history, either in time or emphasis, but which leave out the overall development of our ritual. I looked at the most important books and you will discover, as I did, that most of them were written a while ago. Colin Dyer's *Preston* came out in 1987, Harry Carr's in the 70s/80s, Bernard Jones in 1950 and the Knoop, Jones and Hamer books even earlier. I will look at some books individually, but as far as I can see, no-one recently has tried to write a basic book that covers the history and development of our ritual **within** the history of the Craft itself, so this is what I have attempted to do.

In this Chapter and the rest of the book, I have made many references to quite old books and papers and some you will, no doubt, **laugh like drains to hear that I would like you to examine a 100-year old paper.** I am being very serious – from about 1880 onwards, we saw the emergence of so many highly knowledgeable Masonic writers that it is almost impossible to keep track of them.

I said in the Introduction that five books are the most rewarding and are referred to as *KJH1, HC1, HC3, BJ1* and *KJH2*. All are remarkable in the historical information they provide, but not always very easy for the beginner. Most are out-of-print and getting difficult to find – in a second-hand bookshop (if you can find them) *HC1* and *BJ1* will cost about £25 but you will be very lucky to get hold of *KJH1, KJH2* or *HC3* anywhere except your Provincial Llbrary or a good County library. Try and find them somewhere – they are important and there are really no alternatives to them!

I did Chapter 1 for my benefit as well as that of the reader. In looking at our history, especially from say 1500 to 1750, to understand how and why some of our customs evolved, we need to have at least a feel for the national environment that prevailed. The Chapter only scratches the surface, but should give you a good basis if you want to take English history further. **You can ignore it if you find it boring!**

Chapter 2 is a little unusual but quite important for a general understanding of what did and what does make up our 'Working'. So many Masons forget that a Working is the words **and** the associated ceremonial.

I hope that Chapters 3 and 4 lay a historical basis for all the supposition and guesswork we have all had to make because of the lack of really firm and believable evidence. How did the ritual and ceremonies go from some stoneworkers getting together, presumably to protect their trade interests, with some kind of initiation ceremony and some old manuscripts, to the beginnings of organisation in Chapter 5 and hence to the well-organised and detailed ritual and ceremony specifications of Chapters 6, 7 and then 9 and 10?

Much of the 16th and 17th centuries of our history rely on what happened in Scotland and there is mention of the *Schaw Statutes* in Chapter 3, but it has been difficult enough to trace things in England, so Scotland has taken a back place in the book. This is a great pity, because there are many more early records of Masonry in Scotland than in England and it is believed that a fair amount of Scottish practice was absorbed into England. (Another book perhaps?)

Chapters 4 to 7 show how the ritual went from a simple ceremony to a three Degree complex with increasingly more sophisticated ritual.

Chapter 8 is a sort of interlude, in that it will remind you of various aspects of the Craft, but it will also show you that there is probably no **one** satisfactory explanation for how we developed. The experts have been differing widely for years.

Chapters 9 and 10 then hopefully bring the development of ritual up to the 20th century.

There is no way I can review every ritual - there are far too many. In some cases, I was told that 'our written-down ritual is only available to the lodge members'. Other lodges maintain the traditional 'word of mouth' passing-on of the workings. I have given a small selection of the kinds of variations that many Masons know about, and one or two more that are less well known. From them, you will see that there are very many small and often trivial variations. It would be nice if we could pick all the bits we like and incorporate them into our own working. **Fat chance!**

References generally

There are many references to books, papers and web sites. Where I am quoting from a source directly, I tell you where it came from. If the source is, say, an old manuscript or other document and it is available on many different sites and books, I tell you which document but not always which book/site it came from, because the material, often being 300 or more years old is, in effect, in the public domain.

Similarly, if an author has a view, repeated in different places, I may have said Timothy Ridiculous 'holds the view that ...' or 'often says'. I have tried where possible to minimise the number of references, not from laziness, nor from academic sloppiness, but because I feel that this is an introductory book. Those who will use it as a quick reference guide will probably not be too concerned to go much deeper. Those who use it as a stepping stone to further study will soon find which books to read (if they can get hold of them) and which sites to visit.

Books

These are shown in the code table. Many have already been referred to and the Introduction mentions the use of the code throughout the book. When you look at some of the web sites, you will find that other Masonic books are available.

Code	Authors	Title
KJH1	Knoop, D., Jones, G.P. and Hamer, D. *Manchester University Press, 1963*	*The Early Masonic Catechisms* Not the easiest of book to read but absolutely vital if you want to be sure about the early development of ritual. **Must read.**
HC1	Harry Carr *Lewis Masonic, 1985*	*Harry Carr's World of Freemasonry* A nice readable book with many interesting, though not linked, chapters by one of the most respected Masonic scholars. **Must read.**
HC3	Harry Carr (editor) *Quatuor Coronati Lodge, 1971*	*The Collected Prestonian Lectures 1925-60* It contains some of the most important QC lectures of the century. **Absolutely essential must-read book.**
BJ1	Bernard Jones *Harrap & Co., 1956*	*Freemasons Guide and Compendium* Another readable book, very organised and covering Craft history in all stages. **Must read.**
KJH2	Knoop, Jones and Hamer *QC Correspondence Circle, 1978*	*Early Masonic Pamphlets* Lots of little snippets, from newspapers, periodicals, manuscripts etc., some vital, all of which help to fill in 17th/18th century Masonic history holes.

AJ	A.C.F. Jackson *Lewis Masonic, 1986*	*Early Masonic Exposures of 1760-69* Full details of TDK, J&B and other exposures, together with substantial comments. **A very important book.**
PK1	Pick, F.L. and Knight, G.N. *Frederick Muller, 1969*	*The Pocket History of Freemasonry* Nice, readable little book that covers a lot of history.
PK2	Pick and Knight *Frederick Muller, 1983*	*The Freemasons Pocket Reference Book* A very handy little Masonic dictionary – open anywhere and start reading!
HC2	Harry Carr (editor)	*The Early French Exposures 1737-1751* Heavy stuff. But needed if you want to know how French Masonry influenced ours and vice versa.
CD1	C. Dyer *Lewis Masonic, 1987*	*William Preston and his Work* **Essential** if you are to appreciate just what Preston did and how important he was.
KJ1	Knoop and Jones *QC Correspondence Circle, 1978*	*The Genesis of Freemasonry* The book's sub-title is 'An account of the rise and development of Freemasonry in its operative, accepted and early speculative phases'. A masterly piece of work.
KJ2	Knoop and Jones *Manchester University Press, 1949*	*The Medieval Mason* The book's sub-title is 'An economic history of English stone building in the later middle ages and early modern times'. Good, solid stuff to back up Chapters 3 and 4.
CB1	C. Batham *Australian Masonic Research Council, 1993*	*Freemasonry in England and France* Some interesting material to back up several of our Chapters.

Web sites

Home sites
So many useful sites with so much information. Very difficult to recommend just a few. You will have to search around until one strikes your eye and you can then drill in and see what goodies can be mined.

I have found Wikipedia extremely useful, but many of my collegues and acquaintances are very suspicious. They claim that material is not checked and anyone can put their own rubbish up.

I can only say that as with all web sites, you must decide for yourself just how valid are the contributors and their contributions!

Masonic Trowel – access to many articles etc.	http://themasonictrowel.com/
Phoenix Masonic museum and library – packed with articles etc.	http://www.phoenixmasonry.org/
Grand Lodge of Scotland	http://www.grandlodgescotland.com/
Grand Lodge of Ireland	http://www.irish-freemasons.org/
The Internet lodge	http://www.internet.lodge.org.uk/
Province of British Columbia and Yukon	http://Freemasonry.bcy.ca/info.html
A highly irregular lodge but lots of useful papers especially Tracing Boards and Landmarks	http://www.rgle.org.uk/

Sites for books/papers/document lists
A set of goldmines for Old Charges, Exposures and many other documents.

Wikipedia	A vital site for much Masonic material – try it!
A extremely valuable collection of papers from British Columbia/ Yukon	http://Freemasonry.bcy.ca/texts/index. html
Grand Lodge of South Carolina. Many downloadable papers	http://www.scgrandlodgeafm.org/digital-books.html
A long list of documents from 643 to 2006, many downloadable – a valuable site	http://www.stichtingargus.nl/engelsrom. html
Many downloadable old documents	http://www.rgle.org.uk/RGLE_Old_ Charges.htm
Another extremely useful source of old documents, downloadable.	http://theoldcharges.com/
Yet another downloadable set of documents	http://harmonie699.org/library/historical-documents/
Many downloadable papers.	http://theMasonictrowel.com/Articles/ Manuscripts/manuscripts_main_toc. htm#top
Useful list of papers/books	http://www.theMasonictrowel.com/ Articles/Manuscripts/meaning/early_ Masonic_documents.htm

Pietre-Stones restricted area [ ] contains MD etc. User name and password needed to access MD and other exposures	http://www.freemasons-Freemasonry.com[/restrict.html]
Access to a very wide range of books – navigation is tricky	http://countcagliostrosmasonicelibrary/blog.com
Masonic Wiki. German site with translation available	http://freimaurer-wiki.de/index.php/Hauptseite
Set of AQC lectures + index	http://Freemasonry.bcy.ca/aqc/index.html
Internet lodge WMs papers since 1998	http://internet.lodge.org.uk/wmspapers

Books on line

Remember that some of these are copyright. Nevertheless, if they are on-line, someone is happy for you to read them. I see no reason why any site cannot be viewed (assuming it is not criminal of course), but you need to consider whether downloading and copying is proper.

The Spirit of Freemasonry Hutchinson, later edition	http://www.phoenixmasonry.org/spirit_of_masonry.htm
The Spirit of Freemasonry Hutchinson, 2nd edition 1795	http://www.themasonictrowel.com/ebooks/Freemasonry/eb0131.pdf
A candid disquisition of… Wellins Calcott	https://babel.hathitrust.org/cgi/pt?id=dul1.ark:/ 13960/ t2s47p15n;view=1up;seq=5
History of FM throughout the World Gould	http://www.phoenixmasonry.org/goulds_history_volume_X.htm X = 1-5 for 5 volumes
Illustrations of Masonry Preston 1796 edition	http://Freemasonry.bcy.ca/ritual/preston.pdf
Manual of Freemasonry Carlile	http://www.rgle.org.uk/Manual%20Freemasonry.pdf
Masonic Treatise Finch	http://Freemasonry.bcy.ca/ritual/finch.pdf
Browne's *Master Key* decoded (unfortunately in German!). Can't find one in English	http://freimaurer-wiki.de/index.php/Lehrlingfragst%C3%BCck_nach_Browne_1

General Reference

The Regius Manuscript	http://Freemasonry.bcy.ca/texts/regius.html

Grand Lodge of the Antients Wikipedia	https://en.wikipedia.org/wiki/ Antient_Grand_Lodge_of_England
Laurence Dermott - Wikipedia	https://en.wikipedia.org/wiki/ Laurence_Dermott
Ahiman Rezon - Wikipedia	https://en.wikipedia.org/wiki/ Ahiman_Rezon
Old Charges - Wikipedia	https://en.wikipedia.org/wiki/Masonic_ manuscripts
General Masonic education	http://theMasonictrowel.com/education. htm
List of Grand Masters from 1717 to date	http://www.Masonic-lodge.info/MLI/ mli109g.htm
Many good articles	http://www.skirret.com
Very useful 'private' site. Interesting stuff on Tracing Boards	http://ecossais.net
Review of Tracing Boards	http://Freemasonry.bcy.ca/texts/ gmd1999/tb_history01.html
Masonic education course	https://babel.hathitrust.org/cgi/ pt?id=dul1.ark:/ 13960/t2s47p15n;view=1up;seq=5

USA

Interesting USA lodge giving a comprehensive discussion of the 3 Degrees	http://www.jjcrowder743.com/ threedegrees.html
The Builder magazine from 1915 to 1930. Contains an unbelievable amount of material, not just US.	http://www.phoenixmasonry.org/the_ builder_1915-1930_toc.htm
Lots of US articles for comparison with UK	http://www.Masonicworld.com/
Duncan's *Ritual* for comparison with UK rituals	http://www.phoenixmasonry.org/ duncans_ritual/
Very interesting 'instruction manual' by the Grand Lodge of Maine	http://www.mainemason.org/resources/ instructormanual/index.asp

Other publications

There are numerous journals and monthly/quarterly Masonic magazines, but, like books and web sites, there are so many that it would need a book to review them, even if we restricted the analysis to the last 10 years. I have therefore just listed the ones I read.

The Square	Ian Allan Publishing Ltd
Freemasonry Today	Freemasonry Today Ltd
Freemasonry Today - the best of 10 years 1997-2007	Freemasonry Today Ltd
The Norfolk Ashlar	Provincial Grand Lodge of Norfolk
The Surrey Mason	Provincial Grand Lodge of Surrey

Quatuor Coronati Lodge papers

The pictures show the front page of Volume I and the traditional history of the Four Crowned Martyrs on a Spanish tapestry of 1497.

Fig 11.1: *AQC* Volume I.

Fig 11.2: The legend of the Four Crowned Martyrs.

Many of the papers produced by writers of the Quatuor Coronati Lodge and published in *AQC - Ars Quatuor Coronatorum*, the Transactions of the Quatuor Coronati Lodge No. 2076 - are extremely important and usually very interesting. The annual volume each year gives all the papers delivered in the Lodge and a range of other papers received.

Other than those listed above, you will need to search for yourself to discover the papers most appropriate to your reading and study. The Grand Lodge of British Columbia and Yukon site (see general reference above) has an index of papers and the QCCC (Correspondence Circle) has published an index on CD from 1888 to 2003.

I hope this Chapter and the book as a whole has helped you to go on much further with your Masonic research towards that daily advancement.

Appendix
The Ancient Landmarks

We have seen the term 'Landmark' several times in the book, usually as a quotation 'abiding by the established Landmarks of the order'. All very well, but as in many other Masonic areas, there is a history either of secrecy or of confusion. So we need to think about what actually **is** a Landmark and then what are **the** Landmarks?   I think most Masons will agree that the following are essential:
  • Belief in the GAOTU
  • VSL always open at a meeting
  • Obedience to those in higher office.
They seem pretty obvious (and are), but there are many others that could be considered.

What is a Landmark?
There are lots of so-called definitions and explanations such as:
  • something that represents an **important new development** – an event, idea or item that represents a significant or historic development
  • something preserved for **historic importance** – a structure or site, identified and preserved because of its historical significance
  • highly significant – marking a **significant change or turning point** in something, especially in law.
Interesting that none of these mention 'fundamental' or 'cornerstone' or 'basic', though. Other definitions or explanations of the term which have appeared over the years (some useful, others not very) include:
  • leading and essential characteristics – generally received – the very essence and conditions of Freemasonry
  • ascertained on the authority of ancient documents
  • leading principles from which there can be no deviation
  • existed from a time when the memory of man runneth not to the contrary
  • unchangeable - the universal law of Masonry, to alter which is a heinous offence

Perhaps one of the better ones is
• ceremonies, rules and laws – deemed absolutely necessary to
mark out this distinctive Order.

None of these is entirely satisfactory but you get the general sense.

The Premier Lodge of England in the 18th century claimed the power
to legislate anything Masonic for the real benefit of this ancient Fraternity,
provided also that the old Landmarks be carefully preserv'd.

One of the requirements for the recognition of a Grand Lodge outside
our English Constitution is:
• the principles of the Ancient Landmarks, customs and usages of
the Craft shall be strictly maintained

This explains why Grand Lodge is not in amity (does not accept) some
foreign Lodges, which, although very 'Masonic', do not regard a belief in
the existence of the GAOTU as being essential.

What are our Landmarks?

Hopefully you can accept that it looks as if a Landmark is a kind of
cornerstone of Masonry – something which must be obeyed, followed,
always to be aware of, etc., in order for the traditions of the Craft to be
maintained, indeed its very continuance made possible. Unfortunately, over
the centuries the number of options for a Landmark has increased and what
actually **are** the Landmarks is hotly debated.

An old but important book in its time, called *Masonic Jurisprudence* by
J. Lawrence (A. Lewis, London, 1912) says:
There are certain immovable and unchangeable principles and
doctrines which go right behind laws and regulations and which no
law or regulation can modify.

It lists 24 Landmarks, stating that the first six are unlikely to be disputed:
• a belief in a supreme being
• the VSL is indispensable in every lodge
• the equality of all Freemasons
• the secrecy of the modes of recognition
• the modes of recognition themselves
• certain qualifications are necessary in every Candidate

Others from this source include:
• government by a Grand Master elected by the Brethren
• the necessity for Masons to meet in lodges

- the government of Brethren so assembled by a Master and two
  Wardens

Coming out of all this, there seems to be two fundamental requirements.
Landmarks must:

- have been in existence from the very beginning
- be so important to the Craft that **it would not be the same if the
  Landmark was removed or changed**

You may have noted that in all these definitions or explanations, no-one
seems to have considered it necessary to mention 'charity' or 'relief' within
a Landmark.

We may want to agree with R.F. Gould who, in his famous *History of
Freemasonry*, said:

> 'Of the ancient landmarks it has been observed with more or less
> foundation of truth, that nobody knows what they comprise or
> omit, they are of no earthly authority, because everything is a
> landmark when an opponent desires to silence you but nothing is a
> landmark that stands in his own way.'

Something for you to think about!

Are the following Landmarks, ie. without them would Masonry change, be
worse off or not be able to exist at all, as we practice it now? Be careful! It
is not **'do you consider it essential to Masonry'**. You must ask yourself
'if we scrapped it, would it change Masonry'. The trouble with this is
that the word 'change' needs to be thought about. The last of the 25
Landmarks mentioned above says that no Landmark can be changed and
this is really ludicrous. It implies that if a Landmark is generally accepted,
even if circumstances change, the Landmark cannot. There have been many
major changes in the past, such as the creation of a Third Degree, watering
down the penalties, etc. A change is not always for the better, but many
Masons react to any change (we've always done it this way!) and it always
takes a brave man to try and implement a change, even though no-one can
be absolute as to which really are the Landmarks – look at what Gould said
above.

Before looking at some possible examples, you may recall that the
Obligation of the Master Elect in the Second Degree, contains the
following:

11. You admit that it is not within the power of any Man or any
    Body of Men to make any Alteration or Innovation in the Body of
    Masonry without the consent first obtained of the Grand Lodge.

There is also Rule 155 of our Book of Constitutions – a summary is:
    … that a private lodge can regulate its own proceedings if consistent with the **general laws and regulations** of the Craft but a brother can protest if anything is proposed that is **contrary to the laws and usages** of the Craft.

Do these two conflict? Are they relevant to our views on Landmarks? You must differentiate between what is custom or practice (however long it has been followed) and what is essential and always will be.

Look at these:
1. White gloves
2. The Second Degree Tracing Board
3. The WM and Wardens' gavels
4. Three Degrees
5. The Charity column
6, Masonic fire
7. Tyling the lodge
8. The office of Deacon
9. The rough and perfect ashlar

Many of these have become part of the fabric of masonry through long use and tradition. Some have existed for a long time, while some are quite recent. Having looked at my views on the items above, I maintain that the only real definitions of a Masonic Landmark are as above:

- **have been in existence from the very beginning** – Masonry had to start somewhere and something that can be traced with a degree of confidence, right back to the beginning, surely must be preserved?

- **be so important to the Craft that it would not be the same if the Landmark was removed or changed** – ceremonies, workings, furniture, accoutrements, etc. have developed to support and maintain the basic principles and truths of the Craft. Changing these does not mean we therefore admit that the principles and truths themselves are capable of change.

My views (and many will argue, perhaps with good reason) on the suggestions given above:
1. White gloves are nice but only came in towards the middle of the 18th century. Could we manage without?
2. We have already discussed this in the book (Chapter 10).

3. Very important but essential? Could we manage without? Probably not, but a Landmark?

4. The Craft has stabilised on three Degrees since about 1730. I would say that although not an 'original' Landmark under our definitions, if we added another Degree or decided to merge two of the existing Degrees, the Craft would not be the same. I think, now, it must be regarded as a Landmark.

5. Giving charity and supporting relief is so fundamental to the Craft that, although not always in the form of a column (which is not of Masonic origin anyway!), I believe it should be thought of as a true Landmark.

6. Nice but not vital.

7. This is difficult. Our history of privacy and being a society of secrets, has led to ensuring that our meetings are not 'cowanised'. Is this now a basic Landmark or what might be called sensible practice?

8. Deacons have been around for about 230 years and do a lot of work. In earlier times, it was the Wardens who did much of the work. If someone was prepared to make many changes to the ceremonial and the ritual, I suppose we could manage without them. I don't see them as a Landmark.

9. Our building tradition for the Craft is so strong that these two items, in effect, summarise the work of a Mason – the junior Mason receiving a rough rock and getting it to a finer form for the hands of the more expert workman. The lodge would be poorer without them, but a Landmark?

Finally, an interesting American view of 25 landmarks and well worth visiting. There is an expansion given for each landmark.

http://www.Masonicworld.com/education/files/25%20landmarks%20of%20Freemasonry.htm

Index